# DEINSTITUTIONALISING WOMEN
## An Ethnographic Study of Institutional Closure

An ethnographic study of deinstitutionalisation, this book explores the lives of women living in a locked ward within a large institution for people with intellectual disabilities. Kelley Johnson describes, in rich and carefully-observed detail, the lives of the women in the institution largely through their own stories and experiences. The closure of this institution gave her a unique opportunity to closely examine the impact of deinstitutionalisation on these women. The book raises a number of broad questions about our understanding of disability. It considers the role of professional views of intellectual disability in shaping perceptions. It also looks at the process of deinstitutionalisation, with its paradoxical discourse of rights and management. Finally the book's feminist analysis brings insight to the ways in which institutionalised women are not only locked out of society, but out of their lives as women as well.

Kelley Johnson is Senior Lecturer in Deakin Human Services at Deakin University in Melbourne. She has published widely in the area of intellectual disability, and has worked extensively in advocacy for people with disabilities.

*For Ben*
*and for the women who lived and worked in the locked unit*

# DEINSTITUTIONALISING WOMEN

## An Ethnographic Study of Institutional Closure

KELLEY JOHNSON

PUBLISHED BY THE PRESS SYNDICATE OF THE UNIVERSITY OF CAMBRIDGE
The Pitt Building, Trumpington Street, Cambridge, United Kingdom

CAMBRIDGE UNIVERSITY PRESS
The Edinburgh Building, Cambridge CB2 2RU, UK   http://www.cup.cam.ac.uk
40 West 20th Street, New York, NY 10011–4211, USA   http://www.cup.org
10 Stamford Road, Oakleigh, Melbourne 3166, Australia

First published 1998

Printed in China by Colorcraft

Typeset in New Baskerville 10/12 pt

*A catalogue record for this book is available from the British Library*

*National Library of Australia Cataloguing in Publication data*
Johnson, Kelley.
Deinstitutionalising women: an ethnographic study of
institutional closure.
Bibliography.
Includes index.
ISBN 0 521 62366 9.
ISBN 0 521 62369 6 (pbk.).
1. Mentally handicapped women – Institutional care –
Victoria. 2. Mentally handicapped women –
Deinstitutionalization – Victoria. 3. Mentally handicapped
women – Victoria – Social conditions. I. Title.
362.2082

ISBN 0 521 62366 9 hardback
ISBN 0 521 62569 6 paperback

Publication of this work was assisted by
a special publications grant from the
University of Melbourne.

# *Contents*

*Note to the Reader*                                          viii
*Acknowledgements*                                             ix
*The Women*                                                    xi

1   Entry Points                                                1
      Rationale for the Study                                   1
      The Research Methodology                                  3
      The Positions of the Researcher                           7
      The Structure of this Book                                16

**Part I  Inside the Institution**                             19

2   Life in the Unit                                           22
      Unit N: Its Geography                                    22
      The Women Living in the Unit                             24
      The Women of Unit N: A Snapshot                          27
      The Women Working in the Unit                            30
      Life in Unit N                                           33
      Researcher/Participant                                   43

3   Paths to Unit N                                            45
      The Women's Paths to the Institution                     49
      Paths to the Locked Unit                                 53
      Researcher/Detective                                     58

4 Locked Out/Locked In 60
   The Women of Unit N: 'Failed Women' 61
   How Were the Women Known? 68

**Part II  Coming Out** 79

   The Decision to Close Hilltop 80
   The Stages of Closing Hilltop 81

5 The Unlocked Door 84
   The Women's World 84
   The Wider Context 90
   Researcher/Exile/Negotiator 94

6 Stepping Forward 98
   Client Consultation on Relocation (CCOR) and Matching 98
   Constraints on CCOR and Matching 102
   The Women's Experience of CCOR 105
   Families, Advocates and CCOR 110
   Staff in the Unit and CCOR 111
   The Convenors and CCOR 112
   The Closure Project Team Managers 116
   The Women's Experience of Matching 117
   Families and Advocates: the Matching Experience 122
   Unit Staff and Matching 123
   The Convenors and the Matching Process 125
   Closure Project Team Managers and Matching 127
   Researcher/Advocate 128

7 Leaving Hilltop 130
   The Women and the Last Six Months 131
   Advocates, Families and the Last Six Months 136
   Staff and the Last Six Months 137
   Convenors and the Last Six Months 138
   Closure Project Team Managers and the Last Six Months 141
   Researcher/Story Teller 143

8 Deinstitutionalisation: Managing Subjectivities 146
   Deinstitutionalisation and the Women 146
   Deinstitutionalisation and Rights 149
   Deinstitutionalisation and Management 155
   The Silence of the Women 164

**Part III  Outside** 167

9   Escaping Stories 169
   Objectification of the Women 170
   Functions of the Intellectual Disability Discourse 179
   Conclusion 185

*Glossary* 188
*Bibliography* 190
*Index* 209

# *Note to the Reader*

To protect the confidentiality of those who took part in the research for this book, all names of institutions have been changed. Because the book focuses on the women who lived in the locked unit, they have been given pseudonyms. Care has been taken to exclude information which could be used to individually identify the women living in the unit. Staff and managers are identified only by initials which in no way reflect their real initials.

# Acknowledgements

There are a great many people I would like to thank for their assistance and support during my research. To the women and their families, into whose lives I intruded, I owe a great debt. The staff who worked in the locked unit and those who managed and closed the institution gave very generously of their time and knowledge.

Throughout the four years of work involved in the study, Professor Connie Benn, Dr Bruce Lagay (Social Work Department, University of Melbourne) and Dr Deborah McIntyre were constant in their support, guidance and inspiration.

My partner, Spencer Zifcak, was generous in his support and challenged me to shape my ideas positively. Our son Sam was tolerant and patient in the face of my work and preoccupations. Thank you both.

I am also grateful to staff at Cambridge University Press, particularly Phillipa McGuinness, Jane Farago and Glenys Osborne, for their valuable editorial advice and support.

I would also like to thank the following for granting permission to reprint poetry in this book:

W. W. Norton and Co (New York) for five lines from Part 5 of 'Turning the Wheel' in *A Wild Patience Has Taken Me This Far: Poems 1978–1981* © Adrienne Rich 1981; and for four lines from 'Delta' in *Time's Power: Poems 1985–1988* © Adrienne Rich 1989.

Faber and Faber Ltd (London) for two lines from the poem 'After R. M. Rilke' from *Collected Poems* by Primo Levi © Faber and Faber 1988.

Macmillan Publishers Ltd (London) for two lines from an untitled poem on page 115 and nine lines from an untitled poem on page 63 of *The Echoes Return Slow* by R. S. Thomas (1988).

Carcanet Press Ltd London for six lines from 'ET Phone Home' in *Friend of Heraclitis* by Patricia Beer (1993).

HarperCollins (New York) for two lines from 'The Song the Idiot Sings' and eight lines from 'Title Poem' in *Selected Poems of Rainer Maria Rilke. A Translation from the German and Commentary by Robert Bly* (1981).

KELLEY JOHNSON

# The Women

BRIGID ANDERSON was institutionalised at birth and was 26 at the time of the study. She had spent all her life in institutions and more than eight years in the locked unit. She had no family or advocate. Brigid's first Client Consultation on Relocation (CCOR) preference was a metropolitan house, her second a metropolitan institution and her third a country institution. She was unmatched and went to live in a country institution.

DORA CRAIG was 43 and had been institutionalised for thirty-one years from the age of 12. She had lived for eight years in the locked unit. Her parents visited her irregularly. Her CCOR preference was undecided, and she was matched to a metropolitan institution and went to live there.

UNA HARRIS was 40 and had been in institutions since she was 18. She had spent approximately five years in the locked unit, and was visited regularly by her sister. All three of Una's CCOR preferences were for a country house. She was matched to one and went to live there.

IRIS JAMES was 43 and had spent nineteen years since the age of 24 in institutions. She had lived in locked units for over ten years. Her sister visited her regularly. All three of her CCOR preferences were for a metropolitan house, and she was matched to one and went to live there.

LENA JOHNSON was institutionalised at the age of 64. At 72 she had been living in institutions for eight years, and half of this time had been spent in the locked unit. She had an appointed guardian and visited her elderly mother regularly. Lena's three CCOR preferences were for a metropolitan house, but she was matched to a country house and went to live there.

KIRSTEN JONES was 39. She had entered the institution at 20 and had lived there for nineteen years, spending approximately thirteen of those years in a locked unit. She had no contact with her family. All of her CCOR preferences were for metropolitan houses. She was matched to one and went to live there.

BETTINA JUNISOV was institutionalised at 6. At 25 she had spent nineteen years in the institution, with eight of those years in the locked unit. Her parents visited her irregularly. Bettina's three CCOR preferences were for a metropolitan house in the community, which was also the matching decision and her final location.

JANE KING had spent periods in the community, but had been admitted repeatedly to institutions since the age of 6. She was 30, and although she had been in the locked unit for only six months, she had lived there previously, She had a guardian. Although her first preference was a metropolitan house, Jane was matched to a metropolitan institution and went to live there (her second and third preferences).

ILSE LANE was 56 and had been in institutions since the age of 6. She had lived in the locked unit for eight years. Ilse had a citizen advocate but no family. All three of her CCOR preferences were for a metropolitan house, and she was matched to one and went to live there.

RHONDA LEE was 37 and had spent thirty-one years since the age of 6 in an institution. Rhonda had been in the locked unit for six years, and her family visited her regularly. Rhonda went to live in a metropolitan house early in the institution's closure and did not go through either the CCOR or matching processes.

ROSALIND MAITLAND was institutionalised at 5. At the age of 53 she had spent forty-eight years in institutions. Twenty of those years had been spent in locked units. Rosalind had a citizen advocate but no family. Rosalind's three CCOR preferences were for a metropolitan house, but she was matched to a country house and went to live there.

JUNE MILES was 46. She had been institutionalised for twenty-three years since the age of 22, and had spent seven years in the locked unit. She had a citizen advocate but no family. Although all of her CCOR preferences were for a metropolitan house, June was matched and sent to a country house.

LAURA MITCHELL was 57. She had lived in institutions for thirty-three years since the age of 24, and had been in locked units on and off for thirty of those years. Laura had no family. Her three CCOR preferences were for a metropolitan house, a country house and a metropolitan institution respectively. She was matched to a country house and went to live there.

FAYE MORRIS was 10 when she was institutionalised, and at 47 had spent thirty-seven years in an institution. She had lived thirty of those years in a locked unit. Her sister visited her irregularly. Faye was initially matched to a country house (her first preference), but concerns about her behaviour led to a change in the matching decision. She was matched to a metropolitan institution and went to live there.

INGE ROBERTS was institutionalised at 9, and at 41 had spent thirty-two years in institutions. She had lived ten of those years in the locked unit. Her father visited her irregularly. Although Inge's first preference was for a house on the grounds of a metropolitan institution, she was matched and went to live in a metropolitan institution (her second and third preferences).

JODIE RYAN was 45 and had spent twenty-three years in institutions after first being admitted at 22. She had spent seven years in the locked unit. She had a citizen advocate friend but no family. All three of her CCOR preferences were for a metropolitan house, and the matching committee approved this and she went to live in one.

DORIS SMITH was institutionalised at 3, and at 56 had spent fifty-three years in institutions. She had spent eleven of those years in the locked unit. Her sister visited her irregularly. All of Doris's CCOR preferences were for a metropolitan institution. She was matched to such an institution and went to live there.

ELAINE STONE was 61 and had spent periods in the community since she was institutionalised some thirty-three years earlier at 28. She had lived in a locked unit intermittently for thirty years. Her brother visited her irregularly. Her three CCOR preferences were for a metropolitan house, and she was matched to one and went to live there.

KATE SURREY had been in institutions since she was 28 and had spent fifteen years until the age of 43 in the locked unit. Her mother visited her regularly. Kate's three CCOR preferences were for a metropolitan house, and she was matched to one and went to live there.

JOYCE THAMES was institutionalised at 8. At 39 she had spent twenty-three years in locked units. Joyce's parents visited her frequently, and Joyce had regular home leave. Her three CCOR preferences were for a metropolitan institution. Joyce was matched to one and went to live there.

VERA WATERS was institutionalised at 16. At 59 she had lived in institutions for forty-three years. It was not possible to discover from her records how many years she had spent in a locked unit, but estimates ranged from seven to twelve years. Vera had a citizen advocate as well as a sister who visited her regularly. Vera's three CCOR preferences were for a metropolitan house. She was matched to one and went to live there.

# CHAPTER 1

# *Entry Points*

> I am not neutral, I am not distanced, for being an outsider
> does not mean to be cool and clinical; it must mean to burn
> with those fires which define you as the outsider.
> *(S. L. Gilman, 1991, p.17)*

This book is about women and deinstitutionalisation. In particular it is
about how deinstitutionalisation entered the lives of twenty-one women
who were labelled as having intellectual disabilities and challenging
behaviours. The book grew out of twenty months of field work with
these women, who lived in a locked women's world at Hilltop, a large
institution for people with intellectual disabilities. It describes their lives
there prior to the decision to close the institution and it provides an
account of the way deinstitutionalisation in process affected their lives
and those of the people around them.

Essentially, this book is a collection of voices: those of the women who
lived in the locked unit, their families, the women staff who worked with
them and the people who were responsible for closing the institution.
But these voices and stories are heard through my voice, and for this
reason it is important at the beginning of the book that my biases,
interests and limitations be made clear. This chapter, then, describes my
reasons for undertaking the research, provides a brief account of the
methodology used, and outlines the theoretical and personal perspectives which influenced my work as researcher.

## Rationale for the Study

The study began with my questions and concerns about the impact of
ten years of deinstitutionalisation policies on the lives of people with

intellectual disabilities who continued to live in large institutions. In order to explore this issue I gained access to Hilltop, an institution where 440 people were living. The study began with interviews with the staff and managers working there.

Within six weeks of entering the institution I had based myself within Unit N, a locked unit for women at the institution. My motives for selecting this unit for intensive study were personal, pragmatic and research based. The personal motives were complex and were not at all clear at the time, or even now. From my first sight of the women in the grounds of the institution I was fascinated by their loudness and the respect with which staff spoke of them. Perhaps I hoped to learn something from the women's experience which would help me understand my own position as a woman. Perhaps I was drawn to the unit because of the 'challenge' which these women and their lives appeared to pose for me as an individual. Once in the locked unit, I became enmeshed with the women in a complex set of relationships and emotions. I became committed not only to carrying out my research with them: I had a strong interest in ensuring that during deinstitutionalisation they were treated fairly and I very much wanted the quality of their lives to be improved following the closure of the institution. Further, I wanted to give them a voice: I wanted to be a witness to their experiences and to tell their stories.

More pragmatically, while I was regarded with suspicion by staff in other parts of the institution, staff in the locked unit welcomed my presence. They were ready to accommodate my demands for time and access. They saw my entry to the unit as a way of evaluating the work they were doing and as offering an opportunity for gaining knowledge about research and about the women who lived there.

There were also more traditional research-oriented reasons for my decision. The unit had a fearsome reputation in the institution. From my first day I was warned about the people living there, and staff outside the unit talked with anxiety about the possibility of being rostered to it. Consequently, I reasoned that if deinstitutionalisation had impacted positively on the institutional life of these women, who were regarded as the 'outcasts' within the institution, then perhaps generalisations about its impact could be applied to other, less stigmatised groups and individuals.

Finally, as a woman and a feminist, I was concerned that no previous studies had focused on the lives of women in institutions and I was interested in discovering in what ways institutional practices might be influenced by gender.

Four months after I started working in the locked unit, a decision was made to close the institution. My study instantly changed its focus, for here was deinstitutionalisation in practice. From this point on, my research was shaped and driven by the impetus of events. My contact with the women provided a focus for a study of how the ongoing process of deinstitutionalisation affected them and those around them. Because I had been in the institution for some time I was accepted by senior managers and so gained access to all levels of the closure process.

## The Research Methodology

The research involved four stages. The first consisted of *going into* Hilltop and my initial meetings with the people living and working there.The second stage occurred *inside* the institution. During this stage I gained access to the locked unit, spent many hundreds of hours sharing the lives of the women who lived there, and was involved with the staff who worked with them and their families. The third stage involved *coming out* of the institution. During the closure of Hilltop I stayed with the women and watched how decisions were made about their lives. I was a participant observer in the consultations and meetings held to decide where the women would go after the institution closed, and I interviewed the managers and workers responsible for the closure process. In the final stage I moved *outside* the institution in order to reflect on the experience of deinstitutionalisation and to write this book.

### Going In

The formal process of going into Hilltop was not very difficult. The Chief Executive Officer was enthusiastic about the idea of someone carrying out a long-term study there, and permission was readily obtained from the relevant government department. However, these formal requirements did not really 'get me in'.

Staff at the institution had been under frequent attack from the media because of conditions in the institution and were defensive and resistant to the idea of my research. Consequently, each interview with a staff member was an exercise in careful negotiation. My decision during this time to base myself in the locked unit assisted the process of 'getting in'. Unit N was perceived as one of the most difficult to work in and staff from other units respected those who worked there. My commitment to undertake long-term work in the unit led to a more positive attitude towards my research: I was seen as less of a threat to other staff since most of my time was spent confined within one unit. In their view I was effectively locked away.

To get into the locked unit I negotiated a contract with the staff in the unit which involved assisting them with evaluations of some innovative work which they were carrying out. In return they gave me access to the unit and were willing to allow me to be part of its life. Negotiations about access to the unit with the women who lived there occurred only on an informal basis and this was a constant source of concern to me.

## *Inside*

My time in Unit N consisted of making detailed observations of the lives of the women living and working there. The emotional impact of living and working in a large 'total institution' was profound. I was shocked at the lives which the women lived in the locked unit. They were confined behind locked doors with little access to the institutional grounds and even less to the wider community.

Within the unit there was nothing to do and the monotony of the days was broken for some women only by short periods of occupational therapy or by irregular visits from family. Violence was a constant part of life within the unit. Some women were aggressive to each other or to staff; others sought to injure themselves or attacked the building in which they were locked. I watched this in helpless pain and, as a participant observer in the unit, became part of the means of controlling the women. It was not possible to be in the unit and not be active. At times I was afraid of being attacked or of not being able to 'manage' an incident. At other times I was shocked at the speed with which I became institutionalised.

> L. [staff member] was trying to get Brigid to leave the couch and go for a bath. Brigid seized her by the hair and refused to let go. L. tried to remove Brigid's hand. I saw this happening as I came through the door into the day room. I asked L. if she wanted some help and she asked me to hold Brigid's hand while she freed herself. She then asked me to help her lift Brigid off the couch. I started to do so, then realised that I was actually 'manhandling' someone. I stopped. (Field notes)

Through incidents such as this, I became aware of the strength of the staff pressure to conform to the culture in the unit. Without staff support I would not be able to retain my place there. I also experienced at first hand the powerlessness of staff and families in attempting to change the situation for the women.

I spent much time sitting in the day room observing what was happening around me. I talked with the women and took part in their day-to-day activities. These included going for walks, watching television and looking at magazines or cards. I was also part of the unit's routines. At meal times I assisted people who had difficulty in eating, and I helped people go to the toilet or have a bath. I scrubbed floors and mopped up urine and vomit. The work was physically exhausting and emotionally tiring. The unit was noisy, women screamed and shouted, the television (when it worked) was on, the phone rang loudly and there was the constant threat (or reality) of physical aggression.

As time went on, my knowledge of the women living in the unit increased. It was not possible to hold 'formal' interviews even with the women who could speak, but I did hold many informal discussions and conversations with them. In addition to the time spent with the women in the locked unit I spent long hours reading yellowing files which documented their lives in the institution, and also read their General Service Plans (GSPs).

During my twenty months of field work I formally interviewed all members of staff in the unit at least twice. In addition, my field notes included many hundreds of conversations and discussions. Throughout the research process I kept detailed field notes, slipping away from the unit at lunch times and during breaks to write them up before later transcribing them.

### Coming Out

With the decision to close Hilltop, the complexity of the study increased. I obtained permission to be an observer at all management meetings concerned with institutional closure and also of the decision-making processes about the future of the women carried out during that closure.

I interviewed the six managers responsible for the closure of the institution three times throughout the research and carried out individual interviews with their staff who were directly involved with the women. In addition I facilitated group consultations with all project team staff. During this time I continued to spend time with the women living and working in the unit.

I contacted and interviewed eighteen members of the women's families, or their advocates. The time I spent with the families was extremely painful. None of them had been given any opportunity previously to discuss their daughter/sister. Each told stories filled with the pain and grief of their life with the woman before she went to the institution. These stories gave me a different view of individual women. Sometimes the views a family had of their relative were completely contradictory to my experiences with her. Listening to the families' stories, I came to understand the need some had to distance themselves from their relative, and some of the resistance they felt about de-institutionalisation. I was forced to re-examine my previous assumptions and beliefs about the role of families and the views I held about deinstitutionalisation.

I found the gap between my encounters with closure team members and life in the unit enormous. This increased the stress involved in the field work. Further, because of industrial disputes resulting from the closure decision, I found myself privy to information from groups in conflict with each other. Much of this information could not be shared with anyone. Paradoxically, therefore, as my relationships with people at the institution became closer over time, as we worked, ate and talked together I was conscious of an increasing estrangement.

During this time I watched the dismantling of the women's world. It was an extremely intense experience which evoked strong feelings. At different stages I was angry, joyous, grieving, fearful and outraged. Some of my research data suggest that these feelings were experienced by many others involved in the closure process.

My role with the women changed over time. From being a participant and intruder into their lives in the unit, I became an advocate for some of them during consultations to decide their futures. With staff in the unit I tried to provide some support in the transition time before they left the institution. And I held their stories.

*Outside*

The research concluded as the institution closed. As the final months went by I became increasingly a receptacle for the grief and the stories of others. 'You'll tell the story' was a refrain I heard from different people. Others began to plan their futures, new jobs, new homes, a new way of life. I was left symbolically holding the institution and the thousands of stories which form the basis of this book, for while the institution came to an end for those working and living there, I relived the experience through writing about it. There was a trust from those with whom I had been involved that I would tell 'their story' and tell it as they would want it told. Yet this was a trust that in some instances I was forced to betray, for I had to choose the stories and to make of them a new one.

Nor did I finally get outside. I had formed close links with the women who lived in the locked unit and I spent time in following them up after they left the institution. I became an informant to whom others would come to find out how the women's lives had changed. I also kept in contact with the closure team and with the staff with whom I had worked in the unit.

Sharing information gained during my field work with those with whom I had been involved proved difficult. During the field work I had written a series of reviews of the processes of deinstitutionalisation which had been given back to those managing the closure. There had been acceptance of these 'working papers' by those involved and they had proved to be a useful source of information. However, accounts of life in the unit proved confronting for staff who had worked there. Reading draft chapters they relived the sense of powerlessness and the relationships which were broken by the institution's closure. One staff member commented: 'I don't want to read any more. I just want to forget the whole thing.' There have been times, as I struggled with reliving the experiences of my twenty months with the women, that I too have wanted to forget the whole thing.

## The Positions of the Researcher

At different times during this research I held different positions in relation to those with whom I worked and in relation to the data I collected. I deliberately entered the field with the intention of remaining as open as possible to the experience with which I was engaging, and I eschewed adopting a particular theoretical position into which my data might fit. However, I did take particular theoretical frameworks with me into the field work. These provided themes which influenced the conduct of the research.

As the study developed, further themes emerged from my experiences, from involvement with the data and from reflection and reading. In this chapter these two sets of themes are somewhat artificially divided into 'entering' and 'emerging' themes, and while the latter are introduced in this chapter, they receive much greater discussion later in the book. These themes were not always equally important or relevant to me throughout my field work, but they did influence the positions I held during the research process.

### 'Entering' Themes

> It is precisely the encounter between the social scientist's own beliefs and practices and those of the people he or she is studying which makes up whatever understanding we can have of another social reality. (Outhwaite, 1985, p.29)

The experience and theoretical positions I brought with me to the study influenced the way it was carried out, and some became influential too in the way the data were later interpreted.

### Knowledge of Intellectual Disability

Although I had no previous experience of living or working in a total institution, I had worked as a researcher with people with intellectual disabilities in a variety of community settings (Johnson, Andrew and Topp, 1987; O'Brien and Johnson, 1987; O'Brien and Johnson, 1988; Johnson and O'Brien, 1989; O'Brien and Johnson, 1993). I had a firm commitment to the value of deinstitutionalisation and a concern for the fate of those I saw as unnecessarily segregated from the community.

I was interested in exploring 'the personal, subjective experiences of people with developmental (intellectual) disabilities and those around them' (Taylor, Bogdan and Lutfiyya, 1995, p.1) in order to understand better the meaning their lives had for them. From past research and reading I had learned the research skills of clear, straightforward written and spoken expression, the need to share ideas, to provide a relatively informal environment in which to talk to people, and to listen with care and attention (Bogdan and Taylor, 1976; Munro, 1977; Bogdan and Taylor, 1982; Bogdan and Taylor, 1989a; Potts and Fido, 1991; Ferguson, Ferguson and Taylor, 1992a; Booth, 1996).

I had not worked very much with people who were unable to speak directly with me, but I was aware that participant observation, taking time to be with someone and watching my own reactions to their behaviour and feelings would provide guides to communication (Edgerton, 1984a; Biklen and Moseley, 1988; Gleason, 1989; Goode, 1989; Wilkinson, 1989; Sinason, 1992).

*Qualitative Research*

I began this study with a view that a qualitative methodology was the one most suited to my purposes. This view was quickly confirmed as the focus of the research became the lives of the women. Adopting this perspective in order to research did not just mean a focus on qualitative methods, but involved the adoption of a research paradigm described by Ferguson, Ferguson and Taylor (1992b) as 'interpretative qualitative research'. The consequences of using this paradigm profoundly influenced the goal of the research, the way it was carried out and the assumptions on which it was based.

The goal of this study was essentially to 'describe, interpret and to understand' (Ferguson *et al.*, 1992b, p.7) the processes which were impinging on the lives of the women and to explore reactions to them. The major method used to achieve this goal was participant observation. This included active ongoing involvement in the life of the unit over an extended period, discussions with the women who lived there, and interviews with families, advocates, staff and managers. It also included the documentation of meetings and the analysis of documents and files (Edgerton, 1971; Estroff, 1981; Frankenberg, 1982; Gans, 1982; Burgess, 1984; Jorgensen, 1989; Weiner, 1990; Edgerton, 1991; Richardson, 1991).

The study was based on a number of assumptions about the nature of research 'reality' outlined by Ferguson *et al.* (1992b). In particular I held firmly to the view that reality is created and social, and that 'people as social actors construct the reality or truth of a situation' (Ferguson *et al.*, 1992b, p.5). I also believed that the division, promulgated in much empirical research, between the researcher as an objective observer and the subjects to be studied was artificial and that the experiences, values and ideas which I brought to the study were an important part of the data which had to be acknowledged openly as part of the research process (Rose, 1990). Finally, I believed that the data I obtained during the research would be value laden.

The utilisation of a qualitative interpretative methodology meant that rich data were accumulated from field notes, transcribed interviews and texts which were made available during the research (for example 'client files'). It was an open-ended, interactive form of research which sought to 'bridge the gap between stories and research' (Taylor *et al.*, 1995, p.1) .

*Action Research*

My past experience in research had been that carried out from an action research position. There are differing views about the nature of action research (Sanford, 1970; P. A. Clark, 1972; A. W. Clark, 1976; Susman and Evered, 1978; Brown and Tandon, 1983; Carr and Kemmis, 1986; Kemmis, 1990; Chein, Cook and Harding, 1990; McTaggart, 1991; Schratz and Walker, 1995; Jennings, 1996; Stringer, 1997). These views reflect a spectrum ranging from minimal participation by those taking part in the research, to the integral involvement of all those engaged in it. Within the context of this research I used the following definition of action research:

> [Action research] aims to contribute both to the practical concerns of people in an immediate problematic situation and to the goals of social science by joint collaboration within a mutually acceptable ethical frame-work. (Rapoport, 1970, p.499)

I believed that this approach was ethically necessary in working with people who were disadvantaged and from whom I was seeking infor-mation. It was a means of establishing some form of reciprocity.

I saw action research as involving the following characteristics. First, it is collaborative (Rapoport, 1970; Cherns, 1976), involving the develop-ment of relationships with others at the research site. Second, it is participatory, with people involved in the research taking part in its design and implementation (Cunningham, 1976). Inevitably, this means that it must problematise the relationship between researcher and participants (Finger, 1990). Third, it is change oriented and aims to alter conditions or behaviour. Finally it involves a focus on group inter-actions and relationships (Susman and Evered, 1978).

The nature of the people and the organisation involved in this re-search precluded a full commitment to a participatory action research approach, however the research was shaped and influenced by a com-mitment to that underlying philosophy. In practice, action research became an integral part of the research in the following ways. A num-ber of different forums were developed which involved people in the research process. These included a group of senior managers at the institution who met to talk about work concerns relevant to my study and who provided advice and information. I also participated in staff seminars and joined a planning group which organised a three-day seminar to conclude the closure project.

An informal group of staff at the locked unit initiated and then participated with me in designing an evaluation of an innovation being developed in the unit. In addition to its usefulness to them, this work was helpful in developing my own study.

Later I worked with managers of the deinstitutionalisation process to provide two policy papers about it. These were then fed back to staff and were used to assist in the programme of closure.

*Developing Theory from the Research Experience*

The study was essentially ethnographic in nature. It involved me in twenty months of participant observation and in a study of actions and activities as they occurred (Burgess, 1982; Hammersley and Atkinson, 1992). It was open-ended and flexible in nature and it involved a de-tailed collection of rich descriptive data obtained from many different sources (Bogdan and Biklen, 1992). It also involved a reflexive approach in which my experiences and reactions to them became part of the research data (N. Rose, 1990).

Although I began with a particular focus and a plan of action for the study, the research design developed largely as a result of reflecting on the experiences in which I was involved at the institution. From such reflections arose questions for which I sought answers. For these reasons it was important to keep the collected data as broad and rich as possible. However, my intention was not purely descriptive: I was also concerned to develop from my experiences theories which seemed to best fit them.

*Reflexivity*

There are many voices in this study, but inevitably they are all heard through my voice. For this reason, if for no other, it was important that

I become 'subject' to my own research. The questions I asked, the observations I made, the knowledge and information I gained from others were constructed and interpreted by me as researcher (Steier, 1992; Shakespeare and Atkinson, 1993). Further, examining my own emotional reactions to situations and exploring some of the unconscious means I used to defend myself against the stress of the women's world enabled me to hypothesise about some of the reactions of others in the situation. This was particularly so in interpreting the reactions of the women during the closure process, for they were often not able to articulate their concerns verbally. An examination of my own reactions acted as a signpost to their possible responses (Sinason, 1992).

As a woman, working primarily with women, it was important to recognise as part of the research the mutuality and the differences in our experience if I were to develop a view of the world in which they lived (Oakley, 1990).

This research, then, has been developed from a number of different positions, all of which acknowledge or emphasise the importance of including the researcher as subject in the study. This inclusion was dictated by the positions of the researcher, the goals of the research and the nature of the study itself.

### 'Emerging' Themes

As the research progressed over the twenty months, different themes and theories became important in my ongoing analysis of the research process and the data. While some of these themes originated in an earlier personal interest, their dominance in the research at a particular time was dictated by my efforts to understand what was happening both to the people with whom I was involved and to myself.

### Psychoanalytic Theories and Insights

I had entered this research with an interest in exploring how psychoanalytic theory might be useful in analysing group and organisational practice and behaviour. As I experienced it, life in the locked unit involved a situation in which the women living in the unit and those working with them were locked together in inescapable intimacy, aggression and pain.

The work of I. Menzies Lyth (1988a,b) on defences against anxiety became increasingly relevant and important. Lyth's study in a large hospital setting revealed that many of the hospital practices and staff relationships were governed by the nurses' need to defend themselves against anxieties inherent in their work and relationships with patients. This finding became an important part of my work theoretically and in practice. Further, the world in which I found myself in the locked unit (and later, the world of the dying institution) was a strange one to me. It evoked in me strong conscious and unconscious reactions with which I had to work over the twenty months of my involvement. For example, over time, as I moved through the process of deinstitutionalisation and began to form relationships with different groups, I became aware that I was holding many of the anxieties and some of the pain which individuals and groups were experiencing at Hilltop. It became a matter of personal survival and an important part of my research to examine these reactions.

Exploring the anxiety, depression and anger which I experienced at different stages of the research enabled me to better understand the reactions of those with whom I was working. It also assisted me in examining some of the unconscious processes which were operating both within the locked world and in the wider world of institutional closure. Such a process is well documented in psychoanalytic literature in relation to both understanding individuals and organisations (Dartington, Miller and Gwynne, 1981; Money-Kyrle, 1988; Lyth, 1988a,b,c; De Board, 1990; Sinason, 1992). However, it cannot be done alone. I sought and found a psychoanalytically trained woman to assist me in working through these reactions and exploring how they might assist my understanding of worlds in which the women lived.

### Feminist Approach to Research

While I did not originally intend to carry out research with a specific emphasis on women's experiences of deinstitutionalisation, this rapidly became the focus of the research. Once this occurred, feminist theory and methodology became increasingly important in its development. The women, the social context in which they lived, and the changes occurring for them during deinstitutionalisation were the key focus of the research.

I became increasingly committed as a researcher to revealing (as far as I could) the experiences of the women as they were living them (Harding, 1987; Fine and Gordon, 1992). It became clear from the data I was collecting that an important component in the shaping of these experiences was gender.

To have attempted to treat the women as 'objects' of research would have been unacceptable ethically, for it would have added to the objectification which formed part of their experience. It would also have denied my own position as a woman and as a fringe dweller in the many worlds which I entered during the research; a position which became an important ingredient in the analysis carried out throughout.

The voices of *women* with intellectual disabilities have not been heard clearly within the feminist literature (Hillyer, 1993; Binstead, 1995). They have also not received much emphasis within the disability field, although some stories have been included in anthologies about women and disability (see for example Howe, 1993; Wilmuth and Holcomb, 1993; J. Morris, 1996). The stories of the women living in the locked unit had not been heard. This imposed a responsibility on me as researcher to ensure that I heard such stories and that I was as sensitive as possible to both the common experiences of the group as women and to their unique experiences as individuals (Fuss, 1990; Spelman, 1990).

Discussions which I held with the women living and working in the unit were informal and involved a dialogue which ranged widely across their lives and mine. There was a strong emphasis on story telling and narrative. Such an approach is inherent in feminist approaches to research (Graham, 1984; Roberts, 1990; Davies, 1992; Fine and Gordon, 1992).

*Subjectivity*

This study did not begin with a focus on subjectivity. However, this issue became increasingly important as a result of my experiences with the women in both the locked unit and during deinstitutionalisation. For twenty months I watched as the women were thought about, talked about, written about, documented and dissected by all those involved with them.

From one perspective, the women's subjectivity was reconstituted every time they were spoken about, yet through all of these discussions they remained enigmatic. In the constant revelation of their subjectivity their voices, stating who they saw themselves to be, were silent. My experience with them challenged the traditional humanistic view of subjectivity as a fixed essence which provides a coherent and consistent means of defining the individual. Consequently, the writings of feminist postmodern theorists such as Weedon (1987), Hollway (1989), Flax (1990) and Wearing (1996) became increasingly important in my attempts to understand the constantly changing processes of subjectivity.

My increasing unease at this situation led to questions which became a major concern in this study. How were the women in the locked unit known? And by whom? Why were they in the locked unit of the institution? How did the ways of 'knowing' the women change during deinstitutionalisation? An exploration of these questions had a number of implications for both the methodology of this study and for the way in which the data were interpreted. It led to a focus on the subjectivity of the women as constituted and revealed by others. It also led to a consideration of how the women themselves revealed their subjectivity and how their voices were received by others. I began to explore different ways of seeing and thinking about subjectivity. It was not something held by the women and imparted to others, but was socially constituted by those who interacted with the women either directly or indirectly. It flowed and changed according to time and to the people who held a view about the women. It was always fragmented and disjointed, and sometimes it was constituted by others with a certainty which brooked no questioning. For in a very real sense the women became subject to the ways in which they were constituted by others.

The shifting, complex nature of subjectivity which I experienced in relation to the women was reflected in theoretical conceptualisations which became integral to this book (Foucault, 1976; Foucault, 1980; Henriques, Hollway, Urwin and Walkerdine, 1984; Frosh, 1987; Weedon, 1987; Hollway, 1989; Ramazanoglu, 1993). The definition of subjectivity which best summarises the theoretical approach taken in this book is as follows:

> we use 'subjectivity' to refer to individuality and self-awareness – the condition of being a subject – but understand in this usage that subjects are dynamic and multiple, always positioned in relation to particular discourses and practices and produced by these – the condition of being 'subject'. (Henriques *et al.*, 1984, p.3)

The problematic nature of the subjectivity of the women in the locked unit is a central theme in this book and forms the basis for my analysis of their experiences in the locked unit and during deinstitutionalisation.

*Discourse*

My concern with the subjectivity of the women led inevitably to an exploration of the basis for its constitution by others. Increasingly I became aware that knowledge and the power involved in prescribed associated practices were crucial in determining how the women's subjectivity was 'captured' by others, so the ways in which knowledge, practices and power were exercised in relation to the women became a dominant theme in the study.

These themes find their clearest expression in the work of Michel Foucault (1967, 1970, 1976, 1979, 1991a, 1997a,b,c) and particularly in his exploration of discourse as 'different ways of structuring areas of knowledge and social practice' (Fairclough, 1992, p.3). Of necessity, then, the nature of discourse became an important theoretical consideration in this study. However, discourse is a difficult and ambiguous concept (Ferguson, 1984) at least in part because it has been used in diverse and sometimes contradictory ways by writers coming from different theoretical and disciplinary positions (Fairclough, 1992).

In this research, discourses were defined as:

> ways of constituting knowledge, together with the social practices, forms of subjectivity and power relations which inhere in such knowledges and the power relations between them. Discourses are more than ways of thinking and producing meaning. They constitute the 'nature of the body', unconscious and conscious mind and emotional life of the subjects which they seek to govern. (Weedon, 1987, p.108)

This definition suggests a number of characteristics of discourses which were central to this study. First, discourses specify truth as it is known at any particular time in history (for example the nature of intellectual disability) and they also specify what can and cannot be said in relation to the subjects with which they are concerned. Second, they are concerned with the exercise of power in relation to the subjects which they constitute. Power is constituted in the discourses, for they produce truth and 'we cannot exercise power without truth' (Foucault, 1980, p.93). So the discourse which defines people with intellectual disabilities also specifies practices and rules by which these people will be treated in the community. Third, discourses both constitute and reveal the subjectivity of the people with whom they are concerned. This does not just occur from outside the individual who is subject to the discourse. Rather, the individual also constitutes his or her own subjectivity from within this framework (Foucault, 1978; N. Rose, 1990). Fourth, discourses are themselves subject to change and challenge (Foucault, 1979, 1980; Weedon, 1987; Ramazanoglu, 1993). Finally, discourses involve a diffuse use of power which is not exercised by any one group or individual but which permeates our institutions, our communities and us as individuals.

This study did not involve a detailed discourse analysis of the data (Potter and Wetherell, 1987; Burman and Parker, 1993; Wilkinson and Kitzinger, 1995) but rather adopted a critical approach to discourse in that it was concerned with:

> showing how discourse is shaped by relations of power and ideologies, and the constructive effects discourse has upon social identities, social relations and systems of knowledge and belief, neither of which is normally apparent to discourse participants. (Fairclough, 1992, p.12)

In essence, then, this study became one which focused on the ways in which particular discourses constituted and revealed the subjectivity of the women living in the locked unit. It was also concerned with the limits of such discourses in 'capturing the subjectivity' of the women.

### The Structure of this Book

This book consists of phases of action and reflection. It is divided into three parts which correspond broadly to my experience as researcher. In each of the first two parts are chapters which document descriptively the field work. Each part concludes with a theoretical chapter which is a reflection on the field work. Part 1 focuses on the lives of the women before deinstitutionalisation. It describes their lives in the locked unit and their relationships with family members and advocates. It also explores the paths by which they came to the locked unit. The final chapter in Part 1 (Chapter 4) provides an analysis of the data presented in the previous chapters and examines the nature of the discourses which played through the lives of the women. Part 2 is concerned with the process of deinstitutionalisation as it affected the women living in the locked unit. It concludes with an analysis of the nature of deinstitutionalisation as it occurred at Hilltop and of the ways in which this changed (or did not change) the discourses constituting the subjectivity of the women. Part 3 moves outside the institution to examine the nature of the discourses around institutional life and deinstitutionalisation.

Each of the descriptive chapters consists of a number of voices: those of the women, those of the people involved with them at a particular time, and my own. Each of these voices is of necessity interpreted through mine (as writer), but I have sought to reveal the different cadences, tones and nuances of the stories which individuals and groups told me. However, both the women's and my own stories proved particularly difficult to position within the chapters.

The women who had proved resistant to categorisation and positioning in their lives proved equally recalcitrant in my study. Because it is important that their voices be heard and because I want them to emerge as individuals to the reader, I include in each descriptive chapter one of the women's stories. It was not possible to include every woman's story in detail. Individual stories were included because they appeared to best highlight the themes of a particular chapter. At times these stories disrupt the flow of the narrative. On principle I resisted the temptation to place individual stories in an appendix or to 'box them in' as separate from the mainstream of the study, for it seemed to me that the women's lives had been spent in one or other (or both) of these situations. If the stories appear disruptive to the reader, then you too are experiencing at one level the way the women were perceived and managed by all who came in contact with them.

My own stories too were interruptions to the flow of the narrative. Yet, as should be apparent from earlier sections of this chapter, I was committed to the view that the experiences I had in my twenty months of field work were a legitimate source of data. Each descriptive chapter of this book therefore contains a story which was important to me personally and as a researcher. Similarly, I have written in the first person throughout, both to signal my presence as researcher and to indicate that I too was subject to the research process.

# PART I

# *Inside the Institution*

They don't bother about me. They let me be.
They say, 'Nothing can happen.'
(Rainer Maria Rilke, [1906] 1981, p.123)

To understand the lives of the women living in the locked unit it is important to understand something of the nature of Hilltop itself. This brief introduction provides a description of the institution as I knew it and places it within a historical context.

People with intellectual disabilities had lived and died at Hilltop for 126 years. While the total numbers of people living there varied during that time, it seemed that nothing could happen to alter fundamentally the ways in which they spent their lives. Certainly parents and families who were interviewed during the research for this book believed that in placing their relative in the institution they were making a lifelong 'commitment'. This belief had remained largely unshaken throughout the movement towards deinstitutionalisation in the 1980s.

Hilltop was the archetypal 'total institution' defined by Goffman (1961, p.11) as 'a place of residence and work where a large number of like-situated individuals, cut off from the wider society for an appreciable period of time, together lead an enclosed formally administered round of life'. Its history, the stories of life within its walls and its very appearance epitomised the text-book stereotypes (see for example Goffman, 1961; Wolfensberger, 1975; Radford and Tipper, 1988; Armstrong, 1990; Rothman, 1990; Potts and Fido, 1991). Built in the 1860s, its buildings consisted of twenty-two old bluestone and timber units, which straggled up a hillside behind a monolithic and grand administration block.

The main administration block of solid red brick with a central tower is an ornate piece of architecture. It stands out from the hill, seeming to lean back against the sky. On either side of this building a brick fence stretches into the distance as if the main building is standing guard. The impression of entering another world and my sense of powerlessness in relation to the solidity of the architecture was heightened by the steep steps I had to climb to reach the front door. The building looks as if it were made to last forever. (Field notes)

The institution was situated on a hill some forty kilometres from the nearest city, and the small town which lay at the foot of the hill had provided generations of workers and also supplied the needs of the people living at the institution. In the past, Hilltop had included a farm which was now largely abandoned. The buildings were surrounded by perfectly kept gardens but the institution itself was poorly serviced, for example the central heating system with its hissing, gurgling pipes running around the grounds was not introduced until the late 1980s. Further, in spite of the acknowledged needs of the people living at the institution, there were minimal specialist staff. Occupational therapy could be offered to only a minority of residents on a part-time basis, and there was a small behavioural intervention team and one social worker. A human relations counsellor and a sexual counsellor were available on request.

The reasons for Hilltop's establishment too were similar to those of other institutions built to 'contain' people with disabilities. These included the need to protect the community from those labelled as different and dangerous, and the need to protect people with intellectual disabilities from the rest of the community. Institutions were also seen as a means to train such people for re-entry into the community. In relation to people with intellectual disabilities, institutional development was associated with increasing technical means of identifying people with 'low IQs' and with a corresponding anxiety in the general population and among some scientists that people with such IQs were likely to be poor, dangerous or criminal (N. Rose, 1979; Trent, 1995). The rise of the eugenics movement in the late nineteenth century led to further community concerns that people with low IQs were a possible threat to the genetic health of the wider population. Placing such people within secure establishments offered the possibility of segregating them from the community. Remnants of these views and beliefs could still be found in the knowledge and practices of some staff and in families of people living at Hilltop.

Over time, as in other similar institutions, the numbers of residents and the labels attached to them had changed. For almost one hundred years people with psychiatric and intellectual disabilities had lived there together. However, since the 1960s Hilltop had been designated a training centre for people with intellectual disabilities. In 1966 the institution had had a maximum capacity of 1,500 people but by the 1990s the number of people living there had declined to 440 (Community Services Victoria, undated). This decline was due in part to the ageing nature of the population at Hilltop (Community Services Victoria, 1989; Owen, Cooper and Barber, 1994) and to the decision in 1989 by the Chief Executive Officer not to take new admissions to the institution. Further, throughout the 1980s there had been a steady trickle of people leaving Hilltop to take up new lives in the community. (Such deinstitutionalisation happens first for those who are less disabled, younger, higher functioning and problem-free (Seltzer, Sherwood, Seltzer and Sherwood, 1981).) Consequently, compared to earlier times, the population at Hilltop in the late 1980s was older, had higher dependency needs, displayed 'challenging behaviours' or was more intellectually disabled (Neilson Associates, 1988a). One staff member commented that: 'Those that could live in the community have already gone.'

In the 1960s and 1970s a series of books and articles described total institutions in the United States and the United Kingdom (Blatt and Kaplan, 1966; Blatt, 1970; P. Morris, 1969; Wolfensberger, 1975; Blatt, 1981a). These books were highly critical of the quality of life offered to the people living in such institutions. They documented in words and sometimes pictures a closed world in which people lived in sometimes appalling physical conditions with little meaningful activity, and where abuse and indifference on the part of staff were perceived to be common. This documentation appeared to have had little impact on the lives of people living at Hilltop although there had been increasing criticism of the institution throughout the 1980s. It seemed as if nothing could change the lives of the people living there.

# CHAPTER 2

# *Life in the Unit*

So long as you want her faceless, without smell
or voice, so long as she does not squat
to urinate, or scratch herself, so long
as she does not snore beneath her blanket
. . .
so long as you try to simplify her meaning.
                            *(Adrienne Rich, 1981, p.36)*

The faces, voices or behaviour of the women in the locked unit were the
stated reasons for their removal from the community and from the rest
of the institution. Once they were exiled, it was rare for them to find
their way back to a less restrictive home. Within the locked unit, they
lived their lives in a complex interplay of relations with each other and
with the women staff who cared for them. Outside, little was known
about their day-to-day existence, although stories were prevalent about
the women themselves. Consequently, as a woman researcher based in
the unit, I had a unique opportunity to experience and to gather stories
about a little-known world.

## Unit N: Its Geography

Unit N was the only locked women's unit in the institution. It was near
the top of the hill, hidden away behind other buildings from the rest
of Hilltop and the nearby town. It was situated at the back of the
institution, far from the administration block and the front entrance.
The unit was surrounded, except in front, by a four-foot-high wire fence.
From the outside, the building resembled a nineteenth century rural
school, with a high pitched iron roof, and walls which were a mixture of

timber and bluestone. The building was rambling, with the rear almost at right angles to the front. The old-world feeling was heightened by the peppercorn trees shading the fenced-in lawn at the back of the unit.

> The unit is composed of a large dayroom, dining room, three large dormitories, six single rooms under an open verandah, clothes storage areas, kitchen (where food is served but not prepared), staff office and toilet. There are few pictures on the walls which are peeling and in need of painting. The dayroom is sparsely furnished, and due to the high ceilings and vinyl flooring, sound is amplified. There are two fenced in outside yards with chairs and tables. One has a concrete floor and a rotunda while the other is grassed with two large trees. Clients are unable to move freely around the unit or to initiate activities as staff are required to accompany them to open (unlock) the doors. (Staff member, cited in Warren and Johnson, 1992, p.1)

This description, written by a staff member in 1988, was still generally accurate when I arrived in the early 1990s. However, some changes were occurring as a result of staff pressure for a better physical environment. The open verandah had been enclosed, and during my time at Hilltop further changes were made. Furniture was added to the day room and dining room. The day room and dormitories were painted and partitioned so that smaller and more private spaces could be created. Bright curtains were added to the windows and pictures were on the walls. These alterations made the unit superficially more comfortable, but were not able to change radically the institutional structure and the echoing spaces. Visually, the unit was spartan but clean, and there were signs of some efforts to add touches of comfort. However, there were no personal belongings in evidence in the unit.

As a newcomer to the unit I found the environment chaotic and overwhelming.

> J. [staff member] unlocked the door to the room in which there was a crowd of women. There was no furniture. The noise hit me, a wall of sound, as I went in. One woman was standing in the centre of the room screaming. One was walking around the room holding an old black shoe in her hand.
> Others were shouting. The television was going. Some women walked around the room. Others sat on the floor. Some were undressed. One was completely naked. Others, while dressed, did not have shoes. The room was large. It was difficult to observe much because I was instantly surrounded by women who wanted to touch me or put their arms around me. One, Joyce, asked me to ring her mother. She said she felt strange. (Field notes)

The noise was constant and stressful. The women working in the unit commented that this was its 'worst feature'. The women living there rarely commented about the noise, although Dora would yell at women who were screaming to 'shut up'. Within the day room there was a constant background of shouts, calls and loud voices, interspersed with screams. Sometimes walls, windows or pieces of furniture were banged furiously by a woman. Sometimes they were broken. Doors slammed, people cried or laughed. The intervals of silence were always short. Sometimes the television or music from loudspeakers competed with the noise of the women. The sound of the telephone, which was amplified to the day room, was an intermittent and noisy intrusion.

In addition to the noise, there was a pervasive and unpleasant smell in the unit. The smell was not as bad as in some other parts of Hilltop, but it was present constantly. It was a smell made up of different ingredients; the smell of twenty-seven women living and working in two rooms. It was the smell of food distributed in a closed space. It was the underlying smell of urine and faeces and the disinfectant used to clean them from the floors. It was the smell of breath tainted with drugs. The smell permeated everyone's hair and clothing.

The locked unit was regarded as one of the worst at the institution in terms of its physical environment. Perhaps this was why it had been chosen for a group of women who were exiled from the rest of the institution.

## The Women Living in the Unit

This section introduces the women living in the unit as individuals (through Brigid's story) and as a group.

### Brigid's Story

> Brigid is a slight woman who is under five feet tall. She has short, sparse brown hair (which she pulls out), a round elfish face and brilliant blue eyes. In common with most of the women in the unit, her two front teeth have been removed to prevent her from biting herself or other people. Brigid has a wicked chuckle and shouts and screams loudly. She does not speak or use any sign language. She is always alert to movement around the unit and watches the other women carefully. Brigid has no family, no friends and no advocates. Brigid is one of the youngest women living in Unit N. (Field notes)

Brigid was twenty-six and had lived at Hilltop since she was five years old. I gleaned fragmented accounts of her early history from older staff and from her file notes. Diagnosed at birth as having Down's syndrome, Brigid was left by her mother at a children's home. Approximately twelve months later she was transferred to Lonsdale Lodge (an institution for people with intellectual disabilities). When she was five she moved to the children's unit at Hilltop. Because Brigid was small, staff carried her around until she was about ten years old. She was a favourite with staff working in the children's unit. Some staff saw this treatment of Brigid as the reason for her difficult behaviours: 'We made her the way she is.'

The picture of her as a child within the institution is desolate. She is described as a:

> [m]oderately disabled Downs Syndrome child with no visitors. She has no speech. Requires full care. Doubly incontinent. Hardly joins the others. Behaviour problems from time to time. Aggressive to other children. Doing well on [M]odecate. Attends school on sessional basis. (Unit manager, file notes, 1977)

At some time in the 1980s (unspecified in her file) Brigid was sent to Unit N. Since her final exit from school at twenty-one, she had had no outside activities, however within the day room Brigid had found many things to occupy her time. She had a marked territory which she patrolled, moving from chair to chair. She watched for an open door into the bathroom and would run screaming down the length of the day room to slam it shut, chuckling as she returned to her seat. Brigid spent much of the day removing her clothes and throwing them onto the floor. She would then sit on the couch, touching her genitals or waiting for a staff member to put her clothes back on. Often within three minutes she would remove them again. Sometimes she played with staff: cuddling, playing games of 'Who can stand taller on the couch?' and games of mock aggression. All of these called forth shouts of laughter from her. Such games could degenerate into violence if staff left her, or sometimes for no *apparent* reason. Brigid hit and bit the other women living and working in the unit. She would seize someone else's hair and hang on until the two were separated by a third person.

Brigid sometimes smeared and threw faeces, and was confined to her room at night because of her tendency to get up and attack the other women. She was also aggressive to herself. She headbanged violently, throwing herself backwards into walls or forwards onto tables or the floor. She slapped her head repeatedly with her hands and fists. Efforts by staff to stop this kind of behaviour failed, and Brigid wore scars and marks across her head and face. She also sometimes bore the marks of aggression from other women living in the unit.

In the time I was at Hilltop, I never saw Brigid leave the institution. She rarely went for walks in the grounds, as she had a tendency to sit down and refuse to move once she was out of the unit. Staff were then forced to wait, sometimes for long periods, until she was ready to go on. On one occasion they had to send for a car and extra staff to bring her back.

Brigid was a legend around the institution, and stories abounded about her behaviour, her character and her appearance. She was commonly called 'the devil's child', and older staff claimed that a scar on her stomach was where Satan had entered her. Magical properties were also assigned to this scar by one staff member who commented that it 'had started small but got bigger by itself'.

Within the unit Brigid wielded great power among the women. They were afraid of her, though some also talked of her with affection. Her attacks were difficult to anticipate and were accompanied by laughter once she saw the victim in tears or on the floor. Other women left clear spaces between themselves and her.

Efforts were made to control her behaviour with medication: over the years she had been given Stelazine and Modecate (see Glossary under 'medications'). These had now been eliminated and Brigid was taking 50 ml of Melleril twice a day with more when 'needed'. Staff had no organised programmes for Brigid although her General Service Plan (GSP) stated that there were 'informal programmes to reduce her aggressive and disruptive behaviour'. These programmes consisted of desperate, inconsistent and sometimes bizarre efforts on the part of staff to curb Brigid's 'challenging behaviour'. For example staff sometimes dressed Brigid after she had taken her clothes off; at other times they put her discarded clothing on top of a cupboard and refused to give it to her. Staff dressed themselves in Brigid's discarded clothes in an effort to get her to claim them back. They threatened to tip a cup of water over her if she refused to move (Brigid was very afraid of water). Finally, at times, Brigid was left alone in the day room as punishment and all the other women were evacuated to the dining room. These measures varied depending on who was on duty, and over the years had met with no success. Staff assessments in the 1990s varied little from the note on her file from 1981, which said:

> Brigid's behaviour has always been, and still is, unacceptable. She is constantly seeking attention. She is getting it by spitting, throwing food and faeces, attacking peers and staff. Punishment, withdrawal of food, time out, being ignored, is no deterrent. (File note, 1981)

However, the women working in the unit regarded Brigid with affection as well as frustration. They respected her energy and spirit and were protective of her to other people, commenting that 'Brigid's not so bad', or 'she's just like my little daughter, really'. They talked of how she used to cuddle up with a former staff member for ten hours without moving. They would cuddle her themselves, risking hair pulling and would mirror her loud kisses. They were wary of accepting these kisses, other than at a distance, because of the risk of being bitten.

The sense of desperation and the ambivalence of staff in relation to Brigid are expressed clearly in a statement of her likes and dislikes, which was sent to her new home following the closure of Hilltop:

Brigid enjoys inflicting pain upon others. Brigid enjoys 1:1 interactions with staff. Brigid enjoys eating and going for walks. Brigid enjoys using the trampoline. Brigid enjoys giving and receiving affection. Brigid enjoys cold drinks.

Brigid dislikes being ignored or isolated from others. Brigid dislikes large volumes of water e.g. swimming pools etc. Brigid dislikes noise. Brigid dislikes hot drinks. (Note from Client Profile, 1992)

### The Women of Unit N: A Snapshot

It is 9.30 in the morning. The sunlight is slanting through the windows in the day room, while the dining room remains cool and dim. Four women are down in the dining room. Joyce sits in the lounge area watching the television. Kate, who is blind, sits beside her in an armchair. Kate's knees are drawn up under her chin and are held with her arms, while her head rests on her knees. Rhonda sits in lotus position on the floor of the dining room. She is humming to herself and swaying from side to side. June has been exiled to the dining room because of a fight with Dora. She paces the floor, waiting for a staff member to come through either of the two doors leading into the dining room. When B. [staff member] walks into the dining room [June] rushes to her to show her perpetually sore finger and to say 'My finger, a bit sore.' With this comment, she laughs nervously.

Inside the day room, Kirsten stands by the glass door leading into the dining room. She gazes out through the panes. She holds her hands on either side of her face and whimpers quietly. In one of her hands she holds a plastic mug which she rarely relinquishes. Brigid sits on the central couch in the room. As I watch she strips off her track suit pants, top and undies [briefs], throwing them to the floor and laughing. She then sits down again, looking at the nearest staff member, who after a moment gets up and dresses her again.

Lena sits primly on the couch, her hands folded in front of her and her feet placed together on the floor. She is dressed carefully in a grey and red skirt and jumper. She watches everyone carefully and has an air of waiting expectantly ... for what?

Vera and Ilse, two very small women in their fifties, come hand in hand to ask me to unlock the doors so that they can 'go down' to the staff office. There, they will stand in the cold and chairless passage to escape the other women who 'might beat us up'. Jodie sits in an armchair with her white and black bag looped over her arm. She is looking at the pictures of make-up and hair styles in a torn women's magazine.

Iris, grey-haired and bent, sits with her head down, looking at the magazines which she has held in her hands since she got up and which lay hidden under her pillow all night. Una paces the room, an unseen running track guiding her footsteps around its perimeter. She rarely stops during the day. Faye marches the length of the day room, slumps into a chair, and shouts 'Go away!' as a staff member walks towards her. Rosalind picks up a piece of fluff from the floor and offers it, with a smile, to L. [staff member]. This action will be repeated countless times in a day.

Dora sits, frustrated, in front of the broken television and thumps it in a vain effort to make it work. Inge, back bent, rushes across the room and standing in front of the window, bends over screaming. Laura stands, her arms raised and bent against her head. As I watch she walks stiffly towards a staff member and screams 'Want me dinner', not just once, but time after time after time. Bettina turns circles in the centre of the floor, first one way for several minutes, then the other. She seems oblivious of all around her; her eyes are staring straight ahead and she smiles. Doris is collapsed in a chair. Staff describe her as birdlike and have nicknamed her 'robin'. Apparently she will remain in a state of withdrawn silence for days or weeks, until she begins to enter a manic phase.

Absent from the room is Jane, who after breakfast said she wanted to 'go up' to her room. She generally only reappears for lunch. People rarely go to visit her and she remains distant from the other women. She is probably watching television, smoking or sleeping.

Elaine too has said that she wants to be 'up in the dormitory'. I know that Elaine will periodically come down to ask for cigarettes which she will be given in the staff office, or she will ask to go to the kiosk. The other women are not allowed to go to the dormitory without a staff member because of fears that they will destroy furniture, steal clothes, become aggressive or have an epileptic seizure.

There are three staff on duty in the day room. Two of them are sitting on chairs in the centre of the room and the third has got up to put Brigid's clothes back on. (Field notes)

This introductory account of an individual and the group of women reveals some of the themes and issues which became of paramount concern to me during this research. Although it was relatively easy to watch the women in the day room and to observe their behaviour minutely, they remained an enigma. What was the world for them? What did they know of the world outside? How did they perceive their relations with each other and with the women working in the unit? Why did they do the things they did? These questions were not only those of an outsider. Frequently staff commented: 'I don't know why she does it', for it was not possible to find answers easily to these and other questions by asking the women themselves. Eight of them used no spoken language and their needs were inferred by others living and working in the unit. Six of the women could speak, make their needs known clearly and talk with each other or with staff. However, it was difficult to talk with them directly about their experience of living in the unit as they usually gave only brief positive responses before moving on to other topics. The remaining women had some words and used these repetitively and creatively to achieve many different purposes. However, communication problems were not the only reason the women were difficult to 'know'. To varying degrees, they were locked away by the label of intellectual disability, by their difficulties in communicating (for whatever reason), and because the messages they sent were often not heard. Brigid provides perhaps the most extreme example of this situation. In writing about her, I find it impossible to know what her actions meant to her. When she pulled her hair, was this what she thought she was doing, or was she testing whether it was part of her? Was her head hurting; was this a way of making contact; was it a statement of self-hatred; or was it an inherent part of her disability?

The fragmented account of individuals given in the previous field note reflects the experience of being in the unit. Although I came to have richer and more detailed pictures of the women over time, my observations of their lives as lived in the institution remained disjointed. Living with a group of people in a confined and very stressful space meant that there was little time to spare for any individual. People came and went through the doors of the day room; they sat almost invisibly on the chairs; or they became aggressive and vocal. Only by being aggressive or vocal could they be sure of attention, which would be short-lived and designed to control their behaviour. Yet at the same time, the field note reveals a sense of women leading lives which were separate from their custodians, of having concerns, interests, relationships and a social structure which did not involve the staff. The women made do with what they had in order to create a niche for themselves within their locked world. Within this world they remained very much individuals, exerting will and demonstrating by their behaviour and their appearance that they were unique and, most of all, that they were survivors.

These characteristics led me to have strong and differentiated feeling reactions towards them. For example I felt protective of Kirsten and sought ways to encourage contact with her, waiting patiently with hand outstretched for her fleeting contact. I felt afraid of Brigid for much of my time in the unit, uncertain about when and if she would attack me, and upset when it happened. I found her laughter at someone else's pain particularly shocking and it took a long time to come to some interpretative understanding of the meaning of my reactions. With the fear, as time went on, I became conscious of other feelings towards Brigid – of affection, pain at her life and guilt at my inability to change her lot.

The women of Unit N were isolated women, women who evoked strong ambivalence in those around them, women who were difficult to 'know' and whose lives were played out within complex relationships and group structures within a microcosmic world. They were also women who were subject to constant surveillance both day and night, by each other and by the staff. During this study I too added my gaze. The nature of the gaze to which the women were subject and the way this influenced their lives is a major theme in this study.

## The Women Working in the Unit

Eighteen women worked in the unit. On each day shift, five women were involved in direct care and management duties and two women were involved in cleaning and in providing meals. Two women were rostered for duty each night. It was totally a women's world.

Men were excluded from the unit because some of the women living there did not like them, because of management fears of possible sexual abuse of the women and because of anxiety that the women might 'falsely' accuse male staff of abuse.

> Staff in this unit live their lives with ambiguity. They infer need and anticipate action and trouble from gestures, from inarticulate comments, from a facial expression or a changed location of an individual. They sometimes ignore and often respond to the constant demands, which can be verbal or nonverbal in nature. They stand, rather than sit, ready to separate and soothe when violence or aggression erupts. They manage: the laundry, meals, walks, comfort, bed making, cleaning up, cleaning teeth, washing faces and bottoms, bathing and swabbing the concrete bathroom floors with mops, giving medication.
>
> They wait: for breakfast, for tea breaks, for the opportunity each day to take a group out of the unit, for the phone call which leads to more staff shortages as one of them is called away to another unit. They sit with and hold the clients. They are affectionate, concerned, in control, angry and frustrated, impatient. (Field notes)

The women staff ranged in age from their mid-twenties to their forties. With two exceptions they had not chosen to be rostered into the unit, however they had often been carefully selected to work there by senior managers. One staff member said: 'I had already been told that I was one of those people they could send to Unit N and I would be okay' (Interview with D.). Other staff, finding their way to the unit accidentally, were then selected by the unit manager for permanent positions.

When staff talked about their work in the unit, they saw it as being primarily about caring for the women living there. This care tended to be defined in terms of physical attention: 'The jobs I do are to help with dressing and bathing them, help with cleaning and [to] make sure they're not wet and put out their clothes and make them look tidy and keep them warm' (Interview with I.). This care was also defined in terms of teaching independent living skills: 'I try to teach them manners and that' (Interview with L.). Generally there was a consistent core of staff in the unit, although on a daily basis, there were often absences due to illness or staff shortages in other units.

The unit manager and deputies had been in the unit for approximately two years and the other staff had been there from between three months and six years. If a staff member could cope within the unit, then the unit managers and the senior managers sought to keep them there by re-rostering them and by persuasion. This reflected the difficulty management had in rostering people to Unit N. However, there was considerable kudos for Unit N staff. They were regarded by managers and other staff in the institution as doing a 'good job' and working in one of the worst places at Hilltop. All Unit N staff members, in interviews, expressed a liking for working in the unit. One staff member commented: 'It's interesting, there's always something happening' (Interview with I.). Others commented that they liked the 'ladies' who had 'spirit' and were 'real characters'. Some saw the work there as a challenge to their professional skills: 'If you can work in this unit, you can work anywhere' (Interview with I.). Yet others saw it as an opportunity to develop skills in 'managing challenging behaviours'. While all staff felt positive about working in the unit, they expressed varied feelings about the women with whom they worked. While hesitant about naming her, each staff member had a favourite among the women living in the unit: 'I love Brigid. I give her cuddles but when she's naughty, I don't. Just like a little girl' (Interview with Q.). This allowed for special attention to be given to individuals. However, some women did miss out.

Staff felt frustrated by some of the women's behaviour. They saw it as disrupting the lives of other women and preventing the development of much-needed programmes (for example Jane's aggression was blamed by one staff member for a cancelled excursion which all the women had been looking forward to). However, staff made efforts to understand the women's 'challenging behaviour', usually seeing it as due to frustration over their living environment or as 'attention seeking'.

> [P]utting all these ladies with behavioural problems in one unit to me is a recipe for disaster because you find that once one goes off, all the others will follow ... also, you've got a complete lack of role models other than staff because you can see these ladies are copying each other but not staff members. (Interview with Q.)

The young management team had introduced new practices to improve life in the unit for the women living there and for staff. Staff felt supported by the managers and also felt appreciated by the staff in the rest of the institution. However, the better-trained women felt frustrated by the lack of time which could be given to developing programmes with the women living in the unit and resented the household tasks which took up much of each day. They also resented the custodial nature of much of their work.

I'd like to get more into doing programmes and that, but you can't do that unless all the other stuff is done first ... You're sort of like a security guard or bouncer at times. You spend a lot of the day just trying to break up fights. (Interview with I.)

Just as the women living in the unit demonstrated their individuality, so too did the staff. Some were skilled mental retardation nurses who had been recently trained and who had strong positive views about deinstitutionalisation; others were completely untrained to work with the women and were awaiting entrance to a basic training course. Some were qualified Intellectual Disability Services Officers who had completed a twelve-month course on working with people with intellectual disability. Each staff member had an individual style in working with the women in the unit, and different perceptions of the work and of the women. One staff member commented: 'I bark like a dog at Una, and she answers me. She speaks dog language' (Interview with L.). Another staff member stated:

I just like the ladies. Another reason too over the last year or so, [is] I've done a lot of extra training with challenging behaviours and that's what I feel is my area. Expertise. If you put me in a unit with medical [people] forget it, I've got no idea. This is my area ... I find it easier to implement what I've learned in this unit. (Interview with I.)

This summary of observations of the women working in the unit reveals three important themes which are noted here and developed later in this book.

First, the women staff, like the women living in the unit, were locked in. Except for brief periods during the day, they too were confined to the day room and the dining room, the stresses and the violence. Interaction with people other than those in the unit was limited. There were few opportunities to go outside, and when they did, it was usually with a group of women for whom they were responsible. They had to be self-controlled and vigilant. Becoming upset or emotional was a signal that it was time to take a break. Like the women living in the unit, the staff members faced yawning hours of boredom in their twelve-hour shifts. The monotony of these hours was broken by controlling the violence or aggression, which they saw as one of their most important functions and skills.

Second, within the closed world in which the women staff worked the relationships were intimate, complex and inescapable, both within the group of staff who shared a roster and with the women who lived in the unit. The development of such relationships and their maintenance over time led to a dense web of interaction and feelings which was sometimes confusing and alienating to the outsider but which provided security and consistency to those within the unit.

Finally, the women living in the unit were almost always under the surveillance of the staff. Always within call, and often within sight, the staff watched the women living in the unit throughout their shifts, and in turn the women watched the staff. This mutual gaze was complex and ambivalent. The staff gaze was informed by clearly established bodies of knowledge and related practices, but it also included personal feelings and perceptions of individuals and the group. The gaze of the women was problematic: it was individualised and enigmatic. And to this mutual gaze must be added the complications of my presence, for I watched both groups of women in the unit and I too was watched by the staff and by the women living in the unit.

## Life in Unit N

There were two very different aspects to life in Unit N. The first was a formal one which involved set rituals and relationships which were initiated and maintained by the staff. The second, informal aspect was one in which the women filled in the spaces between such rituals.

### The Formal Life of the Unit

#### The Daily Routines

The morning began early in Unit N. At 6.45 am, those women still asleep would be woken and dressed by the night staff so that all the women would be ready for breakfast before the day staff came on duty. Although rising was governed largely by staff rosters, it was not completely inflexible. Women who were unwell, menstruating or whose waking lives were pain-filled or uncomfortable were often allowed to sleep late.

Breakfast was slightly flexible in time and menu, as it was prepared within the unit. However, like other meals it was eaten in two shifts, with one group of women waiting hungrily in the day room for the first group to finish. Some women were able to collect their own meals and to organise their tables. They were regarded as relatively independent. Others required more assistance.

> Today I helped Kirsten with her breakfast. She sits separately from the other women as she tends to snatch their food. She is always very hungry and finds the awkwardness of using a spoon unbearable. She tried to grab the food with her hands. When I asked her to use the spoon and put it in her hand, much of the food went onto the white bib which she wears at meal times. (Field notes)

Some women were too physically or intellectually disabled or too depressed to eat independently and had to be fed by staff. An important and consistent part of each meal was the administration of medication to individuals. Mostly the women complied with this. When someone did resist, staff presented the medication again and talked the person into compliance, for medication was the basis of staff management of 'challenging behaviours'. Although staff were proud that they had managed to reduce the dosage and number of different drugs taken by the women, in fact only one woman was completely free of them. Of the others, eleven were given Melleril on either a regular or as-needed basis, six were taking Largactil or Neulactil regularly, five took anti-convulsants, and six were taking a mix of anti-psychotic drugs such as Largactil, Neulactil and Valium.

Following breakfast some women would be taken for baths. Some groups had baths in the morning, and others at night. In part this was a matter of choice but the availability of staff and the mood of the women in the unit also played a part in this decision. Bath times could be chaotic: there was no privacy and there was constant pressure to finish from the other women waiting their turn.

A further routine completed after breakfast and each meal was 'toileting and teeth cleaning'. Some of the women were continent and did not require reminders about going to the toilet, while others did. Toothbrushes and toothpaste were locked in a cupboard to which only staff had access. While some staff helped women with their meals, others ensured that the women who had finished went to the toilet, changed and had their teeth cleaned.

The hours between breakfast and lunch were broken by staff breakfast and morning-tea times which were taken in shifts, leaving the unit almost permanently with one staff member short. For the women, the long morning hours would be spent largely in the day room, however a few left the unit on a daily basis. These women, who were granted a measure of independence, went by themselves to the kiosk within the institution. This meant a journey from the day room through two locked doors to the office of the unit, a request for money and then permission to leave. The women who were granted this privilege were trusted by staff not to 'abscond' or cause 'trouble'.

Sometimes a woman made an unauthorised exit from the unit:

> When I arrived today, I saw Elaine vaulting the wire fence around the unit and disappearing down the hill. A moment later S. [staff member] came to the door of the unit and watched her go. She laughed, commenting that Elaine always came back after a while, not like some of the others. (Field notes)

Three women went regularly to occupational therapy classes in another building. Usually these classes lasted only an hour or two, once or twice a week, and the women then returned to the unit. When a woman was judged by the unit staff to be 'unstable' or was disruptive in class she was excluded from participating, either just for that session or for longer periods. Since there was a scarcity of such programmes, only a few women from the unit were chosen to be involved.

Warm or cold drinks were served to the women part-way through the morning. These were always eagerly sought, as all the women seemed to be constantly thirsty, perhaps because drinks were not readily available and perhaps because of the effects of the drugs they were taking.

Lunch time was at 11.45 am and the time (as for the evening meal) was dictated by the arrival of food at the unit in large trucks brought from a centralised kitchen. There was little flexibility possible in the timing of these meals and no choice in the menu. After the women had had their lunch and 'toileting and teeth cleaning' had again been completed the staff began to take their own lunch breaks.

After lunch, the day room and the dining room were cleaned and this was the time on fine days when some women were taken for a walk in the grounds. It was rare for all the women to go together. Usually women went on alternate days, with some women going only rarely. These 'almost daily' walks were eagerly anticipated both by women living in the unit and by staff. For an individual the afternoon might also be broken up by a visit from an advocate or by occupational therapy.

The evening meal was early, at 4.45 pm, and soon afterwards some women were bathed and all began to get ready for bed. Everybody was in night clothes by the time the night shift arrived at 7.45 pm although not all women went to bed early. Lena for example stayed up late, otherwise she woke at three o'clock in the morning; her medication was adjusted to allow this to happen. However, by about 11 pm all the women were in bed. The night staff watched television and made regular patrols along the dormitories to check that the women were sleeping. They responded to emergencies, such as someone having an epileptic seizure, and stayed awake with cups of coffee, craft activities and reading.

Another day began; then night; and then another day.

*The Group Programme*

> My main concern when I went up there first was just everything was done together, like herding of cows ... And I mean the clients were exhibiting all the behaviours that one associates with that kind of thing. There was a lot of violence when I went up there.
>
> A lot of unnecessary medication on tranquillisers ... there was no monitoring of the medication that was being given ... it was quite obvious that some people had been overdosed. (Interview with former staff member)

In an effort to improve staff morale and the appalling conditions within the unit a group programme had been commenced in 1989 by the new unit manager. It involved the formation of five groups, each consisting of four women, who were placed in each group on the basis of their assessed skills, independence and friends. It is doubtful that the women living in the unit understood that the programme actually existed, as no effort was made to discuss it with them.

The group programme operated during each roster, with one staff member being responsible for each group. The most independent group was assigned to the unit manager, who had the least time to spend with them. The introduction of the group programme had done something to remedy some of the worst features of the unit. Reportedly, meals and bath times were both more orderly and more leisurely than previously. Staff had more time to spend with individuals and felt more accountable for their work. Staff also believed that the levels of noise and violence had decreased since the introduction of the group programme. However, the programme was limited in its effects. Staff were transferred from their group at the end of each month, meaning that learning goals and programmes (for example learning to use a spoon at meal times) were rarely transferred across rosters.

Staff found it difficult to make use of the programme at times other than bath and meal times as they were not trained in or experienced at developing programmes, were fixated on a custodial role and were constantly being distracted by other tasks or by meal breaks. Also, the programme relied on all staff being regular and available. This was rarely the case in Unit N and consequently the group programme only worked intermittently.

*General Service Plans (GSPs) and Individual Programme Plans (IPPs)*

Once a year the women's situations were reviewed formally in order to develop GSPs and IPPs (see Glossary). If a woman had a family or an advocate then they were invited to take part in assessing her needs and planning changes in service delivery for the next twelve months. Very few women in Unit N took part directly in the process of developing these plans. Reading through the plans for individuals from the previous three years I discovered that although all the GSPs specified a movement to community living for the women and outlined programme development and service changes to achieve this, little was accomplished in action. The same goals were specified from one year to the next and there was no accountability in the system.

*Recording Life in the Unit*

All formal aspects of life in the unit were recorded, noted and copied by staff across different rosters. Some of these records provided detailed day-by-day descriptions of the behaviour and staff impressions of individual women. Others recorded aggressive behaviour (incident reports) or medical assessments.

The formal aspects of life in the unit were directed at restraining individuals and constraining their lives with the ostensible purpose of protecting them and the other people living in the institution. By its very geography the unit was constraining: locked as they were behind its doors and within its walls even the location of the women in space was subject to other people's wishes. But the routines and the prescriptions of the formal life of the unit added their own constraints of time and tasks.

## The Informal Life of the Unit

*Activities*

While the formal life of the unit served to constrain the lives of the women, the informal aspects of life there sometimes subverted the routines or allowed the women to express their individuality and their feelings. The following account describes the relationships established by the women in the unit and the activities which 'filled' their days. There were no planned activities which arose from life within the unit; there were no books, no magazines, no games. Within the day room the only entertainment through the long hours of the day was the television set, in which only Dora showed a consistent interest. Sometimes staff turned on a radio in the staff office and music (usually light popular music) was relayed through speakers into the room. The women had no choice about the nature of the music, its volume or the times at which it was turned on.

Staff deplored the lack of structured activities in the unit, but did not change the situation. In interviews they commented that they had no training in devising programmes of activities and they expressed fears that some women would injure themselves with any equipment brought into the unit. Some staff talked of beginning gardening or photography with the 'ladies', but these intentions were never translated into practice. However, some women in the unit organised their own activities.

> Iris has a small case in which she carries tattered magazines and a pack of cards. Today I watched her spend two hours looking at a magazine. No one went near her in that time or talked with her about what she was doing. (Field notes)

On one or two occasions during my time in the unit I saw Lena knitting, under the close surveillance of a staff member. Joyce brought a puzzle from home which was held in the staff office. She asked for it and completed it on many occasions while I was in the unit.

*'Challenging Behaviour'*

In the absence of things to do in the unit, the women's 'challenging behaviour' filled much of the day for both them and the staff. It was impossible to know how much of this behaviour was due to frustration, boredom and the constant presence of other women. The term 'challenging behaviour' was used by staff as if all the women's problem behaviour was homogeneous in nature, however behaviour described as 'challenging' revealed great diversity among the women. The following examples give some indication of the range of behaviours that were so described.

> Just after breakfast, Kirsten was standing by the door of the unit. Suddenly she began to scream – short, sharp, high-pitched screams. She began to move around the room, finally flinging herself on the couch. Her screams stopped, then started again. J. [staff member] took her upstairs for a bath, which apparently sometimes stops the screaming. Kirsten's stomach is constantly distended, as she gulps air. Repeated medical visits have failed to find anything wrong, but she seemed to be in physical pain. (Field notes)

Kirsten showed no other behaviours that were 'challenging' and spent much of her day cowering against the walls of the room, afraid of attack from the other women.

> I was sitting in the day room this morning before breakfast. June came in and went up to L. [staff member]. She was swinging a dirty urine-soaked towel in her hand. She offered this to L., with a smile. L. looked at it with distaste and said angrily: 'Put it back, June, it's dirty and disgusting'. June laughed and took the towel into the toilet area. A few minutes later she came back with another towel, equally dirty, which she again presented to L., who expressed considerable disgust. June laughed again and returned to the toilet area. (Field notes)

June was very selective in the items she brought to staff. I never saw her bring a clean towel. She also stuffed items down the toilets and blocked them. She and Dora were very aggressive to each other and there were frequent fights between them.

> Dora came up to me in the day room and pointed to an ugly bruise on her cheek. 'June did that, June did it, it's sore', she said. Staff had separated Dora from June after the bite and she had been sent down into the dining room. Dora was comforted by L. [staff member]. (Field notes)

Jane restricted her aggression to staff members. She had been sexually abused by her family since childhood. She was articulate and independent. She did not associate with the rest of the women living in the unit but spent time talking with staff. Sometimes, however, she erupted into violence against staff, throwing objects at them, throwing them on the floor and punching them. On one occasion she had threatened a staff member with a knife. In the time I was in the unit two staff members were on leave for short periods because Jane had injured them. I never heard of her attacking the other women living in the unit. Staff were at a loss to explain Jane's behaviour but thought it often erupted around frustration of her wants and needs. Staff believed there was a physical cause for her aggression and watched her carefully for signs of an attack. These might include tension in her body and expression, outbursts of anger and 'an expression in her eyes'. When these signs were noticed changes to medication were used to try and avert physical aggression. When asked why she attacked staff Jane would answer 'I was angry'. When questioned further she did not elaborate.

Lena had lived for sixty-four years in the community and had been in Hilltop for eight years. She had been moved to Unit N because she had 'illtreated the older women' in the unit to which she had first been assigned. Talkative and independent, Lena would sit primly for hours on the couch. She enjoyed household tasks and helped with the laundry in the unit. She also enjoyed knitting, however when staff were not looking she would pinch other women or poke them with knitting needles. She stole items very cleverly, secreting them in her stockings or shoes or hiding them around the unit. She had also been known to leave piles of faeces behind the couch in the day room. Staff responded by scolding, by taking away the knitting needles and rarely allowing her to knit, by trying to get her to clean up any mess she made and by searching for the missing objects she had hidden.

These examples suggest something of the range of behaviours likely to occur at any time in Unit N. Staff responded to these behaviours but their meanings were not explored beyond the ubiquitous explanation of 'attention-seeking behaviour'. It was generally recognised that some women did not like others and efforts were made to separate them, but usually only temporarily and after a crisis had occurred. Staff also attempted to reduce such behaviours by informal programmes of behaviour modification. These were rarely carried out consistently because of the frequent changes in staff, because the staff were not always aware that the programme was in place and because of the difficulty of consistently responding to twenty-one people showing different behaviours.

I think that for some of the women there was a set of precise and individual meanings in their behaviour. The women were consistent in the kinds of behaviours they showed, some of which demonstrated great skill in the selection of targets or of particular behaviours. They were also remarkably tolerant of each other's idiosyncrasies. Some women were quick to inform staff if the behaviour of another looked danger-ous, for example Una ate cigarette butts, and other women would immediately tell staff if they saw her do this. Acts of aggression were usually watched silently by those women sitting in the chairs in the day room. No other woman ever intervened either to stop the violence or to join it. Such violence was always restricted to two people with others watching as an audience. Those not watching would continue with their own activities. The victim of violence would often have repeated conversations with staff about the injuries she had received and ask for the offender to be punished. An act of violence committed in the morning would still be discussed at night and would be reiterated to staff coming on duty in the evening.

*Relationships Between the Women Living in the Unit*

Some women lived their lives essentially alone in Unit N, but there was also a complex web of relationships between individuals. While these relationships were sometimes noted in passing by the staff, and while obvious friendships were accommodated within the group programme discussed earlier in this chapter, many of these relationships continued without note. The most apparent relationships were those between women who could express their desires and needs verbally. For example Ilse and Vera slept near each other at night and spent the days together holding hands and talking with each other. They sought protection together from more aggressive women living in the unit and were joined in their friendship by Elaine who was articulate and strong willed. The only other overt friendship was between Bettina and Kate who spent much of each day holding each other on a large chair.

Some women protected or 'mothered' others in the unit. Jodie, who was in her mid-forties, cared for 'Baby Betty' (Bettina), helping to dress her and to ensure that she was comfortable. Other relationships were unnoticed or subtle.

> Rosalind picks up a piece of fluff from the floor and gives it to Iris who is sitting looking at a magazine on the couch. Iris takes it, looks at it carefully and slides it down between the cushion and the edge of the sofa. Rosalind wanders away, returning after some moments with another piece of fluff, which Iris again deposits in the couch. This interaction continues for some time. (Field notes)

There were also strong negative relationships established in the unit. There was no escape from the other women living there, and so minor irritations could quickly erupt into violence. Some women just did not get on with each other but were forced to live in close proximity for twenty-four hours a day. Dora and June were constantly arguing and seeking opportunities to fight or hit each other.

Within the unit, women took on different roles with each other or with the group. Brigid was powerful through her unpredictability and aggressive attacks and because she would push over or fight larger and stronger women. However, she did not attack Jane or the other women who were articulate and were close to staff. Those women who could speak had a status and power denied the rest (except for Brigid). They could make their needs known easily, could attract staff attention and were more likely to have positive interactions with staff. For example, Jane rarely spoke to the other women living in the unit and avoided contact with them, so her relationships were restricted to staff and visitors.

Some women were constant victims, for example Kirsten, who was unable to respond physically to aggression and would stand crying, huddled by the door, her cup in her hand, her hair wrapped around Brigid's fist. She spent much of the day sidling around the walls of the room, never sitting with anyone and only allowing fleeting contact from staff.

## Relationships with People Outside the Institution

Some women did have relationships with family or with advocates, however most of these people restricted their visits to the area around the staff office. The women would go away with their respective advocate or family and little was known about what happened during the time they were away. Staff could only know what the women or their visitors chose to tell them upon the woman's return. In one instance, after Lena reported sexual abuse by a relative she was placed under a guardianship order which denied that person access to her and allowed Lena only limited access to another relative.

In the two years prior to my entry to the unit, there had been a campaign to increase the number of citizen advocates in contact with the women. Six of the women had since gained advocates who visited on a regular basis. When interviewed during this study, the advocates commented on the difference in behaviour they noticed when the women went outside the unit. All advocates commented that the women were happier and more sociable outside. Only once had an advocate been forced to take a woman back to the institution because she found her behaviour 'unmanageable'.

*Relationships with Staff*

Relationships between staff and women living in the unit were complex and ambivalent. Staff expressed this ambivalence verbally as dislike for some of the tasks they had to carry out and for some of the characteristics of the women. It contrasted with their admiration for the 'spirit' of the women who lived in the unit. The relationships established between the staff and the women living in the unit were characterised by physical affection and control. There was a physical closeness between the staff and some of the women, for example women working in the unit would sit beside one of the women living there, hold her hand, put an arm around her and comment 'Do you want a cuddle?' Reciprocal back massages were frequent expressions of affection between staff and women in the unit, but some women were more likely than others to receive affection. Women who seemed self-sufficient, who had a close friend or who indicated that they did not like their privacy invaded were not included in the staff's affectionate embrace. Women who sat for long periods of time, those who indicated a desire for affection and those able to respond were more likely to receive it.

Contrasting with this physical affection was the control and power exerted by staff to contain violence and aggression in the unit. Interventions ranged from speaking to the woman concerned, to physically intervening to separate people and segregating them either at opposite ends of the room or downstairs. In more extreme situations, staff administered additional medication or isolated the woman in question for a period of time.

While staff in Unit N did not seem very skilled in preventing violence from occurring they were skilled in containing and stopping it. They were proud of this and had a reputation for it around the institution. To some extent, then, the violence in Unit N defined the unit's uniqueness and gave staff status among their colleagues. Staff did regard some of the women living in the unit as dangerous, and this seemed to be assessed quite directly in terms of the kind of threat these women posed to staff safety. For example Jane was regarded with some fear by staff and was constantly watched for signs of an 'aggressive attack'.

For the women, relations with staff ranged from an acceptance of their usefulness in providing food, clothing and shelter to an acceptance of their comfort and friendship. For some women in the unit, staff seemed to be peripheral figures, shadowy and unknown.

> I noticed today that June calls all of the staff by one name: Beryl. She knows the names of all the women living in the unit but does not differentiate between the staff at all in spite of repeated efforts to teach her individuals' names. (Field notes)

For other women living in the unit, staff were the main source of relationships and affection.

Staff control over the women appeared to be total, however while the women appeared compliant to this, they all set limits to its degree. For example when Dora said 'fuck off' to a staff member, the staff member usually did, perhaps with a parting verbal retort. When Rhonda *really* decided to go downstairs and a staff member blocked her way, it was usually the staff member who gave way with a comment such as 'Oh, all right then'. When confronted by anger and frustration, staff tended to try to soothe the woman by talking with her or diverting her attention.

Staff used each other to release tension, sitting together for periods of the day, talking about their families or outside activities and often recounting stories about the women living in the unit. The women living in the unit were not included directly in such conversations unless they asked specific questions which were then answered in an aside. Much of the interchange between staff and the women living in the unit revolved around instructions, reprimands or questions asked of the women by staff.

It was actually difficult to carry on a conversation with the women living in the unit, because their world was confined largely to two rooms in which staff were witnesses to the detail of their lives. What was the point in discussing it? Sometimes conversations would arise about things that had happened when other staff were on duty, but generally conversation between staff and the women living in the unit was restricted.

There were clear and sometimes subtle distinctions between the women working in the unit and those living there. The women living in the unit were called 'clients' or more usually 'the ladies'. This differentiated them from the women staff.

> At a meeting this morning, in the office, the unit manager asked all the 'ladies' to leave. All of the women who lived in the unit instantly got up and left, leaving the women staff behind. (Field notes)

Staff drank from china mugs, the women living in the unit from plastic ones. Staff drank better coffee and never ate their lunches in the dining room, but rather in the staff office. Perhaps the clearest distinction between them was that staff carried the keys to the unit.

## Researcher/Participant

I found being part of the life of Unit N to be intense and stressful. It required constant vigilance and energy to cope with the noise, the movement and the aggression. It was an environment in which pain was ever present, whether psychological or physical, and where there were few available strategies to change the environment. It was an enclosed world with its own rules and routines and its own certainties and insecurities. It seemed unchangeable and inviolable.

Becoming familiar with the unit took time and patience. I gradually came to know the staff and to gain some sense of their work and the stress they were under. It was much harder to know the women living in the unit, partly because of the difficulty of communicating. For example it took time to learn how creatively June used her few available words.

By the same token, my world outside the unit seemed remote and unreal to the women living there. When the women could speak directly to me, our conversations were limited by the constraints of the unit, the noise and the disruptions, and by a seeming wariness of talking about anything other than superficial reactions to situations. Staff sometimes regarded my efforts to spend time with individuals with amusement or bewilderment, for example on the day that Joyce and Lena used my pens and paper to write letters and draw pictures, staff present expressed astonishment that they could do so, but also tended to see my participation in the activity as a waste of time. It was difficult to sustain activities in the face of such dismissal.

I found the work in the unit physically exhausting and emotionally depressing, but I also found the unit to be a place of strong emotions and relationships which were intensified by its locked nature.

# CHAPTER 3

## *Paths to Unit N*

At thirteen he was taken
Away to an asylum.
For three days he wailed one word:
'Home, home, home' ... Nobody heard.
Then sedated he fell dumb
Leaving the air shaken.
*(Patricia Beer, 1993, p.22)*

The women's paths to Unit N began with relationships and experiences outside the institution and ended behind locked doors. Some came to Hilltop in infancy or childhood, others in adolescence or adulthood. One came in old age. It was difficult to obtain a clear view of the path each woman took: consequently, this chapter is based on fragmented stories which were pieced together from discussions with the women in the unit, from interviews with staff, families and advocates, and from an analysis of institutional files. These sources reveal both the uniqueness of each woman's journey and some of the common elements which accompanied it: relief, confusion, ambivalence, fragmentation, pain and grief.

### Dora's Story

Dora is isolated and withdrawn, spends most of her time in purposeless moving around the ward, moving head and arms in bizarre stereotyped movements. It is difficult to gain her attention, but a few one or two word replies are to be gained. Oblivious of the nature of her environment or circumstances. Illiterate. Clinical impression is that her cognitive functions are in the range of moderately severe retardation. (Superintendent's report, 1966)

The superintendent's account of Dora contrasts oddly with Dora as I came to know her in the locked unit. She was a tallish woman with light

45

brown hair who walked a little awkwardly and who had some difficulty
going up and down stairs. Her front teeth had been extracted leading to
some slurring of her speech. She was very clear about her needs and
wants and was able to state these forcefully to staff and to other women
living in the unit. She was regarded as very 'independent' by staff
because she chose her own clothes, dressed herself and managed her
own life within the formal restrictions imposed on her. She had a very
expressive face, a wide smile and a hearty laugh. She had a good sense
of humour and enjoyed a joke, particularly attributing farts to staff.
Dora was loud and her voice could be heard echoing around the day
room. She was kind-hearted, encouraging those lagging behind on a
walk or comforting someone who was in pain.

Dora was forty-three years old and had lived at Hilltop for twenty-six
years. It was difficult to know how many of these years had been spent in
locked units, but she had been in Unit N for at least eight years. Until
the age of twelve years she had lived at home with her parents and three
brothers and sisters. Her parents did not know the causes of her intellectual disability and received little support in caring for her; she spent her
days at home with her mother. Dora was 'difficult to manage' and
became increasingly 'impossible to handle'.

> [T]he doctor told us the longer you have Dora with the other children
> she'll bring them down to her level. And when she started to throw things
> around ... we decided the doctor was right and we gave in. (Interview with
> Dora's father)

'Giving in' led to Dora's certification and her admission to an
institution for people with intellectual disabilities (Lonsdale Lodge),
where she stayed for the next five years before moving permanently to
Hilltop. The decision to send Dora to an institution raised complex
feelings for her parents. They saw it as 'heartbreaking for all of us',
however, it did allow them to lead a 'normal' family life.

> That was one thing that I noticed when she went into Lonsdale – the first
> night that we could sit and talk normally as a family. (Interview with Dora's
> mother)

Yet this relief was accompanied by guilt and pain:

> and that was something that worried me, that I should be appreciating that
> [the peacefulness of life without Dora]. I mustn't say the first night, because
> I don't think I stopped crying for about ... I couldn't tell you how long ...
> (Interview with Dora's mother)

It is impossible to know how Dora experienced separation from her
family at the time, but over the years there are repeated file reports

about her expressed need to go home and her distress after her parents' visits. She frequently asked me where Mary Vale was (the suburb where her parents lived). To my reply that it was in the city she would say 'Oh, it's too far to go'. She had some vivid childhood memories: her dog and the colour of her parents' car. Her life radically changed after her admission to Lonsdale Lodge. There must have been a gulf between the quality of life she experienced at home and that in the institution. Her mother commented that:

> This particular day I was visiting and I don't know where they [the women in the unit] had been; they were just marched back and they had only bottoms on, they didn't have any tops on and they just had potties under the stairs and these were big grown-up girls. They got absolutely nothing. (Interview with Dora's mother)

While the conditions in Unit N were not as bleak physically as those at Lonsdale Lodge as portrayed by Dora's mother, Dora indicated strongly that she 'got absolutely nothing' in the way of activities to fill her days. She constantly begged staff for walks, for the television or for anything to fill the hours. She was interested in people and their lives but had no friends among the other women living in the unit. She directed all her attention to staff, filling her days with talking to them, with scratching her head and talking about the results, and with constant changes of her clothes. She went to occupational therapy two mornings a week, however sometimes she was excluded from this because of her 'disruptive behaviour'. When given the opportunity, Dora enjoyed carrying out household tasks and cooking. She had few opportunities to do this.

Over the years, her contact with her family became less although they continued to visit on a regular basis in spite of early discouragement from institutional staff.

> Yes, we went up every week for years and years and years. And Dora was a problem because 'My mum and dad are coming up, not yours, go away', you see. And she knew every week we would be there and, uh, she made life a misery for everybody else. So we were asked if we would ... they suggested that we break it down a bit, so we gradually got it down and we might go six weeks now which, when you look at it, it's a pretty normal thing for a grown-up to visit another one of their children in a normal circumstance ... (Interview with Dora's father)

Dora had not been home since her admission to Lonsdale Lodge, as her parents were afraid that 'we would never get her back [to the institution]'. Her parents did not know why she had been locked up but assumed it was because 'she has always been very boisterous'. Nor was Dora able to tell me why she was in Unit N. Her files record that she was moved from Lonsdale Lodge and into a locked unit at Hilltop at the age of seventeen because of 'aggressive behaviour'. She seemed to have lived most of the next twenty-six years in such units, although during the 1980s she spent some time in an unlocked unit; when this closed down she was moved temporarily to Unit N for 'administrative reasons'. She had not left it since.

In the locked unit, Dora's behaviour was regarded by staff as difficult. In the past she had been given Modecate and Stelazine for extended periods to 'control' her behaviour. She was now taking 300 ml of Melleril each day with anti-convulsants. She would sometimes hit other women living in the unit who came too close to her, and she would shout 'shut up' or 'fuck off' to those staff or women whose noise or intrusions bothered her. She rarely hit staff. During my time at the unit she smashed several windows, putting her fist through the glass.

> I walked into the dining room. Dora was sitting at a table with her arm encased in bandages from the hand to the elbow. I asked what had happened. 'Hurt my hand,' she said. 'Broke a window.' She laughed as she said it. (Field notes)

On some occasions Dora became enraged and was unstoppable. In such a situation she was likely to hurt herself or others in the unit. Staff had worked out strategies to deal with these situations and regarded Dora with respect and caution.

> Some old staff, they don't really know. I mean they've been here, but they still don't know how to be with Dora when she's off ... Not only will she hurt herself, she'll damage something and sometimes whoever is near her; she'll hurt them. Like, for example, they know Dora if she plays up, just ignore her, but they [don't] know they [have] to be close to her because Dora, she'll bang her head you know, so if you're sitting here and she's over there, it takes a while for you to get there to stop her. (Interview with Q.)

Dora had a reputation among the staff for being a 'hypochondriac' and would constantly ask staff or visitors to inspect her latest wounds. Though usually 'superficial', they were never imaginary. Some were inflicted by other women in the unit, some by Dora's own scratching. During the time I was at the unit she suffered bites, scratches and bruises mostly inflicted by June.

Dora's parents knew little of Dora's day-to-day life in Unit N but believed that: 'they get very good meals, from what I see. They look comfortable in their beds ...' (Interview with Dora's father). Dora's parents' criticism of life in Unit N was mediated by their own experiences of frustration in living with her. Dora's mother commented that:

You always had to be careful because you're inclined to get up in arms you know if you think 'Oh, she's got this dreadful sore place on her and somebody's been cruel to her' but ... and I've been cruel to her myself. I've hit her so hard ... (Interview with Dora's mother)

Essentially, Dora's parents saw her life as relatively unchanging over the twenty-six years of living at Hilltop.

The only difference between then and now is that the staff had more *children* to look after then than they have now. But the staff have been very good and they would sit down like *human beings* at the table and someone would come out and set the table, one of the *pupils*, one of the *inmates*, and go about their business just as any average *family* would ... (Interview with Dora's father; my italics)

They also believed that the life Hilltop offered was the only one available to her.

We've been very happy with the unit, yes. I mean what can you do? She's either among normal people or she's not. And she can't cope with living at home with us, so ... (Interview with Dora's mother)

## The Women's Paths to the Institution

Dora's path to the institution provides an entry point to exploring the other routes by which women came to Hilltop.

### *Problems in Managing a Difficult Daughter*

Dora's institutionalisation was precipitated by her parents' fear of her effect on her siblings and by the increasing difficulty of managing her behaviour at home. Four other women had entered the institution in childhood because they proved too difficult for their parents to 'manage'. Parents were particularly concerned about the perceived effect of the child's behaviour on her siblings, although Inge's father expressed concern about her tendency to run away from home.

Interviews and files both revealed parents' desperation at the point of their daughter's admission, for example a letter on Faye's file from her mother stated that:

I find now it is getting beyond me. At times I feel desperate, especially when I am out shopping in the street she will not walk with me and she goes and grabs them [other children?] and they fall over; she takes their hats and icecream and dollars whatever she can get ... by the time I get home I am done ... (Letter from Faye's mother requesting placement at Hilltop)

All families who had admitted their daughters because of difficult behaviours had retained some contact with them over the years, though this varied from once or twice a year (Inge) to every six weeks (Dora).

### Birth of Another Child

Two of the women were admitted to Hilltop following the birth of another child. This appeared to make existing family difficulties unbearable. Bettina was admitted at the age of six after her mother had a second child and found it impossible to care for Bettina at home.

> Everything in the house had to be put away. She turned circles all the time, sometimes falling over ... She screamed a great deal and moved around a lot. She was very heavy and became unmanageable when Mrs J. was pregnant. (Field note from interview with Bettina's family)

The degree of family involvement varied with these women. Bettina's parents visited three or four times a year, while Rhonda's family visited once a fortnight.

### Allegations of Abuse

Three women entered the institution following allegations of abuse or of 'immorality'.

Rosalind was admitted at the age of five following confused but strong allegations of cruel treatment towards her by one or both of her parents. One medical reference in the records suggests that her intellectual disability was caused by this ill-treatment. Jane first went to an institution at the age of six. She moved from one to another, with long periods at home. Now, as an adult, she had been placed on a guardianship order which prohibited contact with her family (except for a sister) because of repeated long-term sexual abuse by her father and brothers. Ilse was taken into care at the age of three by the then Child Welfare Department. The reason given for her removal from her family was 'a background of deserting mother and immorality' (File notes).

For two of these women, admission to the institution effectively removed them for life from their families, and Jane saw her sister only intermittently.

### Increasing Age of Parents

Seven of the women lived at home with their parents until adolescence or adulthood. Final separation from their families came for these women as their parents became frail or old. Una for example came to

Hilltop at the age of eighteen after her mother became too ill to care for her.

> Mum was trying to battle on with her herself ... it came to that decision because I moved out and got married, so Mum was faced with that; there was no other option. (Interview with Una's sister)

Kirsten's mother found the strain of caring for an adult twenty-four hours a day without support impossible to maintain, and so Kirsten entered Hilltop at the age of twenty. She was one of nine children, two others of whom were disabled and lived at home. Her mother commented that:

> Some nights she wouldn't want to go to bed and some nights I'd have to sit up till three or four o'clock in the morning till she decided to go to bed. Because if she didn't want to go to bed she'd keep getting out, well even if you lock doors you just can't go to bed and leave a child like that wandering around the house ... I mean she could fall in the dark and lie there bleeding while you're sleeping and not knowing; and you had to stay up. (Interview with Kirsten's mother)

Contact with family members for this group of women was variable. Some older parents (for example Kirsten's mother) found it too difficult to travel to the institution and 'unbearable' when they got there. Others maintained weekly contact or visited on a monthly or two-monthly basis.

### Death of a Parent

Both Jodie and June entered Hilltop in their twenties following the death of their parents. Both women were now in their early forties; both had advocates but no links with surviving family members.

### Unknown Causes

Information about Elaine's entry to the institution was ambiguous. She was diagnosed at the age of twenty-eight (in 1958) as being schizophrenic and as having: 'many previous admissions to Victorian and NSW mental hospitals over the past five years' (Medical Superintendent). During her thirty-three years of institutionalisation Elaine had moved in and out of Hilltop, sometimes living with family members (for periods no longer than six months) but always arriving back in the institution. She rarely had visitors and had no advocate.

*Summing Up*

These accounts of how the women found their way into Hilltop indicate both the uniqueness of each person's path but also reveal some common threads. As found in previous literature (Bayley, 1973; Dokecki, Anderson and Strain, 1977; Brantley and Gemill, 1991) the precipitating factors leading to institutionalisation seemed to be the increasing inability of the family to cope. Sometimes this occurred in childhood, sometimes in adolescence and sometimes in adulthood. The decision to institutionalise the woman was caused by a change in family circumstances or the increasing difficulty of managing the woman's behaviour. This decision often reflected tensions and strains in the family and the lack of support available to them and is consistent with other research findings (Hand, Trewby and Reid, 1994; Barnes, 1997). In all of these instances it was not the woman's intellectual disability *per se* which led to her institutionalisation. Frequently it was the increasing age or the illness or death of the woman's mother which led to her final institutionalisation in adulthood. For these families:

> There were no formal, systematic methods of support: no in-home assistance, no relief. Since all of these families were traditional, in the sense that child care was seen as primarily the mother's role, the mother shouldered all of these unusually heavy child care responsibilities. (Lord and Hearn, 1987, p.9)

Mothers had been the main care givers of the women in Unit N during their time with their families (see also Bowman, 1991; Traustadottir, 1991; Roth, 1992; Bowman and Virtue, 1993). There was no ongoing support for the families from professionals, and the only option they were offered as an alternative to family care was the institution. All parents interviewed talked of the pain of making the decision to send their child to an institution, for example Kirsten's mother said:

> Oh, it was very hard ... my husband sat me down and talked to me and said 'Isn't it about time; you need a rest, you're looking tired' and you know ... it took me weeks to come to the decision. They held the vacancy for about a month longer than they should've while I made the decision ... I used to go to bed of a night and bawl all night, keep thinking about it. (Interview with Kirsten's mother)

But as indicated by Dora's parents there was also acceptance, even relief, evident in the voices of the parents. The task of caring for their daughter had been hard and largely unsupported. The decision to institutionalise enabled them to care for their other children and to continue with their own lives.

## Paths to the Locked Unit

Once they were institutionalised the women came by divergent paths to the locked unit. Although their entry to Unit N had usually occurred some time after they had come to Hilltop, I found it very difficult to discover how or when the transfer from more 'open' units had occurred. Only Jane was confined there by a guardianship order which regulated her housing. No one else was being compulsorily detained. Senior managers, when asked about the situation, commented that the women were there because of a 'duty of care', however they were unable to state what this actually meant in relation to individuals. Staff in the unit did not have information about why many of the women were in the unit. In some instances where people showed aggressive behaviour to themselves, others or property, staff *thought* that this behaviour was the reason, but in relation to other women staff were uncertain or did not know why they were there. One staff member commented: 'I have no idea why Bettina is here. She never does anything.'

None of the families or advocates of the women had ever been given reasons why their relative was placed in a locked unit, and there were no formal documents available to them which stated why she was there. Sometimes they had no idea why she should be, for example Una's sisters said: 'She's always been in one.'

Other families guessed that the reason was the woman's behaviour. Kate's mother commented that:

> One unit was lovely and I said to my husband 'Oh, this would be lovely for Kate to be here.' I mean, I was used to her being at home. Well it's just a home, but it's always clean and we did the best with it and that's what I wanted for Kate ... And when we went to Unit N, I was horrified with all the beds. As it was I was horrified. But Kate was aggressive and that was the only place for her to go. (Interview with Kate's mother)

Reading through the files of each of the women seemed to provide the best hope of finding some account of their placement in Unit N. The files were voluminous, going back sometimes forty years. The stories which began to emerge from them were ambiguous but suggested a number of reasons for the admission of the women to the unit.

*Alleged Aggressive Behaviour Towards Other Residents or Staff*
*in Units at the Institution*

There was no documentation about investigations of incidents involving alleged aggressive behaviour when they occurred prior to 1987, nor about the context of such behaviour. Nor was there any evidence to suggest programmes designed to change the behaviour or to review it. Rather, the woman involved was simply moved to the locked unit where she could be contained. Thus Lena, having lived her life in the community until she was sixty-four, entered a unit for older women where first reports indicated that she 'got on well with the other residents'. However, over a twelve-month period there were reports of Lena's aggression to other people in the unit, efforts to control her behaviour through the use of Melleril, and a final report which stated:

> Still extremely aggressive towards older patients – has caused many unnecessary [sic] falls and injuries to others. Does not listen to what is said to her and becomes nasty if she does not want to do it [sic]. Generally speaking Lena is at this point in time unsuitable for these residents. (Unit manager's note on Lena's file)

Two months later Lena was moved to Unit N, where she lived for four years.

### Absconding

Women with a history of leaving the institution without permission were placed in the locked unit. The files rarely indicated *why* they tried to run away, nor were there any reviews of this behaviour. Ilse for example had repeatedly tried to run away from Hilltop: the reasons given in her file for this included not getting on with other residents, throwing a temper tantrum, and a stated, repeated desire to return to the institution which had formerly been her home. A note on her file summarises her behaviour in the following manner: 'Her only drawbacks are that she is not always even tempered and is an escapee to boot. Ilse will take off on the least provocation' (Unit manager's note on Ilse's file). Ilse's 'escapes' had previously been punished by increasing her dosage of Largactil and by sending her to bed. In 1983 she was transferred to a locked unit, with no reasons given on her file. Once there, she managed to 'abscond' on at least one occasion, finding her way to the local police station where she complained about her treatment at Hilltop. At the time of the study Ilse had lived in a locked unit for eight years.

### At Moral Risk

Being 'at moral risk' was a particular gender issue which I doubt arose for men (this issue is explored in more depth in Chapter 4). Three women in the unit were believed to be there at least in part because they were 'at risk' sexually. Kirsten was transferred to the locked unit because she 'leaned against people' and entered a man's bedroom in a male/female unit. These actions were seen as provocative and as putting her at risk of sexual abuse. Bettina was seen as sexually vulnerable because of her severe disability. Concern was expressed in Jane's file that she 'sold herself for beer and cigarettes'. Her advocate believed that sexuality had been one of the reasons why Jane had found it difficult to live in the community.

> My understanding was that part of the difficulty around Hamilton Hostel [where Jane lived] was that Jane would have a relationship with men at Hamilton Hostel and that would cause arguments and disagreements among other residents so that Jane was identified as causing the trouble. (Interview with Jane's guardian)

### Screaming or Making a Noise

The files revealed that there was little investigation of the reasons for such behaviour as screaming or making a noise which irritated staff or other clients in a unit. Rather, the woman was moved to the locked unit where she was isolated from other staff and clients. Laura was transferred to a locked unit after a note on her file which read: 'Laura is not suitable for Unit I [an unlocked unit], she's like a caged lion though there's no real vice in her, just noise' (Unit manager's note on Laura's file).

### Smashing Windows or Furniture in a Unit

Smashing windows or furniture in a unit was quite commonly recorded for the women of Unit N. None of them was explicitly confined to the locked unit for this behaviour alone but it was a contributing factor, for example Joyce was confined to a locked unit after repeated reports of aggression, disobedience, 'throwing chairs', 'breaking fifty louvres in a temper tantrum' and 'destructive behaviour'. In this account there is no analysis of the context in which the behaviour occurred, nor is there a review of Joyce's behaviour.

### Diagnosed Psychiatric Illness

The unit was explicitly labelled as one for women with 'challenging behaviour'. While the literature (Emerson, Barrett, Bell, Cummings, McCool, Toogood and Mansell, 1987; Harris, 1991; McBrien and Felce, 1992) makes a clear distinction between challenging behaviour and psychiatric illness, three of the women in the locked unit were there primarily because they had been diagnosed as having psychiatric illnesses. Elaine was believed to have chronic schizophrenia, while Vera and Doris had been diagnosed as having manic depressive illness. All three women had been given electro-convulsive therapy repeatedly during the 1960s and all had spent much of their time at Hilltop on Modecate, Stelazine or Largactil. Their confinement to the locked unit was related to their 'difficult behaviours' rather than to the presence of a psychiatric illness *per se*.

### Administrative Reasons

Dora was moved from an open unit to the locked unit for 'administrative reasons'. In this case the term meant that no other place was available to her at the time. One woman was moved to the locked unit to make room for a new person who was perceived to be better suited to an open unit. However, 'administrative reasons' could also indicate that a particular staff member had taken a dislike to the woman. For example Rosalind's reports in an open unit were positive over an extended period of time, then the handwriting changed and negative comments about her became prevalent, culminating in the statement: 'Rosalind has not fitted into Unit C at all. After discussion with AHN [Assistant Head of Nursing] she is to return to Unit F [locked unit]' (Unit manager's note on Rosalind's file).

### Guardianship Order

Lena and Jane had state-appointed guardians because of difficulties experienced by the institutional staff with both women's family relationships. Lena's guardianship order restricted her access to her sister but did not involve Lena's housing. Jane's guardian, however, was responsible for Jane's accommodation. This meant that he determined her place of residence, in this case Unit N, and that without his permission she was unable to leave it. She could appeal this decision but had not done so.

Jane's guardian relied on reports from staff in the unit and occasional visits to inform himself of Jane's situation. On one occasion when Jane left the unit without permission, he contacted the police who brought her back. The Office of the Public Advocate for whom he worked prevented Jane from moving from the locked unit because she was regarded as a danger to herself or others.

### Self-Injury

None of the women in Unit N appeared to have been placed there because of self-injurious behaviour alone, however their files revealed that this was a common characteristic ascribed at varying times to nineteen of the women. The label 'self-injurious behaviour' included many different manifestations: Una pulled out her hair and ate cigarette butts; Jodie had smashed windows and scraped her wrists across the broken glass; Brigid banged her head; Kate and Dora scratched themselves. Such behaviour varied among the women in both its frequency and intensity.

Few of the women showed only one of these behaviours. For example Kirsten screamed, 'irritating other clients', and was perceived to be sexually vulnerable; Jane was perceived to be promiscuous and to be aggressive to staff; and Dora was verbally abusive and hit other people in the unit.

### Summing Up

It was often difficult to determine what particular incident precipitated a woman's entry to the locked unit. In the files none of the behaviours was described in context or in terms of its frequency or intensity. At most, the decision to send someone to the locked unit merited a one-line comment; at least, the unit identification letter was changed at the top of the file page with no reason being given for the transfer in the written notes. The women were sent to Unit N on the basis of the decision of staff in other units only. None of the women had committed a crime for which she had been sentenced by the courts and none had been sent to the unit by any form of independent tribunal. The notes on the files did not indicate that transfers were made in the women's best interests. Rather, there was a strong implicit message that each woman was moved from more open living because her behaviour was unacceptable or difficult to control. No suggested programmes went with the women to the locked unit, nor was there a time-limit on their stay there. While it was sometimes difficult to establish precisely how long a particular woman had been in the unit, all except one had been there for more than twelve months.

Further, in other open units, there were other women with 'difficult' behaviours. The woman's behaviour alone seemed not always the only factor which led to her confinement in the locked unit, but it was often impossible to decipher from the files what the other factors were.

The purpose of Unit N seemed to be to contain these women for 'the good of the rest of the clients'. Although staff working there expressed the hope that the women would move to more open living environments, and this was stated each year in their General Service Plans (GSPs), there were no consistent programmes in place to assist them to do so. If the women were to leave Unit N they had to change their own behaviour, alone. While the unit manager believed the women should not be in the locked unit, she also believed that behavioural change should precede their departure.

> I would like every client to have a daily occupation whether it just be an educational service where they actually left this unit and went out for the whole day to another environment. Most of these clients need to be within the centre to reduce their challenging behaviour and increase their social skills, and that would be an ideal set-up. (Interview with unit manager)

Such a view appeared to contradict staff beliefs that the environment of the locked unit militated against the women being able to change. For some of the women, being sent to Unit N was quite explicitly a punishment. Jane had been sent there after attacking a staff member, after having been threatened previously with such confinement.

Once women were in the unit it was extremely difficult for them to move back to more open living. The length of time they spent there was determined by the concern and capacity of the unit manager to get them out and the willingness of other unit managers to accept them into other units. Other unit managers generally rejected the women for admission to their unit because of the women's terrible reputation and because they had all been excluded at some time from other units in the institution. Unit N was the end of the line at Hilltop: there was nowhere else for the women to be placed.

The women could have appealed against the decision to lock them in Unit N. The Office of the Public Advocate, the Guardianship and Administration Board and the Intellectual Disability Review Panel all offered opportunities for an appeal against the decision made for each of the women. Also, doubts had been expressed by some of these groups about the legality of confining people in locked units.

> Because there is nothing to do at Hilltop, many residents want to leave. Unless they have been placed under guardianship, there is nothing in the Intellectually Disabled Persons Services Act that would permit any person to restrain them. Any locked door would prima facie constitute illegal imprisonment. (Borthwick, Kennedy, Mallia and Marshall, 1988, p.9)

None of the women appealed the decision to lock them up. Only Rhonda's family fought through the appeal mechanisms to have her released not only from the locked unit, but from Hilltop. They succeeded after a struggle. The other families I interviewed saw no alternative to the locked unit in the institution for their relative.

### Researcher/Detective

As I came to know the women who lived in the locked unit, the question of how they came to be there assumed great importance to me. I was bewildered by staff responses which suggested a lack of clarity about the reasons for the women's admission, and I was outraged that, unlike people in locked wards in psychiatric hospitals, there was no automatic review of their situation. Informal discussions with the women living in the unit revealed that only one of them was able or willing to give me a clear recollection of how she had come to the unit, and two others shared fragmented memories and stories.

My search for an answer to the question led me to the files, some of which went back fifty years and which provided fragmented, unsatisfactory pictures of why the women had been institutionalised and why they were in the locked unit. Superintendents' annual reports, medical certificates, psychological assessments and incident reports were separated into sections within manila folders. The nursing notes which contained each woman's history in the institution were handwritten fragments, the content and structure of which seemed to obey only the whim of the writer. Some described only the physical state of the woman over time; others concentrated on her behaviour. Consequently, it was difficult to gain an overall sense of the individual or her history. Having read these files I understood better why staff were so uncertain: nobody in the institution really had a clear idea of why many of the women were there. The experience of reading the files was frustrating and upsetting. I became angry at the attitudes exposed in them – conscious of how institutional language and practices were used to contain and deny the women – and shocked at the bleak and restricted lives they had lived. Sometimes reading the histories was almost unbearable.

I turned to families to assist in my search for an answer. But while they were able to tell me stories of their relative and how she had affected their lives, they did not answer my question. Rather, I came to an understanding of why they did not ask the question themselves, for I found that families' views of their relative were ambivalent and ambiguous. They knew little of their relative's life in the institution and were often afraid to ask questions which might jeopardise her placement there. These interviews were often long and emotional; for me they were haunting and painful. I identified with parents' struggles to live with their daughter at home, their ambivalence about the decision to institutionalise her and their subsequent separation from her. This identification was made more complex by my knowledge of and feelings towards the woman they were discussing.

In the interviews I found myself carrying out different roles. I provided information about their daughter to parents who had lost contact with her, I sat with people who cried (and sometimes cried with them), I supported people, and in at least one case I tried to remove a historical burden of guilt.

# CHAPTER 4

# *Locked Out/Locked In*

> I thought how unpleasant it is to be locked out; and I thought
> how it is worse perhaps to be locked in.
> *(Virginia Woolf [1929], 1994, p.29)*

Virginia Woolf mourned both her exclusion from privileged worlds
where men were accepted without question and her confinement to a
narrow world which defined her roles as a woman. I chose her statement
as the leading theme for this chapter for a number of reasons. It summarises evocatively the physical, psychological and emotional locking in
and out which the women in this study experienced in their lives. It
emphasises the social constitution of gender (see for example Deaux,
1993; Gentile, 1993; Unger and Crawford, 1993; Clements, Clare and
Ezelle, 1995) in which women are subject to power which categor-
ises them and shapes their lives and their subjectivity. Finally, Woolf's
statement stresses the importance of gender in any discussion of
women's lives: an importance which is frequently ignored when the lives
of women with intellectual disabilities are considered.

The women living in Unit N were locked out of particular forms of
community life and they were locked into a narrow and highly
prescriptive life-style. What was the impact of gender issues on these
processes? This chapter explores how the gender of the women was both
denied and simultaneously (and paradoxically) affirmed by those
around them. It demonstrates how gender discourses influenced the
women's exclusion from their families and communities. It also reveals
that gender was integral to the discourses of intellectual disability and
challenging behaviour which constituted the subjectivity of the women
in narrow and particular ways.

### The Women of Unit N: 'Failed Women'

'One is not born, but rather becomes, a woman' (de Beauvoir [1949], 1988, p.249). This view that the position of 'woman' is culturally determined and implies a set of known characteristics, behaviours and roles different from men's is important when viewed in the context of the lives of the women living in the locked unit.

As Spelman (1990) comments: 'If being a woman is something one can become, then it is also something one can fail to become' (Spelman, 1990, p.66). The field work for this book revealed that in the eyes of those around them the women who lived in the locked unit had 'failed' to become women. Yet their gender remained an often unacknowledged but constant concern to these same people and to the women themselves.

### *The Women as Failed Daughters and Sisters*

As some theorists (Danziger, 1990; N. Rose, 1990; Danziger, 1996) have pointed out, throughout this century we have become increasingly subject to psychological discourses which have produced particular views of normality for children and adults, and girls and women. The evidence from my field work revealed that the perceived failure of the women to take up a position within discourses which frame our view of normality as applied to girls and women made it difficult for their families to identify who they were or their place within the family.

Parents' confusion about their daughters seemed to originate with the diagnosis of intellectual disability by medical professionals. While this differed in time and kind from one family to another it was accompanied by professional opinions which indicated that a particular child 'would be no good' and that there was nothing that could be done for her. For example, Kirsten's mother commented that:

> at the Children's [hospital], once they told me she was retarded I never went back again. He [the doctor] said that there was nothing they could do for her so I thought 'What's the good of going?' and I just didn't want them to do anything for me. She was mine, she was my responsibility. (Interview with Kirsten's mother)

At this point, Kirsten became a 'responsibility' and remained so until she became too difficult for her parents to manage. Once the diagnosis was made, parents no longer expected their daughters to pass the developmental milestones prescribed by psychologists, the community and themselves, and they had no other knowledge by which to come to know their daughters. Further, the women not only challenged the prevailing knowledge and expectations about intellectual development, they also challenged the view that daughters would be 'emotionally stable', affectionate and obedient.

When I interviewed parents, they spoke of their daughter's time at home as a great struggle to communicate with her and to understand what appeared to be her unpredictable and irrational reactions to people and events. Such behaviour was difficult for families to cope with when it was directed to other people in the community, for example Faye's behaviour when out shopping with her mother (see Chapter 3), but it was even more distressing when it was directed at other members of the family.

> My family gave her so much love but she couldn't respond to it. You couldn't go to Kate and put your arms around her. She wouldn't accept it, that sort of thing. (Interview with Kate's mother)

Rather than their daughters moving towards increasing independence from their parents, in all cases the families were confronted with a person whose dependency upon them remained the same or actually seemed greater as time went on: 'I never went more than a hundred yards from home for more than ten years' (Interview with Kirsten's mother). This continuing dependence was one of the key reasons given by families for placing their daughters in an institution.

The failure of the women to take up an expected gender position had traumatic and life-changing consequences for both them and their families. There appeared to be no other discourse in which families could easily position their daughters. Consequently, family views of who or what their daughters were seemed confused, and this was expressed forcefully in the words family members tried to find to describe them. Thus Dora's father seemed uncomfortable with any designated label for his daughter (see Chapter 3). Similarly, other parents described their daughters as 'sick', 'patients', 'children', and 'insane'. These labels suggested that the only alternative to regarding their adult daughter as a highly dependent child was to see her as a sick individual or to fantasise that hidden deep inside her was another person.

> I always used to have the belief or the wish that she was tricking us, and one day she was really going to say 'Hey, you know I've been tricking you all these years; I really can talk.' And I always lived with that belief . . . for years and years . . . (Interview with Una's sister)

The difficulty which parents (and other family members) had in identifying who or what their daughters were removed these women from a position of being a family member and a woman to a position of

being 'other'. Kate's mother therefore talked of her 'daughter', referring only to her nondisabled child and excluding Kate as a family
member. Such exclusion was exemplified physically in the decision to
admit the woman to an institution. Yet paradoxically some parents saw
this decision in gender terms, for example Inge's father saw her admission to the institution as the means to safeguard her physically and
sexually. Parents also saw this decision as necessary for their own well-
being or for that of other family members. Like Dora's mother, all the
families interviewed spoke of their pain and despair over the living conditions present in institutions, yet they felt they had no other choice.

A woman's entry into the institution exacerbated her family's confusion and ambivalence about her and made her position as a woman
even less likely to be sustained in their eyes. Families knew less about
their relative's life once she entered the institution, for example both
Inge and Faye's families were advised not to visit for some months after
admission so that Inge and Faye could 'settle down'. Also, as documented in Chapter 2, family visits occurred at long intervals for short
periods of time and did not occur within the unit, meaning parents and
siblings knew even less of the woman's life.

Further, the records and my interviews with staff and families revealed
that institutional staff did not acquaint themselves with a detailed family
history, so, for example, the fact that Bettina came from a non-English-
speaking family was ignored in staff discussions of her abilities. The lack
of knowledge which staff had of the women's history or of the roles the
women may have played within their families led both staff and records
to focus very much on behaviour and on the fragmented and immediate
presence of the women. It also prevented staff from establishing links
on a day-to-day basis between the women's 'past lives' and their present
situation.

All the families I interviewed had loving stories to tell of their relative
but also expressed pain and fear at what they saw as her 'destructiveness'
to the family. The decision to institutionalise their relative provided
a point at which these feelings became particularly obvious (see for
example the reaction of Dora's mother to Dora's admission to an
institution in Chapter 3).

The confusion and ambivalence felt by families was mirrored in the
responses of some of the women. All of those with parents (with the
exception of Jane) showed unique affectionate responses to them on
visits, but these could also shift easily into anger, abuse and in the case
of Kate to physical attack directed at her mother on her weekly visits.

Sinason argues cogently that at least for some people with intellectual
disabilities the hurt and pain felt over the anger and rejection of their
parents may have contributed to a secondary intellectual disability, to

self-hate and to anger (Sinason, 1992, 1993). My observations suggested that the families' reactions did in some cases shape the subjectivity of the women. For example Lena saw herself as needing care and commented that she was in the institution 'because Mum is too old to look after me so I had to come to hospital'; however, once in the institution, her behaviour appeared to have become increasingly aggressive to the other women in the open units and led in twelve months to her being admitted to a locked unit and placed on tranquillisers. This would seem to suggest that a possible interpretation for some of the women's challenging behaviour related to a sense of exclusion and loss.

While the women may have been seen as 'failed daughters', both they and their families recognised a unique relationship, an inescapable 'locking in'. Some women made repeated requests to go home years after admission to the institution; all parents spoke with strong emotion of the separation of their daughter from the family; and some families had made repeated efforts to reintegrate their daughters into family life. Joyce went home for frequent holidays, and Elaine, Vera, Laura and Jane had lived for periods with members of their extended families.

### 'Failed Women'

> The income earning opportunities of women with disabilities are severely constrained. So, too, are their opportunities to be nurtured and to nurture, to be lovers and be loved, to be mothers if they desire. Women with disabilities are less likely than nondisabled women or disabled men to fulfill roles customarily reserved for their respective sexes. Exempted from the 'male' productive role and the 'female' nurturing one, having the glory of neither, disabled women are arguably doubly oppressed ... (Asch and Fine, 1992, p.151)

The women in Unit N did not take up any of the positions available to them in traditional gender discourses. They were not seen by their families or by the people at the institution as employable in any sense. On fifteen of their files, past doctors' assessments indicated that they would not even benefit from education. The most that was expected of the group was that Jane might attend an industrial workshop for two hours a week. But even this was subject to staff views about her psychological state on the day. The rest of the women did not have access to any kind of work on a paid or unpaid basis inside or outside the unit. Yet in the past, Vera, Elaine and Jane had held jobs in the outside community for varying lengths of time.

The confusion and ambivalence about the nature and subjectivity of the women was most clearly shown in the way in which their sexuality was 'managed' by those around them, and it was in relation to this issue that the paradoxical nature of the women's gender was most clearly in evidence. Sexuality was rarely discussed openly in the locked unit and it took some months for it to emerge as an issue of consideration for me as a researcher. However, its implied presence in part defined the world in which the women lived and informed the practices to which they were subject.

> Although services present themselves to parents in terms of their educational, training and habilitation agendas, there is ample evidence to support the notion that one implicit responsibility which parents expect services to discharge is the protection of their son or daughter from both sexual expression and sexual abuse or exploitation. (Brown, 1994, p.15)

While Hilltop may have had different service agendas to those described by Brown (1994), staff and families regarded the women's sexuality as a serious problem which had to be managed. And it was a serious problem primarily because the women were labelled as intellectually disabled.

The debate about eugenics which shaped discourses around intellectual disability early this century constituted people with intellectual disabilities as a risk to the community both because of attributed negative characteristics and because of the possibility that they would have children with similar disabilities (N. Rose, 1979; Bogdan and Taylor, 1982; Pfeiffer, 1994). For parents of the women, elements of this debate were apparent in their concerns about their daughters' sexuality: they were afraid of the consequences of their adult daughters becoming pregnant and they saw them as individuals whose intellectual disability left them vulnerable to exploitation. There is some justification for this fear as previous research has revealed that women with intellectual disabilities are particularly vulnerable to sexual exploitation and abuse (Johnson *et al.*, 1987; Sobsey, 1994; Brown and Turk, 1995; Heyman and Huckle, 1995). The women's sexuality was thus constructed by others in terms of either the threat of pregnancy or exploitation. It was not perceived as an expression of individual desire and an internal fantasy life (Brown and Barrett, 1994).

Evidence that a woman had been involved sexually with a man was taken very seriously by staff as a possible breach of their duty of care. Panic-stricken notes on Rhonda's file revealed a medical examination following her discovery in a yard alone with a man. The file goes to some lengths to vindicate staff in their care of Rhonda and to stress the improbability of 'anything' having taken place. Kirsten was promptly removed to the locked unit and placed on contraceptive pills after staff thought that she might have been assaulted in a 'mixed' unit.

Locking the women into Unit N provided some assurance for both staff and families that the women's sexuality would be managed and controlled. Both Jane and Kirsten were in part confined there because of their 'sexual activity', although for each of these women this was expressed very differently. In both instances it was the women who were removed from the situation, and whose behaviour was seen as unacceptable.

Further action was also taken to ensure the 'protection' of the women. The construction of their sexuality determined who cared for them and the kinds of relationships which they could have. No men staff were allowed to work in the unit, and they showed considerable reluctance to do so anyway, even in emergencies. It seemed that only women could control the sexual dangerousness of the women who lived in Unit N.

All community advocates were women, also. Consequently, the contact which the women in the locked unit had with men was restricted to members of their families and to chance meetings in the grounds. The ambiguous nature of the women's sexuality in the unit was translated into ambiguities in practice, for while the women were perceived as dangerous to men, leading to the creation of a world in which men had no part, they were also encouraged to 'look like women' (sic), and to look 'pretty' or 'sexy' by the staff in the unit.

Within the unit the sexuality of the women was rarely discussed except when it appeared to be a problem. Jane for instance was sometimes visited in the unit by a man with whom she had formed a relationship during one of her periods of community living. Her lover was later banned from seeing her because of a possible risk of HIV/AIDS and, ironically, Jane was then sent for sexual counselling to assist her in developing relationships with men. Both Joyce and Jane were regarded as difficult because they had made accusations of sexual abuse by men staff members. Consequently, they were watched closely. Lena was banned from seeing a relative after she accused him of 'touching' her on a visit to his home. All of these incidents led to the women being sent for sexual relationship counselling. This form of counselling was not seen as appropriate for the other women in the unit.

The lack of privacy within the unit ensured that all sexual expression was open to surveillance by the staff. Masturbation or genital touching was not treated as sexual behaviour but as an integral part of intellectual disability and as a 'dirty habit'. Women were reprimanded for this behaviour or told to stop it. They were not taught when and where it might be appropriate. However, Jane did have a 'private' room and there was explicit recognition by staff that this was in part because of her need for sexual expression.

It was impossible to know if sexual relationships existed between the women in the unit. Staff never discussed this and although there was evidence of warmth and affection between Kate and Bettina this did not appear to include an overtly sexual aspect.

The sexuality of the women in Unit N was therefore construed as a problem related to their intellectual disability which could be dealt with by isolating them from contact with others, containing their dangerousness and establishing strict measures of control over their behaviour. However, it was not only the sexuality of the women which was constituted in confusing and ambivalent ways: their behaviours both breached and confirmed the stereotyped views of women held in the wider society. The key issues for admitting the women to Unit N, as shown in the files, included loudness, sexual vulnerability or promiscuousness, aggression, running away and self-injury. None of these characteristics is regarded in our society as 'womanly', however Daston (1996) argues that these kinds of behaviours are seen in the wider community as an expression of uncontrolled and dangerous emotions characteristic of women. From this perspective the locked unit served to control and contain the women and to protect others in the institution (including other residents and men staff) from their destructive behaviour.

The failure of the women to take up positions in dominant gender discourses made them difficult to position. Staff in the unit and their families regarded the gender of the women with ambivalence. Informally within the unit, the women staff formed relationships with them which were complex and related often to gender issues but which often also seemed confused. My observations suggested that some staff took on a mothering role while others spoke sadly of the women's failure to live lives like their own. Sometimes staff fantasised about a different kind of life for them: one more in accord with traditional women's roles. The unit manager for example expressed regret that Dora had had so little opportunity to be involved in the household tasks which she seemed to enjoy, yet staff saw little possibility of enabling the women to take up such roles.

Informally, the individual members of staff related to some of the women in terms of commonly shared 'women's' issues. For example they encouraged Jane to 'lose weight' so that she would 'look pretty', and one staff member joined with her in a television exercise programme. Staff took time and care in doing the women's hair and applying make-up and frequently complimented them on their appearance. Yet staff in the past had played a part in making the women's bodies 'unwomanly', for example the women's front teeth were removed to prevent them from biting, Lena and Faye's legs were frequently swollen with cellulitis, and no efforts were made to assist those women with ungainly gait or with difficulties in communication. While the latter may also have been true for men living in the institution, its effect on the women was to distance them further from the traditional expected image of a woman.

While staff often related informally to the women as 'ladies' or as 'daughters', they also sought to distance themselves from them as women. As described in Chapter 2, these distinctions related in part to the routines of the unit and to the labels assigned to the women.

Personally I was ambivalent towards the women. I identified strongly with them as women who were oppressed by the system in which they lived and by their past experiences, and I felt a great deal of 'protectiveness' and affection towards them. I also felt considerable respect for them as survivors of an oppressive system. Such feelings related to their marginality and to their energy and were, I suspect, gender related. However, I did find it difficult to relate to them as peers and I found it easier to talk with staff about common family experiences and to talk of their 'work' than to talk with those women who could speak. These responses to the women seemed to be echoed in their relationships with staff and with their families.

Although these women had been locked out of traditional gender positions, some of them did try to place themselves within this discourse. Joyce and Dora were interested in families and in children, and Jodie adopted younger women in the unit and cared for them. Dora changed her clothes frequently in an effort to 'look nice', and Lena, Jane and Dora were conscious of their appearance and their looks. Jane was the only one of the women who was known to be involved in a heterosexual relationship, but some of the women (for example Dora) expressed strong and ambivalent feelings about men.

Gender issues informed the ways parents and siblings saw the women in the locked unit, but they did so in terms of what the women were *not*. The inability of others to position the women within the discourses of becoming a woman left the women largely unknown and ambiguous figures. It is hardly surprising then that the focus of knowledge of the women and the practices that arose around them were grounded in professional discourses of intellectual disability. There was, after all, certainty in diagnosis and professional knowledge. These enabled families and staff to 'understand' the women in the absence of other certainties. My field work revealed that the constitution of the women as intellectually disabled and as having challenging behaviour governed relations with them and excluded from consideration other aspects of their subjectivity.

### How Were the Women Known?

The question 'How were the women known?' and the additional one 'And by whom?' became increasingly important as I considered the women's situation over time. Consequently, the ways in which they were subject to power and knowledge became key concerns for this study. Conversations with them, with their families and with the staff gradually revealed the ways in which they had been locked out of, and locked into, the discourses which played through their lives.

My participation in and observations of life in the unit revealed the interplay of knowledge and power in the women's lives. Here were bodies of knowledge and practices which provided means of 'knowing' the women and which permeated the work of the staff in the unit, the methods by which the women were dealt with by senior managers in the institution and the ways in which families saw themselves in relation to their relative. These discourses also shaped the way the women saw themselves and the people around them; they allowed certain kinds of knowledge of the women and excluded others.

### *Knowing the Women: Intellectual Disability*

The aspect of the women's subjectivity most easily identified by those involved with them was their 'intellectual disability'. Their relationships with their families, their location in the institution, the formal documentation about their lives and the public responses of staff to them centred on this issue. It offered an assurance that the women were known and that they could be understood and related to. It also provided a rationale for their exclusion from both community and institutional life, for there was a professional certainty in the 'truth' that was spoken about their disability.

The majority of the women were sent to the institution at a time when the nature of intellectual disability, the capacity of psychological and 'scientific' means of identifying it and the practices to manage it were largely unquestioned (N. Rose, 1979; Pfeiffer, 1994; Danziger, 1996). IQ tests were seen as a valid and reliable means of measuring intelligence (Jensen, 1972; Terman, cited in Kamin, 1974), and intelligence was seen as a quantifiable and largely unchangeable characteristic. Once a person was identified as having an intellectual disability, the choices open to them and to their family were limited to largely unsupported 'care at home or institutional care' (Hand *et al.*, 1994). Institutional care was seen as the best option since it effectively removed a burden from the family and enabled more effective management of the individual. This was particularly important in relation to women, who were seen as a possible threat to the social and genetic health of the wider society, both because of attributed negative characteristics and because of their capacity to have children.

These certainties were apparent in the way the women were treated and managed. Thus the families I interviewed had been told that their daughters possessed a fixed and unchangeable characteristic: intellectual disability. Institutional care therefore was the best option available.

Institutional superintendents' reports relabelled the women annually with the terms appropriate to IQ levels: 'moron', 'imbecile' and 'idiot'. In more recent times the women were redefined as having 'borderline', 'mild', 'moderate', 'severe' or 'profound' disabilities. For neither form of categorisation was there evidence on the files that the women had been formally tested; the labels floated free from their anchor of IQ assessment. But the certainties integral to the diagnosis determined the way in which the women lived their lives, the ways they were perceived by staff and families, and the kinds of practices to which they were subject in the locked unit.

By the early 1990s, however, the discourse of intellectual disability had begun to change. Experts had questioned the validity and reliability of IQ tests and the values which underlay them (McClelland, 1972; Kamin, 1974; Hanson, 1994; Fraser, 1995; Goleman, 1996). Debates were developing in the literature which fundamentally questioned the nature of intelligence itself as defined historically in the psychological discourse (Hernstein and Murray, 1996; Jacoby and Glauberman, 1995; Goleman, 1996). From a strong focus on the IQ test as a means of identifying levels of 'intelligence', and promoting the belief that people with low scores on such tests constituted a threat to the community, experts progressively began to question the use of such tests as the sole arbiter of 'difference'. As a result, people with intellectual disabilities were reconstituted from 'villains' to 'victims' of societal oppression (see for example Wolfensberger, Olshansky, Perske and Roos, 1972; Hayes and Hayes, 1982; Hattersley, Hosking, Morrow and Myers, 1987; Ryan and Thomas, 1987; Leighton, 1988).

The impact of this new knowledge and these new 'truths' about intellectual disability led to a questioning of all that had been previously believed to constitute it. The unease with the old 'truths' of intellectual disability and the problematic nature of the new ones were reflected in the definition of 'mental retardation' developed in 1992 by the American Association on Mental Retardation (AAMR).

> Mental retardation refers to substantial limitations in present functioning. It is characterized by significantly subaverage intellectual functioning, existing concurrently with related limitations in two or more of the following adaptive skill areas: communication, self-care, home living, social skills, community use, self-direction, health and safety, functional academics, leisure and work. Mental retardation manifests before 18. (AAMR, 1992, p.1)

This definition reflected a shift from a substantial reliance on IQ tests as the principal means of diagnosing intellectual disability to the inclusion of 'adaptive behaviours'. The AAMR definition was further qualified by establishing the need to place these behaviours in the cultural and social context of the individual and the need to recognise the possibility of changes in adaptive behaviours. However, the changing discourse still maintained the focus on the 'difference' of people with intellectual disabilities and it continued and even amplified the fragmentation of their subjectivity into objective, measurable characteristics.

Within the locked unit the women were caught between these two different discourses of intellectual disability. Since 1986, by law, the women's adaptive skills, their strengths and their weaknesses had been reviewed annually by staff and family or advocates in their General Service Plans (GSPs) and Individual Programme Plans (IPPs), however the information provided by these plans did not challenge the prevailing views of staff or families about the nature of the women's intellectual disability. The plans provided tightly structured assessments which focused on predetermined skills and which were carried out not in a community context, but within the restricted living arrangements of the unit.

Other skills possessed by the women which lay outside the prescribed focus of the formal process of assessment were acknowledged informally by staff but were not considered in terms of the women's adaptive skills. Staff joked about Lena's real ability to drive a car and to ride a bicycle, commented on Elaine's skill in extracting cigarettes from reluctant staff members and reiterated a view that Brigid 'knows more than she lets on'. These skills were seen in the context of an existing, unchanging intellectual disability, and were usually viewed by staff as a tactical manoeuvre in a battle of wits between them and the individual which was split off from a consideration of that individual's intellectual abilities. Some skills which the women possessed, for example Vera's ability to play the piano, were outside the boundaries of even informal consideration.

Staff did consider identifying and developing independent living skills (adaptive skills) as an important part of their assessments of and work with the women. But it was difficult to consider these effectively within the context in which the women lived when this had not significantly changed. (This fundamentally undercut staff efforts to develop skills.) The group programme (see Chapter 2) was designed to assist the women in learning such skills, however it achieved little success, as the programme was inconsistent, staff had little training in teaching the women new skills, and the environment of the unit prohibited any attempts to show initiative or to practise newly acquired skills. Nor did the staff seem to have much faith in the programme's capacity to change the women's lives, for example the group of women with the most skills received least help from their staff leader (who as unit manager was preoccupied with administrative matters). Given this situation it is hardly surprising that the same learning goals appeared year after year in the carefully inscribed GSPs and IPPs. Thus the view of the immutability of intellectual disability was sustained in practice.

The original discourse of intellectual disability was predicated on the IQ results obtained on a narrowly defined test which relied on individual comparisons. From this result, a global picture of a person with a certain level of intellectual disability was developed. The negative stereotyping which resulted from this process has been amply documented in the literature (Wolfensberger *et al.*, 1972; Bogdan and Taylor, 1982; Bogdan, 1988; McGill and Cummings, 1990; Stainton, 1992; Wolfensberger, 1992). Examples of such stereotyping were revealed in my interviews with families and with staff, for example the women were individually described as 'monster', 'devil', 'child' and 'patient'.

In spite of the emphasis in the newer discourses of intellectual disability which sought to identify people with intellectual disability as citizens with rights, these negative stereotypes continued to underpin the way in which the women in Unit N were constituted by those around them. While the new and originally 'neutral' terms 'clients' and 'ladies' were used in referring to the women who lived in the locked unit, these continued to differentiate the woman and to define them as other.

The discourses of intellectual disability identified the women as one homogeneous group. The attribution of this category to the women camouflaged their individual differences in skills, interests and capacity, and finally constituted their subjectivity according to particular knowledge and practices.

### Knowing the Women: Challenging Behaviour

The women in the locked unit were regarded by those around them as dangerous to themselves and to others. This categorisation of them lessened the impact of new discourses of intellectual disability on their lives, for they were regarded as 'too dangerous to live in the community'. It also allowed staff to know them as individuals, for they were defined in knowledge and practice in terms of their behaviour.

Unit N was designated a unit for women with challenging behaviours. Staff knowledge and practices were centred upon this concept and it governed the way the unit was run, who was in it and how they were treated. It was integrally related to the discourses of intellectual disability, its meanings and practices identified, shaped and refracted through the prism which these provided. It was also closely related to the gender of the women.

The term 'challenging behaviour' is one which is used frequently and almost exclusively in the literature about people with intellectual disabilities in the United Kingdom and Australia and less commonly in the United States. It is a descriptive term which has a variety of meanings attached to it (Holt, 1995). It has emerged from attempts to find a non-pejorative term for 'problem' behaviour.

> Severely challenging behaviour refers to behaviour of such intensity, frequency or duration that the physical safety of the person or others is likely to be placed in serious jeopardy, or behaviour which is likely to seriously limit or delay access to and use of ordinary community facilities. (Emerson *et al.*, 1987)

Within this context the women in the unit showed all forms of 'challenging behaviour'.

> Challenging behaviours may be apparently 'unpredictable' or occasioned by a wide range of everyday events. They may be challenging because they occur with a high frequency, are particularly violent or distressing. They may be very difficult for relatives or staff to understand or have sympathy for and may be very difficult to control when they occur.
>     They may be associated with psychiatric disturbance but may equally well be associated with poor or inappropriate communication skills or with disturbance of social relationships. For the most part they will be of a chronic nature, having persisted over a long period of time. (Blunden and Allen, 1987, p.15)

Challenging behaviour is an omnibus term, like intellectual disability. Similarly, within the unit, it camouflaged a wide range of different behaviours while at the same time allowing staff and families to relate to the women in the unit as individuals.

Further, challenging behaviour also has nuances and double meanings, some of which are explicitly revealed by the literature and all of which were demonstrated in the locked unit. First, it 'challenged' service providers to find effective means of helping people who exhibited it (Blunden, 1990; Harris, 1991). In the case of the women at Hilltop this had led to the establishment of a specialist unit within the institution in which they could be 'contained', 'protected' and ostensibly rehabilitated.

Second, the term challenging behaviour has been described as subtly demeaning both to people with intellectual disabilities and to those involved with them; a term given to children's behaviour, not to the serious aggressive and self-injurious behaviours which it often describes (Hillary Brown, personal communication, 1992). In the unit, for example, the language of challenging behaviour reduced the high and frightening levels of violence and aggression to those which could be 'accepted' and 'managed'. In using this description of the behaviour it was as if women with intellectual disability were incapable of expressing unmanageable or dangerous behaviour even though their lifestyle was predicated on the belief that they could.

Finally, challenging behaviour can be seen as a challenge to service providers, families and advocates. In the unit the women's challenging behaviour shaped the staff reactions and gave them some control in their world, for the threat of violence was ever-present. As a consequence staff tended to be conciliatory in dealing with individuals. They watched each woman carefully and tried to take evasive action if she showed signs of anger or frustration. Further, the women were able, through their behaviour, to manage or alter the routines of the unit, for example bed-times could be altered, or women could through particular behaviours force a separation for a period of time from someone they did not like.

In some instances, challenging behaviour was also perceived by staff as the result of wilful or bad intent on the part of the individual. In the past, the presence of Unit N at Hilltop had meant people were sent there when their behaviour was regarded as unacceptable in other units. The behaviour was decontextualised and the 'problem' was moved on; the locked unit was the end point of this movement. As a consequence Unit N was perceived as a punishment unit by some staff, and challenging behaviour was perceived as 'bad' behaviour in relation to some women (implying both intentionality and choice). Thus Jane was told that if she could control her anger for three months she would be allowed to live elsewhere.

For staff in the unit, the presence of challenging behaviour was a 'challenge' both to them and to the system. In interviews, staff commented that they liked working in the unit because the women posed a challenge or were 'real characters', yet at the same time staff were anxious about being attacked by some of the women. However, the very threat of attack was also a source of pride to the staff: pride in their capacity to avoid it or to contain uncontrollable behaviours or to wear scars and continue to work within the unit. The presence of challenging behaviour thus motivated staff in their work and gave them credit in the wider institution. Staff therefore found themselves in a double bind. Their task ostensibly was to rehabilitate the women, but if they were successful in this, both their skills and the status which they held within the institution would be lost or devalued.

As with intellectual disability, challenging behaviour was also used by staff as a camouflage for their lack of understanding or their inability to infer meaning from some behaviours. It became an explanatory device, and once it was used, further exploration of the behaviour did not really need to occur. It offered a description, a diagnosis and a position from which staff could act in relation to the woman concerned, for by its very nature and definition challenging behaviour focuses on easily observable external responses. Staff knowledge and training consequently led them to concentrate their attention on *behaviour*, precluding from formal consideration the difficult task of inferring the emotional or psychological state which a particular woman might have been experiencing.

While staff implicitly recognised a number of different meanings in the women's challenging behaviour, in their work they explicitly and formally saw such behaviour as an integral part of intellectual disability and/or as a result of institutionalisation. There is evidence within the literature that some forms of 'challenging behaviour' may be due to biological imbalances associated with particular kinds of intellectual disability (Presland, 1989; Holt, 1995), however there is little evidence that staff or the women in the unit had access to the kind of sophisticated diagnosis which would enable such links to be established clearly for individuals. Rather, staff used their training and the literature as a basis for the postulation of a general causal connection between behaviour and intellectual disability. This in turn led to a staff view that challenging behaviour was largely unchangeable and out of the control of the individual concerned. Staff also saw challenging behaviour as being due to the effects of institutionalisation. In particular, they saw some of the women's behaviours as resulting directly from their admission to the locked unit. Boredom, frustration, loneliness, the need for attention, and limited access to other people and ways of behaving were perceived by staff to be precursors of some challenging behaviour, but once the women were in the unit, staff found it difficult to move them out and were also unsure as to what should be done with them.

As with intellectual disability, it was difficult to know how the women viewed the behaviour that others regarded as challenging. Jane said she 'got angry' when she was aggressive. Lena turned away and refused to answer when asked about her removal of others' property or her attacks on other people. But no one really sought answers from the women themselves, as the knowledge and practices around challenging behaviour confirmed that it was 'known' and 'understood'.

Given these attributed meanings of challenging behaviour it is not surprising that staff practices in relation to it were both guided by the prevailing literature and were narrow in their focus. They also rested on assumptions about the nature of intellectual disability and the presumed incapacity of many of the women to be active agents.

The diverse meanings given by the staff to challenging behaviour had a profound impact on the practices used to 'manage' it within the locked unit. There is evidence in the literature that medication may be useful in managing some forms of challenging behaviour (see for example Heistad, Zimmerman and Doebler, 1982; Aman, 1985; Crabbe, 1995). However, there has also been concern expressed at the over-use of such medication (Aman and Sing, 1988) and at the side-effects of drugs such as Melleril and Largactil, which when taken over time lead to lapses in concentration, memory losses and physical side-effects such as tremors and shaking (Estroff, 1981; Kelly, 1991; Hubert, 1992a,b). Within the locked unit almost all of the women were on such medication and it was the main method used by staff in controlling challenging behaviour. Staff were critical of the use of such medication and stated that they wanted to reduce its consumption, but doses were increased when this was regarded as necessary and reviews of medication were irregular. The long-term side-effects of some forms of medication were an unacknowledged part of life in the unit and were not postulated as contributing factors to the women's disability.

Aversive methods of behaviour modification described in the literature (Conway and Bucher, 1974; Bailey, 1983; Carr and Lovaas, 1983; Donnellan and Cutler, 1991) were rarely used as a conscious strategy, with 'time out' being the method used most often (Brantner and Doherty, 1983), but they were sometimes used as a measure born of desperation, for example threatening Brigid with water (see Chapter 2). However, there was a strong emphasis on behaviour modification and analytic strategies (Goldstein and Keller, 1987; Presland, 1989; Helstetter and Durand, 1991; Horner, 1991; Gardner and Graeber, 1995). Such programmes were outlined in each IPP but were never consistently carried out in the chaotic environment of the unit, where they were euphemistically described as 'informal'. The Behaviour Intervention Support Team (BIST) was used to assist staff in developing such strategies but there was little follow-up owing to a shortage of resources.

Methods such as gentle teaching (McGee, Menousek and Hobbs, 1987; McGee and Menolascino, 1991), with its emphasis on the need for 'bonding', 'mutual respect' and 'acceptance', were not used in the unit. Psychotherapeutic methods based on a view about the internal life of the person and on assumptions about the capacity of individuals to change or to be active agents (Sinason, 1991, 1992; Waitman and Conboy-Hill, 1992; Bicknell, 1994; Hollins, Sinason and Thompson, 1995) were not discussed or used by staff. Indeed 'counselling' was a euphemism used for reprimanding an individual after they had engaged in unacceptable behaviour. Some efforts were made to teach people alternative strategies for dealing with stress and anger, but these had little success.

In spite of the acknowledged failure of existing methods to change the women's behaviour, staff did not question the usefulness of them. No other options were available to them within the prevailing discourse. My observations suggested that the use of these methods controlled and sustained behaviour which was labelled challenging. There was no prospect of escape by the women without a change in their behaviour, and there was no hope of a change in their behaviour while they stayed in the unit.

The discourse around challenging behaviour constituted the women as the problem. Once the woman was labelled, her removal to the locked unit ensured that the behaviour would become the focus of staff attention and surveillance, for its problematic nature was the *raison d'être* of the unit. My observations suggested that this discourse served to provide a way of 'knowing' the women which contained them, and it served in some instances to sustain and even to exacerbate their behaviour.

Gender has not usually been considered as an issue in analyses of challenging behaviour although as Clements *et al.* (1995) describe, the failure to do so can both precipitate and exacerbate such behaviours. For the women who lived in the locked unit gender was an unspoken but ever-present issue. It defined the challenging behaviour of some women; and for others the staff's failure to consider gender issues led to a superficial view of aggressive behaviour. For example Jane had been sexually abused by both her father and brothers throughout her childhood, yet in her admission to the locked unit, her visits to psychiatrists and her admission to a psychiatric institution, this issue was never taken into account, nor was she offered counselling for the psychological and physical trauma she had experienced. The gender of the women determined their physical location, who cared for them and the ways in which they were treated. The particular form of challenging behaviour which they showed seemed largely to define their individuality for staff working in the unit and also for families. They were 'known' by their behaviour, so while challenging behaviour identified them as a particular group it also separated them as individuals.

*Summing Up*

Historical and prevailing discourses of intellectual disability permeated and suffused the lives of the women. Their lives and their subjectivity were defined, shaped and managed by these discourses. The life of the unit, the meanings staff gave to their work and the ways families related to the women all depended on the maintenance of a construction of the women as a homogeneous group of women with intellectual disability who were dangerous and who required protection from themselves and the community. It is hardly surprising then that the practices in the unit, while ostensibly designed to rehabilitate, instead emphasised management and control. It seemed inevitable that the women would remain subject to this discourse for the foreseeable future.

# PART II

# *Coming Out*

We are in the society of the teacher-judge, the doctor-judge, the educator-judge, the social worker-judge; it is on them that the universal reign of the normative is based; and each individual, wherever he may find himself, subjects to it, his body, his gestures, his behaviour, his aptitudes, his achievements.

(Michel Foucault, 1979, p.304)

Four months after I began my field work in the locked unit, and eighteen months into my research, the government decided to close Hilltop and to do it within twelve months. The decision was to bring the women to the attention of the guardians of the 'normative' and to change their lives forever.

This introduction places the institutional closure within the wider context of deinstitutionalisation and describes the way in which it was designed and implemented.

The decision to close Hilltop was a profound shock to staff and families of people living there. However, it was clear that preparations for the closure had been undertaken over time and in considerable secrecy. The staff received a package of materials outlining the closure process on the day that a media announcement was made. A consultation process with families, staff and people living at the institution had been developed over two years, and negotiations with the central branch of the union were under way.

As with institutional closures in other countries the decision to close Hilltop was motivated by a mixture of ideological and pragmatic issues. Over the past ten years there had been increasing community and media criticism of the care given by institutions.

The cost of renovating the institution was believed to be higher than the cost of closing it and the decision was believed to be a popular one in an election year. However, the decision was primarily motivated by a growing belief that institutions were not the best places for people with intellectual disabilities. The government's commitment to deinstitution-alisation had developed during the 1980s. It was reflected in new legislation designed to establish the rights of people with intellectual disabilities (*The Intellectually Disabled Persons' Services Act 1986*) and in the establishment of a public advocate (ombudsman) to ensure that these rights were protected. The government had also moved to decrease the numbers of people admitted to institutions over this time. While not explicitly defined in government policy the elements included in deinstitutionalisation appeared to be:

> The reduction in the number of admissions to public institutions, the development of alternative community methods of care, the return to the community of those individuals capable of functioning in a less restrictive environment and the reform of public institutions to improve the quality of care provided. (Willer and Intagliata, 1984, p.3)

In adopting deinstitutionalisation as a policy the government was following trends occurring in Western Europe, the United Kingdom and the United States (see for example Steer, 1986; Korman and Glennerster, 1990; Collins, 1992; Tossebro, 1996). However, deinstitutionalisation in Australia as elsewhere has not been without difficulties. Large institutions have proved difficult to close because of the cost involved, community fears about people with intellectual disabilities and resistance to the closure by staff and parent groups.

### The Decision to Close Hilltop

The closure process included four major political decisions which were to have important implications for the women living at Hilltop. The institution was to be closed within twelve months and this was to happen regardless of union opposition. This time-line was to ensure that there would be little opportunity for the development of a campaign against the closure by the union or other people. Setting such a tight deadline also affirmed, to staff, the government's commitment to finally close Hilltop, however it gave little time for a detailed consideration of individuals' needs.

Of the 440 people living at Hilltop, 216 would find a new home in the community. Approximately twenty-five were expected to be relocated to nursing homes because of their age and dependency, and the remainder were to be relocated at other training centres around the state. This decision was made on economic grounds. Discussions which I held with people working within the relevant government department revealed that the cost of housing all Hilltop residents in the community was perceived by the government to be too great. In effect, this set the people living at Hilltop in competition with each other for scarce community places.

Although the closure document indicated that some 'high support' people would move into the community, the factors which appeared to be important in deciding on a community placement were listed as client preference, the availability of regional support services, day programmes, other services and suitable housing. These factors, with the exception of the first, militated against people with high dependency needs or difficult behaviours moving to the community.

All people at Hilltop were to move to accommodation and services which were equal to, or better than, those which they currently experienced in the institution. This meant that those people living in the best accommodation at Hilltop, for example in the houses on the grounds, were in a privileged position in relation to people living in the worst accommodation. While this was an unintended consequence of a decision which was meant to establish some form of quality assurance, it had ongoing repercussions for people throughout the closure process.

Finally, the package promised that permanent staff at Hilltop would be employed in the new community houses, in other training centres or in other areas of the public service. An enhanced resignation package was to be offered to staff who wished to leave the Department. This strategy meant that staff would begin to leave the institution during the process of closure, though in some cases their relocation or resignation could be negotiated to suit the needs of the people at Hilltop.

### The Stages of Closing Hilltop

While early responses to the decision to close Hilltop were chaotic at both a project management and an institutional level, some months after the decision a clear series of stages for its closure had been defined. Details of each of these were only worked out as the stage itself was entered, but a broad outline of the process was formulated through the use of a critical path which was developed in consultation with all managers involved in the project. This resulted in a step-by-step analysis of tasks and objectives through the process of closure. Essentially, there were five stages to the process.

### Stage 1: Formation of the Project Team

The first three months of the closure project involved the establishment of an independent project team and detailed planning of the project. This was led by a manager who had skills in project direction but no knowledge of the field of intellectual disability. Working with him were managers who were skilled in this area. Key areas of responsibility for these managers included planning and resources, client relocation regional liaison, capital works, and staffing services and training.

### Stage 2: 'Client' and Staff Consultation on Relocation

The second three months involved extensive consultation which aimed to establish three preferences for each person in relation to their future living arrangements. 'Clients', their families and/or advocates, staff, and members of the client relocation team participated in a series of meetings from which information about the individual and their preferences were gathered. At the same time, following the signing of an industrial agreement, staff received information about redundancy packages and redeployment opportunities. They were asked to specify preferences for their future work.

### Stage 3: Matching

Following the establishment of preferences, a process of matching people living at Hilltop with particular future living arrangements was carried out. Decisions were finally made during matching about whether a person should go to a house in the community, to another institution or to a nursing home. A similar process was carried out with staff, who were gradually matched to vacancies becoming available through public service bulletins. During this time staff began to leave the institution – some to take up enhanced resignation packages early in the process and others as new jobs became available.

### Stage 4: Transition

At the completion of the matching process families and clients were notified of the decisions which had been made. Avenues of appeal were made available for those unhappy with the decision. Following the final matching decision, work with regions and institutions increased. Negotiations around funding and development of services were carried out by the regional liaison team. Assets of the institution (and of the people living there) were assessed and reallocated. The transition stage saw the gradual movement of people into their new homes and staff to new jobs. This was also the period when the institution itself began to close down.

### Stage 5: The End of the Institution

Stage 5 was concerned with the final 'mopping up' of the project. This included the sale of assets of the institution and its final decommissioning. Closure-team staff completed a final monitoring of people who moved into their new homes.

# CHAPTER 5

# *The Unlocked Door*

These adults – like children – need care and protection.
But will they be left without care and direction?
Plans to remove them from their home so secure –
Some of these plans are a pile of manure.
A house on the outside, they say, that's the best,
But will they be lost and abused like the rest?
Instead of fun and hugs and treats,
Will they be out wandering the streets?
As for the clients who aren't so nice
If they moved next to you, you'd move out in a trice
They yell and fight or make a mess,
Wander or steal, or destroy more or less.
Would you want them living next to you?
*(Anonymous staff poem written on the
announcement that Hilltop would be closed.)*

The announcement of the decision to close Hilltop immediately divided staff, families and people living at the institution into those supporting its closure and those resisting it. This polarisation continued throughout the closure and had implications for how it occurred and for its end results. For the women in the locked unit the decision offered an opportunity for release from their narrow world. This chapter is an introduction to the women's 'coming out'. It describes the reactions to the closure decision both of the people in the women's immediate world and of those less directly involved: people in the institution and in the wider community.

## The Women's World

The time immediately following the decision to close the institution was chaotic and anxiety-provoking both for the women and for those involved with them.

84

*Vera's Story*

Vera was a tiny woman with grey-brown shoulder length hair often worn in a bun. She had a thin attractive face with bright dark eyes and a gentle rather high-pitched voice. She shook a little, probably from the long-term effects of medication. Her reaction to the announcement to close Hilltop was unambiguous and forthright, as evidenced by my field notes.

> I unlocked the front door of the unit and walked into the passage. I was feeling anxious as this was my first visit to the unit after the media coverage of the closure. Vera and Ilse were standing in the passage. Vera ran towards me and took my arm. She said in a soft, excited voice: 'Hilltop's going. I'll be going home. Soon. I want to go home.' (Field notes)

'Going home' meant being with her sisters and having things to do: watching television, reading magazines and playing cards. She ended our conversation with the comment 'I've been here a long time.'

Vera had certainly been at Hilltop for a long time. Her citizen advocate stated that Vera had lived at Hilltop for forty-one years, on and off. It was thirty years since her final admission and prior to that she had spent varying amounts of time there for either months or years. She still had vivid pictures of what home meant and always and unavailingly asked her family to take her there when they visited her.

'Going home' had always been elusive for Vera, even in her childhood. She was one of twins and she lived with her four brothers and sisters on an isolated farm. When she was five, she and two other sisters contracted polio. They were sent to a large country hospital some hundreds of miles from home. She did not return to her parents for five years and during this time her schooling was very limited. While the polio did not affect her mobility, it did completely disrupt her childhood.

Retrospectively, Vera's sisters commented that they thought she and her twin had been 'different' from when they were very young but that this only became really evident in their teenage years. Vera refused to eat, began to hallucinate and spent her nights talking and singing, keeping the rest of the family awake for weeks at a time. Her behaviour included hitting her sisters who were her main carers. Vera managed to obtain a number of jobs, none of which she kept very long. She was sent to Hilltop when her family could no longer cope with caring for her. Her twin sister, who showed similar behaviours, continued to be cared for by her family until her death.

Diagnoses differed about Vera in her file notes. In 1955 the doctor at the institution commented that: 'She is a congenital mental defective with schizophrenia. She is probably in the low grade moron class but may be lower than this' (Doctor's report on Vera's file). A later diagnosis stated that Vera was:

> A borderline intelligence [sic] woman of thirty-two with apathy and withdrawal occasioned by perceptual isolation and poor schooling due to polio as a child together with frank schizophrenia intervening at age fourteen. Her mental retardation is undoubtedly due entirely to these factors and not to any genetic defect. She is now a chronic schizophrenic. (Superintendent's report on Vera's file)

Vera's file later indicated a diagnosis of manic depressive illness for which she was treated with lithium. It was now impossible to differentiate between Vera's original condition and the iatrogenic effects of the treatment she had been given. Vera had been treated repeatedly with electro-convulsive therapy on her first admissions to Hilltop and she had been on large doses of Largactil and other anti-psychotic drugs for long periods. Staff in the unit said they did not really know why she was in Unit N. Her file stated that:

> Vera was placed in Unit N as she suffers from hypomania. When Vera is in a manic phase she hallucinates, strips off her clothing, urinates, hits others and runs away. (Unit manager's note on Vera's file)

Vera's manic episodes were now infrequent and were usually controlled with medication. Perhaps the main reason for her continued stay in the unit was the difficulty in finding another place for her.

Following the decision to close Hilltop, staff were concerned that Vera would be separated from her close friend Ilse during the relocation. The two had a very close relationship, sharing all their waking hours and sleeping near each other at night. They spent much of each day in the passage outside the staff office, where they stood hand in hand, sometimes asking for coffee or money to go to the kiosk. Both had advocates and were often taken out together.

Ilse and Vera interpreted each other to staff. Because Ilse was deaf, she sometimes did not hear what staff were saying. Vera would answer for her or reinterpret the words. Ilse had a strong sense of her rights and would protect Vera from other women or staff. Ilse and Vera were also very friendly with Elaine, who was protective of them, would save treats to share with them and was anxious if they were away for any length of time.

Vera frequently said that she wanted to go home and her life at Hilltop seemed to offer her little in the way of activity. She and Ilse were very afraid in Unit N. 'We want to go downstairs; they [the other women] might bash us up here,' was a frequent comment. However, while Vera spent much of her time afraid, she could become angry and aggressive, shouting at other women whom she believed had offended her, and in some instances, though very rarely, hitting them. When in a large group Ilse and Vera tended to sit on the edges, not getting involved in fights or arguments. They tended to make many requests of staff, which while generally tolerated were perceived as demanding. Vera had a great liking for nice clothes, and could play the piano and sing. Her advocate commented that she could read very well. None of these skills was registered in her files nor could she use them in the unit. Her family recognised this and wrote in distress to management at Hilltop, commenting that:

> Institutions having large numbers of inmates are unable to allow much enjoyment of the everyday activities to which they were once accustomed. In Vera's case, kitchen and house duties, indoor games and puzzles, singing music of her own control [sic]. (Letter from Vera's sister on Vera's file)

It is hardly surprising that after forty years of institutional life in which she had held strongly to her desire to leave, Vera should regard the decision to close Hilltop as an opportunity to escape. In fact, the door of Unit N opened sooner for her than for many other women. Soon after the decision the unit manager negotiated for Ilse and Vera to move down the hill to a more comfortable open unit with other older women in the hope that this would increase their chances for community placement. They remained in this unit for the remainder of their time at Hilltop. In the new unit they showed me their beds (still in a dormitory), the caged birds and plants in the living room, and the magazines. There was even a piano in the corner of the room. While Vera said intermittently that she did not like the new unit, her visits back to Unit N were restricted to standing in the passage with Ilse and talking with Elaine and the staff. She never again ventured into the day room.

### The Women's Responses to the Unit N Closure Decision

Following the decision to close Hilltop, each of the women received a letter from the government informing her of the institution's impending closure and reassuring her that alternative accommodation would be provided. However, my observations revealed that this method of providing information was useless. Only one of the women could read and none was able to understand the formal language. The women found out about the decision either by staff interpreting the letter or through informal comments and discussion within the unit. Some staff were visibly upset and shocked by the announcement and conveyed this to the women. This sometimes led to confusion and anxiety:

> I walked into the day room [on the day of the announcement]. Dora rushed up to me. She said: 'They're pulling down the buildings. It's all going. Where will we go?' (Field notes)

Ilse commented to staff members: 'They'll kill us out there [in the community].' The fear and anxiety experienced by some of the women was heightened by staff reactions.

> Joyce said happily: 'Hilltop's gone, so I'll be going home.' N. [staff member] said: 'No, you won't be going home, Joyce. You'll have to live in a community house with lots of people you don't know.' Joyce looked anxious and walked away. (Field notes)

One staff member, obviously anxious and upset about the decision, gave Jodie a hug in the day room and said: 'You don't want to leave us and go into the community do you?' Jodie said 'No' (Field notes).

Reactions from other women varied. For example Vera spoke of going 'home' to live, and immediately following the announcement Jane was involved in several acts of aggression against staff which led to her isolation for some time (no one suggested a possible link between the two events). Some of the women were not able to communicate how they felt about the decision and others were not aware of it.

The decision to close the institution also had an immediate direct effect on the women's lives. Initially the decision to open the doors of the institution further restricted the lives of the women. Industrial bans, which were introduced within a few days of the closure announcement, prevented the women from leaving the grounds in the company of staff except for medical treatment, meaning that even their infrequent excursions into the nearby town were curtailed. Rhonda, who was about to leave the institution to take up a community placement, was only allowed to do so after much discussion with the union.

### Families

All the women's families had been notified by letter of Hilltop's closure, however these letters did not arrive until some time after the public announcement. The majority of the parents heard of the closure through the media or friends. All of the families I interviewed expressed initial reactions of shock, anxiety, fear and anger on hearing of the decision.

> So it was a bit of a shock, but it's up to the government to do something towards it ... which they have. But I was thinking of all those poor people, me included, who'd have to take their children home. Well, I thought that at my

age ... I was afraid. Under normal circumstances I would, but I can't ... I thought of me and all the people who are older than me ... I was really worried because they virtually sent us a letter ... saying ... that ... there was nothing in the letter saying anything about future accommodation ... Just that you'd be consulted, but what were they going to consult about? Were they going to consult you about you taking her home, or you finding somewhere? (Interview with Kirsten's mother)

In the interviews, all parents and families said that they had felt certain that their relative would be in Hilltop for life. This certainty had now gone and old guilts, fears and terrors as well as memories resurfaced. The families were uncertain about what the short-term consequences of the decision might be and were also distrustful of government promises to provide continuing services to their relative. Such anxieties and concerns were exacerbated by the campaign run by the Hilltop Parents and Friends Association at the institution, which urged families to resist the closure process. Siblings who had taken responsibility for their sister upon the death of parents seemed less afraid of the decision than did parents. The former, after the initial shock had been reduced, thought that the decision offered a new opportunity for the women to begin life in the community and they expressed the view that Hilltop should go. But even when families later supported the move of their relative into the community the initial response was universally one of shock and denial.

### Staff Responses to the Unit N Closure Decision

The closure announcement came on the day that the dormitories in Unit N began to be subdivided into more private bedroom spaces. The irony of this was not lost on the staff who had fought hard for the renovation. One staff member commented that on the day the announcement was made: 'Everyone was very depressed. We did nothing all day, just sat around and talked about it' (Interview with B.).

All staff in the unit were concerned about their future job prospects and their security, however they also expressed a great deal of concern about the women in the unit. The managers in the unit, in particular, were concerned that the women would simply be moved *en masse* to other institutions because of their bad reputation. They were also concerned that an industrial strike might be called by the union (there is a full discussion of the union reaction later in this chapter) and they had horror stories of how the women had been treated during the last one. As in the wider institution, staff in the unit were polarised in relation to industrial action, with food and domestic services staff and less-qualified direct care staff supporting it and staff with greater training and responsibility opposing it.

The days following the closure decision were frenetic. Staff had little information about the closure details, and parents, families and advocates flooded the unit with anxious queries. There were frequent union meetings, which meant that the unit was chronically short staffed. Staff anxiety and concern also led them to be preoccupied, so at a very stressful time staff were unable to offer the women their full attention and support.

In an effort to prevent the removal of the women to other institutions, the manager instituted some changes to the unit. Plans for Rhonda to move into the community were accelerated in spite of tensions with the sub-branch of the union. Ilse and Vera were transferred, and unsuccessful efforts were made to encourage Elaine to go also. A small evaluation of the group programme in the unit (see Chapter 2) was concluded quickly and its recommendations included a process to assist the women in adjusting to the closure. This was submitted to senior management at the institution but no action was taken on it. Efforts at increasing independent living skills, at least in relation to meal times and bath times, were increased.

The unit manager tried unsuccessfully to gain more access to a house on the grounds to provide the women with some experience of living in the community. She began a pilot project which involved unlocking the doors of the unit at specified times during the day, hoping to prove that the women could live in more open situations. It was ironic that it took impending closure to initiate such reforms in the unit. Unfortunately, at the same time the unit manager was trying to carry out these changes, staff rosters became fragmented as staff left for further training or to take up new jobs. Her experienced core staff were in demand in other units as those with most experience began to leave. The initiatives foundered to some extent on the lack of resources and support.

## The Wider Context

With the decision to close the institution, the number of people concerned with the women living in the unit and their future increased. In particular, institutional and project team managers and the union sub-branch held differing positions in relation to the closure. These positions were to have an increasing effect on the lives of the women as deinstitutionalisation gained momentum.

### Institutional Managers

Senior managers at the institution had known some weeks previously that the decision to close Hilltop was going to be made. At that point their main concern was to ensure that the decision was not 'leaked' to the staff because they wanted to maintain the initiative in relation to expected industrial action. Yet in spite of their foreknowledge of the decision, senior managers were still shocked by it.

> Oh, it was still a surprise. I knew ahead of the announcement. I knew ahead of time, but when it was actually said to the public ... it was still a sort of surprise, like somebody dying. (Interview with institutional senior manager A.)

Following the announcement of the closure the senior managers were primarily concerned about the possible industrial issues and about the mechanics of the actual closure process. They had a vested interest in making sure that their areas of responsibility were managed well during the closure in order to maximise their future career options, so there was a mixture of determination and preparation for battle in the way in which they discussed the decision. When asked about the future of the people living at Hilltop, they expressed anxiety about the effects of moving people internally prior to the final closure, concern about difficulties which some people might experience in going into the community and a belief that some people should not leave institutional life.

> With the best will in the world and the best technology available in IDS [Intellectual Disability Services] there are people here who I would not be at all confident about going to live in a house because of the risk they represent to themselves, to their fellow clients and to staff and potentially to the community. And the risk we would run in placing some of these people in houses is [to] ... set up isolated mini-institutions rather than isolated monolithic institutions like this one. (Interview with institutional senior manager C.)

It seemed that the issue of perceived 'dangerousness' and 'challenging behaviour' would be a key criterion in deciding the future of the people living at Hilltop.

### The Closure Project Team Managers

The closure project team leader saw the Hilltop closure as a challenge in negotiating change with politicians, the union and other interested parties, and he saw his role as one of managing change and intrusion.

> Because any project becomes an intrusion: either it's an intrusion here [at the head office of the responsible government department] or it's an intrusion in the way Hilltop is operating on a significant scale. (Interview with project team leader)

When asked how he saw the outcomes of the project his response was pragmatic:

> If I'm being really idealistic, they'd be, I guess, the clients accommodated in their new accommodation, the same with staff, and that things are actually operating in a reasonable way. (Interview with project team leader)

The cool and strategic way in which the project was portrayed by the team leader contrasted strongly with the sense of personal commitment to deinstitutionalisation at Hilltop which was voiced by three of the project team managers responsible to him. For these people it was the culminating project of ten or more years' working in the field. They had risked job security or promotion or their health to take on the task. Those directly concerned with the development of new services and the relocation of Hilltop residents and staff indicated strong views on institutions and their future.

> I don't think that there should be institutions. They should be bombed. And in institutions staff talk about what's a 'good' institution and what's not and you try to explain to them that they are not good, there is no gradedness; like, they're all the same. (Interview with project team manager Q.)

The remaining two managers held a pragmatic view of the closure and one which was more consistent with that of the team leader, but for all of the project team managers the decision to close Hilltop was the beginning of a challenge: to succeed where others had failed before, and to achieve a milestone in deinstitutionalisation.

### The Union

The response of the union sub-branch to the announcement of the closure of Hilltop was swift. Within twenty-four hours of the announcement, it had called a meeting of all staff. Present at this meeting were the senior members of the federal union and almost all the staff at the institution. The meeting (which I attended) was angry and frustrated. Lack of trust in the decisions made by the central branch of the union was expressed by staff who felt that they had been 'betrayed' by a proposed industrial agreement between the union leaders and the government. The meeting unanimously passed a resolution condemning the decision to close the institution. Particular concern was expressed at the decision to move Hilltop residents to other institutions and, more forcefully, at the possibility of job loss for union members. The following day a series of industrial bans was introduced by staff at the institution. These included a decision not to co-operate in any way with the closure project team, bans on excursions for people living at Hilltop, and bans on transferring people from the institution to community placements or to other institutions. The bans also included a refusal to complete any General Service Plans (GSP) or Individual Programme Plans (IPPs) and a prohibition on any research being carried out in the institution. All of these bans, with the exception of the last one, were kept in place for almost six months.

Yet beneath this action were divided loyalties and differences between staff which in part prevented more radical industrial action. For example direct care staff were anxious at the possible implications of extended or militant union action to oppose the closure decision. They had better opportunities to obtain work than the non-direct care staff and were legally responsible for the welfare of the people living in the institution. Non-direct care staff who wielded most power in the union sub-branch were vehemently opposed to closure and were anxious about possible loss of their jobs. Staff were therefore not united; further, they differed in their views on deinstitutionalisation. The official union sub-branch view was:

> We've known that Hilltop is going to close eventually and we've worked with them [politicians] towards community housing. Close slowly. (Interview with union sub-branch representative)

In line with this position, the sub-branch argued against the 'trans-institutionalisation' of people from Hilltop and for the provision of what they termed 'adequate' community supports. Some staff, however, were totally opposed to the closure of the institution, while others believed that it was time for it to go.

While the official union view was that community living was a good alternative to Hilltop for some people, the union representative I inter-viewed believed that some people were either too 'vulnerable' or too 'unpleasant' to live in the community.

> We've got people that have got behaviour problems in the sense of social behaviour problems ... I'm a great believer in ... I know it's going to come out wrong, but look – leave them where they are and work with the kids of today. (Interview with union sub-branch representative)

### The Hilltop Parents and Friends Association

The Hilltop Parents and Friends Association represented about 200 individuals who were mainly relatives or advocates of people living at Hilltop. Its response, like that of the union, was swift. Throughout the closure process it ran a campaign to gain support for a cluster village to be sited on the grounds of Hilltop. The campaign opposed the trans-institutionalisation of people from the institution.

The Association also argued for a much stronger say in the futures of the people living at Hilltop than it had done in the past. Over a period of about six months it sent letters to parents and families urging them repeatedly not to co-operate in the consultative process in relation to their relative and to lobby the Minister for Community Services and the managers in order to change the closure decision.

Representatives from the Association expressed their concerns directly to the Minister and paid for a consultant's report, which supported cluster village living. The Association stated that it was not opposed in principle to the closure of the institution but wanted services which would be aimed at the security of people with intellectual disabilities and which would be individually designed. It also felt that there was one group of people for whom community living was not appropriate: these were people with psychiatric and/or behavioural problems.

> You see, you've got to look at the broad spectrum of intellectual disability and coupled with that you've got to look at what other problems physically, sensorily or psychologically ... they have. (Interview with Hilltop Parents and Friends Association representatives)

Among the motivations Association representatives attributed to the government in its decision to close Hilltop were the money to be gained from its sale, and current government policies and ideologies.

> The ideological drive ... that's the whole thing, the government, bureaucrats, aided and abetted by well-meaning but misguided individuals in the field of intellectual disability are hooked on the ideology that's behind the state plan. That ... deinstitutionalisation. (Interview with Hilltop Parents and Friends Association representatives)

### Researcher/Exile/Negotiator

Although I had known that the announcement to close Hilltop was pending for some two weeks, reading about it in the weekend papers was still a shock. There was a solidity about the place physically which seemed to defy change and which made the thought of its disappearance difficult to grasp. I was excited at the positive implications of the decision for the women in Unit N and for my research, but I was also shocked at the realisation that my relationships with people would be severed, and that the routines which seemed so timeless and secure were doomed. This mixture of feelings and thoughts carried me through the first two days at Hilltop. I was afraid that staff might refuse to speak with me or that there would be trouble about my research, but this did not at first seem to be the case.

Staff were angry, upset and stunned at the suddenness of the decision. They seemed pleased to have someone to talk to. However, this all changed when the sub-branch of the union decided to ban all research at Hilltop.

> R. and I were having a cup of coffee in the unit office this morning. J. came in and said to me 'I'm awfully sorry, I've got some bad news for you. You've been banned. You've got twenty-four hours. You can't come back on the grounds until the bans are lifted.' At first I couldn't believe it. The room started to spin around me and I felt dizzy and ill. In part it was the rejection and exclusion and in part the loss of relationships with the women and staff in the unit. In part too it was the loss of nearly two years' work. It was devastating. (Field notes)

Staff in the unit were shocked at my exclusion and offered sympathy and some hope. The institutional senior managers suggested that I obey the ban and 'wait and see' what would happen. They could not see any possible course of action which would be useful and, after all, the ban on research was a minute incident compared to some of the other events which were occurring around them.

During the week of my exclusion, I spent time talking with the one sub-branch executive member I had met and writing letters to the other office bearers, explaining again the nature of my research and reasserting my independence from all government departments. I also contacted people in the central branch of the union, from whom I received advice and some support. I was contacted by the union sub-branch and asked to attend a meeting the following week to discuss my situation. I drove to Hilltop afraid that I might be seen as breaking the ban, that the meeting would be unsuccessful. I was eager to visit the women in the unit, and managed to do this briefly before the meeting. Staff at the unit again expressed their support for me and their disappointment at my exclusion.

The discussion with the sub-branch executive was difficult. It was held in the union office, which was a small building with limited space for a meeting. We crowded around the table and I explained that my research was being undertaken independently, that it would not be published for some time (if ever) and that I was responsible to the university for ensuring that it was carried out ethically. I also indicated that I was carrying out research work for the staff at Unit N and would provide them with these results as soon as they were complete. It became clear during the meeting that three factors had influenced the ban on

research. Staff were anxious that I might acquire and publish information which was negative both about Hilltop and about the lives of the
people living there; they saw this as further evidence of 'institution
bashing'. They were also afraid that I might be a spy sent by the
government and management to find out information about the staff.
Finally, they were unclear about the nature of my work, primarily
because I had not interviewed all executive members of the union
during my research time at Hilltop. After considerable discussion the
executive members agreed that they would recommend to the next
meeting of the sub-branch that I be allowed back to the institution. As I
had been banned by a meeting of members the executive could not
rescind the decision.

Staff at Unit N began a campaign to ensure my return. They lobbied
each unit at Hilltop and talked with the people who had moved the
motion for my removal. At the next union sub-branch meeting, which
was held some days later, I was allowed to return to continue my
research. However, no other bans were lifted and all other research was
excluded.

There were a number of implications which could be drawn from
this experience. In my months at Hilltop I had become institutionalised:
I had spent time in the unit, got to know the staff and the women
who lived there and I had begun to develop a role as an observer and
as a researcher and support person. Now within one day I was
deinstitutionalised. I was shocked at the speed with which events moved.
I felt disoriented and grieved by my removal from a work place where I
had colleagues and friends.

In microcosm, this experience reflected that of many other people at
the institution. Some people living there and some staff had been there
for thirty years or more; some knew no other home and had no contacts
outside the institution. Perhaps one of the hardest parts of my exclusion
was the knowledge that I could not go back with any role at all, not even
as a friend. Yet this too was to be faced by those leaving Hilltop when it
closed.

I also realised how important it was to have a base within the
institution. I was perceived as being valuable to the people at Unit N and
they were prepared to fight to bring me back. (I also think that this
struggle was seen as a legitimate form of opposition to the union bans in
general.) Had I been an observer only, I doubt if there would have been
sufficient concern to warrant my return. My role as an action researcher
had been an important component in ensuring my survival. I recognised with a new awareness how important it was to have clear communication with all the power brokers in the institution.

My relationship with staff and managers at Hilltop changed on my return. I think the institutional senior managers regarded me with some respect because I had negotiated my way back into the field after the exclusion. Staff were better informed about the nature of my research and they had made the decision that I would continue with it. I was no longer there because of a management decision: I now had some sort of mandate from the staff. I also had a debt to staff at Unit N who had worked hard for my return, and this was a source of some anxiety to me as I feared it might interfere with my independence.

# CHAPTER 6

# *Stepping Forward*

It's OK for the rich and the lucky to keep still;
no one wants to know about them anyway.
But those in need have to step forward,
have to say: I am blind,
or: I'm about to go blind,
or: nothing is going well with me,
or: I have a child who is sick,
or: right there I'm sort of glued together.
*(Rainer Maria Rilke, [1906] 1981, p.111)*

For the women living in the locked unit the process of deinstitutional-isation involved two steps: the establishment of three preferences in relation to their future living arrangements; and matching, which involved the actual decision about where they were to live. This chapter describes these processes and explores the impact of each on the lives of the women, the staff working with them, and their families.

## Client Consultation on Relocation (CCOR) and Matching

### *CCOR at Hilltop*

The women's first step towards deinstitutionalisation involved them in becoming subject to the CCOR process. Client consultation had been developed and trialled over a two-year period prior to the decision to close Hilltop. It was designed:

to minimise the sense of confusion and anxiety experienced, and to maximise the participation of adults with an intellectual disability in the process of relocating. (Cashin, 1992, p.1)

Each person living at Hilltop was taken through the eight steps which made up CCOR (Hills, 1991a; Cashin, 1992; Johnson, 1992a):

Step 1   identified the individual with intellectual disabilities and gathered information about them from their General Service Plans (GSPs) and from other sources.

Step 2   established the communication methods used by the person who was being relocated.

Step 3   involved a meeting between the person with intellectual disabilities and the key people in their life.

Step 4   involved planning the type and method of information provision required in order to fully inform the person about moving out.

Step 5   implemented step 4 by informing the person about moving out and thoroughly recording all activities carried out to achieve it.

Step 6   involved a decision as to the person's ability to make an informed decision about moving out. An appeal mechanism was included if a dispute arose as a result of this decision.

Step 7   involved the relocation decision being made independently by the person with an intellectual disability if they were assessed as able to do this. If they were judged as unable to make independent decisions then relocation was determined either jointly with the person and others, or by substitute decision makers on that person's behalf.

Step 8   consisted of the final establishment of three preferences for future living arrangements using the methods outlined in steps 6 and 7.

It took three months to take all the people living at Hilltop through the process, and by its completion preferences for future living arrangements were established for each individual. Prior to the commencement of relocation it had been decided that approximately half the individuals would go to community placements in different regions across the state and half would go to other institutions within the state (nursing homes and other training centres).

CCOR was to provide the information on which specific matches could be made between particular people and their new homes. Information obtained from old GSPs was used as a basis for planning services with the regions. Using this information a questionnaire was developed to provide data on the regions' capacities to develop new services. CCOR was then used to consult with people living at Hilltop, families, advocates and staff about which kind of location they would prefer.

The CCOR process was carried out using convenors who worked with the client relocation manager. The convenors were drawn from a number of different sources. A core staff of six was seconded from the relevant government department, others were drawn from regions where people living at Hilltop were likely to be relocated and still others were seconded from Hilltop staff. Core staff on the team worked with those individuals who did not have clear community preferences, who did not have family representation or who were judged as having challenging behaviours or high dependency needs. It was hoped that the core team would offer more consistent, individualised and skilled support to this 'difficult' group of people than would be possible with part-time seconded staff.

An orientation programme was implemented for members of the client relocation team. This programme was repeated by the manager as new members of staff from the regions were added to the team. An implementation manual was prepared as a guide to the convenors (Cashin, 1992).

It was central to the CCOR process that everyone who was subject to it had an advocate independent of institutional staff. Families were traced and included in the process wherever possible. The local citizen advocacy organisation was requested to provide 'action advocates' for those people without either family or advocates.

When a person already had a citizen advocate, the advocate was involved in the consultation. In some instances where a guardian had been legally appointed for the individual, the Office of the Public Advocate was asked to provide an advocate for the CCOR process. Contact was also made with self-advocacy groups to encourage them to provide on-site support for clients at Hilltop. Money and a room were provided to support this but the self-advocacy groups did not make their appearance at this stage. Finally, a geriatric assessment team was contracted by the closure project team to assess all people over sixty-one years of age for eligibility for nursing home care. This was implemented concurrently with CCOR.

*Matching at Hilltop*

Unlike CCOR, matching was developed during the closure of Hilltop. It involved the allocation of individuals to their new homes, either in the community or in other institutions. CCOR preferences formed one part of the information to be considered during matching. More than half the people at Hilltop gave as their first preference a home in the community, and some regions were particularly popular, for example those close to the institution. Consequently, a set of criteria had to be developed (in addition to the CCOR preferences) which would allow people carrying out the matching process to 'choose' who would get their first preference. The establishment of such criteria proved very difficult, and a number of different ones were considered by the closure teams during the development of matching. The criteria eventually selected were the preferences established by CCOR, the proximity of the individual's preferred living place to a relative or advocate, the preferences of friends, and the capacity of services to provide support for the individual.

The main part of the matching process occurred over three weeks in a house at the bottom of the hill at Hilltop. The house had a number of large rooms in which regional meetings could occur. Each morning, cars would arrive from a number of different regions, there would be a briefing and the panels would begin to meet. Each panel was made up of regional representatives, members of the Hilltop closure team and Hilltop staff members. In some instances the panel's work was completed in half a day because there were a only a small number of people to consider. Other panels met from early in the morning till 6.00 pm or later, sometimes returning for a second day.

The files of people with first preferences for a particular region were placed on a table in the room and the panel worked through them. The houses available in the region were generally listed on a white-board and as each file was read, preliminary decisions would be made about the individual's allocation. Factors taken into account in making these decisions included the person's possible compatibility with other members of the house, the proximity of the house to advocates or family and whether or not the person had friends with whom they wanted to live.

The panels also discussed whether the services available in the region could meet the needs of the individual. Sometimes the files were read aloud by the convenor of the panel. At other times all members of the panel took files and were then responsible for leading the discussion around a particular person. It was rare for all members of the panel to read all the files for their particular region due to the time constraints. Some individuals at Hilltop were allocated a house early in the pro-ceedings, while others were moved between the options during the day. Some remained on a list which was unmatched. If they were still on this list at the end of the day they would then be considered for their second or third preference. Some of the panels dealt with more than eighty people in one day; others with no more than fifteen. The panels worked very hard, with only a brief break for lunch. By late in the day people were exhausted.

The managers of the client relocation team and the regional liaison team co-ordinated the day from a central room in the house and were available to provide assistance if required.

The chairperson of the committee on challenging behaviours kept a separate file of people who had been diagnosed as having varying levels of such behaviours and would provide information about individuals on request from panel members.

### Constraints on CCOR and Matching

A number of constraints affected the ways in which CCOR and matching were implemented and also, to varying degrees, the quality of the information about individuals which was obtained and used.

#### Time

It was crucial to the closure project that CCOR and matching be completed by predetermined times because, on the basis of this information, regions and other institutions would begin to plan services around the needs of the individuals chosen. It was also important that the relocation of people from Hilltop be dovetailed into the capital works programme which was already under way. While time constraints restricted the capacity of those involved in CCOR to spend extended periods with individuals or their families the impact of these constraints on matching was even more noticeable. There was no time to trial it comprehensively although staff did try it out with some client files to identify problems. Further, matching had to be commenced immediately following the completion of CCOR, and for a few individuals this meant that it went ahead before their preferences were established.

There was limited time for the panels to make the decisions as the entire operation was completed in three weeks, although confirmations to families went out some time afterwards, which allowed for some discussion of the decisions and some revisions when these were perceived to be necessary. Finally, there was little time to brief panel members.

#### The Staff Involved in CCOR and Matching

The use of seconded staff from the institution and from other regions impacted heavily on both CCOR and matching. The provision of independent and skilled convenors was essential for the successful implementation of CCOR, for they were responsible for managing the process for each individual. The use of Hilltop staff as convenors jeopardised the independence of the convenors, for some had known the people with whom they were working previously and some knew the staff in the units. The use of regional staff as convenors meant that people with varying degrees of skills and commitment were employed.

The closure project team had no control over who was sent from the regions. These staff were sent at different times throughout the process, making effective orientation to the process difficult. Some regions were able to release staff quickly while others took longer to do so. This bore no relation to the number of people who were likely to state preferences for a particular region. Some staff from the regions were released on a full-time basis enabling them to make a full commitment to the project, while other regions released numbers of staff on a part-time basis, making co-ordination and follow-up difficult for both staff and those they were serving.

The success of the matching process was highly dependent on the skills and knowledge of those people comprising the decision-making panels. However, in some instances representatives from the regions did not have adequate information, were insufficiently briefed at a regional level or were not familiar with the situation at Hilltop. Sometimes representatives were sent to the panels with particular regional agendas, for example only to take people who were young or who had few behaviour problems.

Hilltop staff representatives were not chosen on the basis of their knowledge of the individuals being matched by a particular panel. Rather, efforts were made to select senior staff who knew unit managers and who were available on the days set aside for matching. These people were responsible for contacting unit managers by phone if panels indicated that they required further information about a particular person. In some panels it was clear that there was more information available about the people being considered than in others. Individuals who were known to either the regional staff representative or the Hilltop staff representative were given more informed consideration.

### Staff Availability

The industrial bans prohibited staff from providing assistance to any people involved in the closure of Hilltop. Effectively, this meant that the information which could be obtained about individuals from staff was limited in those units where the bans were strictly enforced. While the bans were not always strictly adhered to (conservative management estimates suggested that fifteen per cent of staff and two–three units were completely committed to the bans), they proved to be an obstacle for the people working on CCOR and matching. In some instances convenors had to read people's files and their GSPs in order to obtain information. When staff did break the bans, confidentiality had to be maintained and meetings had to be held discreetly. Further, by the time matching began, many staff had left Hilltop and many units had temporary or new staff. Consequently, at times panels found it difficult to locate staff who knew the person under consideration.

### Competition Between Individuals for Scarce Community Places

The decision made at the beginning of the closure that approximately half the clients would live in the community and half in other institutions had a profound effect on matching. In regions for which many people had indicated a first preference, panels were forced to choose between them, accepting some and rejecting others. Individuals were 'sifted' through a number of different selection panels according to their first, second and third preferences.

Those who missed out on their preferences or who had placed an institution as a third preference sometimes found themselves relocated in an institution rather than in the community. More popular regions, particularly metropolitan ones, had more choices about the people they took, so people judged by these regions as less suitable were likely to be finally matched to less popular country regions or institutions. Further (as noted earlier), because of a government commitment to providing equal or better quality of life for people following deinstitutionalisation, some people located in houses on the grounds at Hilltop were given priority for houses at other institutions. This reduced the chances of other people to be matched to this option.

### Availability of Services in the Community

A political decision made in the planning of the closure that the people moving to the community would be housed in forty-three houses, most with five bedrooms, restricted the range of options available to individuals in a number of ways. It meant that some people could not take up a community option as the kind of accommodation provided was not suitable for their needs (for example if they did not want, or were unable, to live with a group of four other people). Further, some families were extremely hesitant about the kind of accommodation being offered and in some instances chose an institutional placement instead. In order for the housing to be complete by the time Hilltop closed, the capital works programme had to be under way before CCOR and matching could occur.

Although efforts were made to base the capital works programme on the information from old GSPs, it became clear that this information was inadequate. It was not always possible to allocate people to the places they wanted because of an insufficient number of houses. Further, some regions were very popular and were unable to absorb the numbers of people wanting to go to them, so they rejected some people with first preferences. Finally, some people were assessed as needing twenty-four hour active staff care but only a few regions could offer this kind of service. These people were likely to be rejected for community placement and matched to another institution.

## The Women's Experience of CCOR

The CCOR experience was unique for each woman. However, without exception, their most immediate experience of it was the one or two meetings which were held with either families or advocates present to establish their preferences. Prior to this direct involvement, the convenor had gathered information about their history and their perceived current skills and needs. This information came from three sources: the convenor's reading of the institutional file for each woman, discussions with staff (usually the unit manager or her deputies) and interviews with the woman's family. Little information came directly from the women themselves.

### Kirsten's Story

C., the unit manager, asked me to go upstairs to get Kirsten for her CCOR meeting. Her mother and two sisters had arrived at the unit. I walked into the dayroom and went up to Kirsten, who was standing, holding her cup near the door. 'Your mum's downstairs: come and see her, Kirsten.' She moved quickly to the door and went down into the dining room. She did not hesitate but went to the table at the far end of the room where her mother and her two sisters were sitting with the convenor and a unit staff member. She was very excited: she walked around the table and stood near her mother, not venturing too close in spite of efforts at persuasion. She rocked back and forth, holding her cup. Then she began to move quickly around the table, stopping always near her mother and rocking again. She would not come too close but smiled constantly. Her eyes were on her family as she continued to pace around the table. She put her hand out and her mother held it. She withdrew, moving around the table, before coming back to stand again near her mother. Her mother tried to talk with her: 'Come on Kirsten, sit on my lap. Do you remember your sisters?' Kirsten did not respond. Her mother started to cry and her tears fell onto the table. She wiped them away with her handkerchief. (Field notes)

This was the first time that Kirsten and her mother had met for six years, for her mother's increasing ill-health had made trips to the institution by public transport difficult.

Kirsten's CCOR meeting was held in the unit dining room, which had no privacy as it was a through-way for people going between the office and day room. Her family did not spend any time alone with her as they were late arriving for the meeting and the convenor and staff were already present. At the meeting it was decided that substitute decision making should be used as Kirsten was unable to make independent decisions.

Throughout the meeting Kirsten remained totally focused on her mother. The latter wiped away tears and tried to participate in the meeting but part of her attention was fixed on her daughter and she made repeated efforts to draw her closer. She knew little about Kirsten and wanted to know a lot more. She asked about her eating habits, about her health, about whether she was toilet trained. She asked how much money Kirsten had and who was responsible for it. Her anxieties were about Kirsten's physical security and the necessity to safeguard her money and possessions. She said at a later interview that she was content to leave the decisions about where Kirsten should go to the staff who were with her twenty-four hours a day as they would know her best. However, she did express a desire for Kirsten to live in cluster housing as she would be safe there. This was ruled out as an option by the convenor of the meeting and Kirsten's mother expressed surprise as she had received a letter from the Hilltop Parents and Friends Association advancing this as a possibility. By the end of the meeting Kirsten's family was satisfied with three preferences for community living in the region where her mother lived. Her mother summed up her own reaction to this decision:

> Well, I think she'll go into one of these houses and she'll be happy. It'll be a bit strange for her at the time because she'll wonder where everybody's gone. She's going to have to learn to adjust to a smaller crowd than what she did before. But then she'll probably get more attention which she'll find strange, but apart from her wandering I'm all for it ... Well, I'll be able to see her a bit more. (Interview with Kirsten's mother)

For her mother, the day was traumatic: a broken-down car, a long walk up the hill to the unit, difficulty in breathing during the walk (she had emphysema) and the shock of seeing her daughter, now older and changed in appearance. As well, she had to absorb the information which she was given about the closure of Hilltop, the possibilities for her daughter's future, and basic information about Kirsten's skills and needs. Finally, on the same day, she had to make decisions about the future living arrangements for her daughter. Kirsten's family did not visit again while Kirsten remained at Hilltop.

Staff in the unit were angry with families who did not visit their relatives. It was difficult during Kirsten's CCOR meeting for the convenor to manage her mother's fragmented knowledge of her daughter, however a knowledge of the history of Kirsten's family revealed the difficulties under which they had lived and the uniqueness of their experience. This history was not known either to the staff or to the convenor of CCOR.

Kirsten was the third of ten children. At three months of age she caught meningitis from a neighbour's child. She recovered, but her mother noticed that 'she didn't seem to concentrate or focus like other children'. Repeated visits to the Children's Hospital concluded with a diagnosis of 'severe mental retardation' and a prognosis that Kirsten would 'never be able to do anything'.

Kirsten then lived at home with her family until she was twenty years old. She was never toilet trained and could not feed herself, so much of her mother's time was taken up with her physical care. Kirsten also had difficulty sleeping and her mother recalled many sleepless nights as a result. During this time Kirsten's mother worked shifts at the local market and cared for the other nine children, two of whom also had disabilities. On Kirsten's file, reports from social workers stated that there was a loving but somewhat chaotic atmosphere in the small house. At the age of twenty Kirsten was sent to Hilltop because her father had a heart attack and her mother was 'very tired' and could 'no longer cope'. Kirsten had been in Hilltop for nineteen years, thirteen of which had been spent in locked units. For the first six years after Kirsten's admission her mother visited regularly: at the end of each visit Kirsten would cling to her mother's clothes and cry.

Just as staff knew little of Kirsten's family history, her mother knew nothing of Kirsten's life in the unit or of her past experiences at Hilltop. This knowledge was not shared with her during the meeting.

I first met Kirsten at the door of the day room where she stood for much of each day looking out into the dining room. She had light red hair, fair skin and green eyes. Her figure was slim except for her bulging abdomen which was said to be the result of gulping in air. She never mixed with the other women. She would move around the walls of the room rather than cross the space, and when she did cross the centre of the room it was usually at a run. She was very much a victim in the unit (see Chapter 2). Other women in the unit would sometimes strike her and she would rarely hit back, usually crying her pain.

She was very quiet with staff but would follow them around at a distance, sometimes responding to a quiet voice or outstretched hand with a quick touch or smile. Kirsten did not talk, but moaned, whimpered and screamed. Her screams usually commenced soon after a meal and continued for some time. She sounded as though she were in pain and staff had referred her for medical opinions without receiving any help. They now sought their own interpretations and remedies, some of which seemed to relieve Kirsten temporarily. Perhaps more than any of the other women her files showed repeated negative comments from the staff she had encountered in the past. An early superintendent's report described her as follows:

> She has an ungainly gait with marked muscular inco-ordination. Her facial expression is vacant and she spends the day aimlessly shuffling about the ward. Remains mute and inaccessible and is totally dependent on nursing care for all her needs. (Superintendent's report on Kirsten's file)

This description was repeated for almost ten years without variation. Throughout her years at Hilltop Kirsten was described negatively as having 'dirty habits', 'being aggressive', and 'having a dirty habit of playing with herself'. She was also described as 'a greedy and overactive girl' who 'can be very stubborn and cruel to other clients' ... 'Feeding and toilet habits are filthy. Won't sit on the toilet. Steals from others at every opportunity.' To stop her from 'playing with herself', staff in the past had tied her hands behind her back or knotted her cardigan sleeves together. The picture which the files gave of her was different from that given by her mother. She remembered Kirsten as loving and wanting to 'cuddle you all the time'. Kirsten liked sitting on people's laps and was affectionate with all of her family.

Kirsten was moved to Unit N after an ambiguous encounter (in which her face was scratched) with a man who was resident in another unit. Staff reported in the files that they thought she might have been sexually abused and that she was 'tested for pregnancy', with a negative result. For some time she was placed on the pill because staff believed she was 'sexually active', however they also saw her as vulnerable and unable to defend herself. This episode was not known to current staff in Unit N, or was ignored, for they were unsure why she had been placed there and attributed it to her screaming.

### Establishing Preferences

It is not possible finally to know what the consultation meetings meant to individual women. However, some inferences can be drawn from the women's behaviour and from my observations of their meetings. The meetings were often held at short notice, making it difficult to attend; this was particularly the case when neither advocates nor family were present (three women). This section describes the consultation process for the nine women whose meetings I was able to attend.

For Kirsten, CCOR involved a meeting with a long-lost family, and her excitement and stress were visible in her behaviour throughout the meeting. Similarly, Brigid renewed a relationship with a former staff member to whom she had been very attached and who became her action advocate. M. spent time with Brigid before the meetings, gathered information about her current living situation and gave her many 'cuddles'. Inge's father made one of his rare visits to see Inge for the CCOR meeting and she too showed excitement at his presence. The meetings did not have any task-oriented meaning for any of these women.

For some of the women, particularly Kate, the meeting was an adjunct to regular visits from family. Kate's mother made one of her weekly visits and at the end of it went down the hill to the liaison house for the CCOR meeting. Kate was not involved in this at all. Brigid, Inge, Bettina and Laura were also absent for all or most of the meetings concerning them, either because they were regarded as too disruptive by the convenor, staff or their family and/or because the preferences were to be decided by substitute decision making.

Only Jodie, Jane and June participated to some extent in establishing their preferences at the meeting. In the days preceding it, Jodie and Jane had talked about it and expressed excitement about the possibility of moving out of the institution. Jane saw it as an opportunity to live once again in the community. She knew the suburb in which she wanted to live and the kind of life-style she would have, saying: 'I'll have my own flat and a job. I'll see my friends and my sister.'

Jodie said clearly that she wanted to live in the community near her advocate. Both Jodie and Jane were carefully dressed on the day and expressed anxiety and excitement about the meeting, however Jane was banned by the Public Advocate from living in the community and her preferences were overridden by the other members of the meeting. Jodie's preference matched with those of the others participating in the meeting and were established. June did not show any foreknowledge of the meeting but clearly established what kind of housing she wanted after Hilltop closed:

> J. [convenor] drew a large house on a sheet of paper and a small house on another. He showed them to June and asked which she would prefer to live in: 'a big house like Hilltop', or a small house. She smiled broadly and said 'this one', pointing to the small house. He expressed some doubt as to her capacity to make the choice and tried again. Again June pointed to the small house. (Field notes)

This was the extent of June's involvement in the meeting. She became restless soon after and left the room. Both Jodie and Jane, however, described in more detail the area in which they wanted to live.

Little consideration was given to what they might do once they moved out of Hilltop.

The convenor said 'What sort of things would you like to do when you move into your house, Jodie?' 'I'd like to learn to type and get a job.' The convenor laughed and said: 'Well I don't know about that, what about pottery and painting?' (Field notes)

The convenor checked if there were people with whom each of the women would like to live. Jodie commented that she would like to live with Lena. The unit manager shook her head and said 'But you don't like Lena'. Jodie repeated her preference, but it was not noted on the file.

At the conclusion of CCOR, Dora's preferences were still undecided, Joyce and Doris had institutional first preferences and all the other women had been given first preferences for community living.

### Families, Advocates and CCOR

Unlike the women, families were generally involved not only in deciding whether their relative should live in the community or in an institution but in what region or local government area they might live. They were also involved in making more detailed decisions about the possible future life-style of their family member, including those with whom they might live. Further, they were responsible along with the convenor and staff member for assessing both the ability of their relative to make decisions independently and her capacity to communicate.

Families and advocates differed in their responses to CCOR. They also differed in the way in which they responded to their family member during the process. For families and advocates, CCOR was an emotional experience: it reactivated feelings of grief, pain, anger and love. In the absence of current detailed knowledge of the woman and her life, families and advocates relied on fragmented pictures of the woman in order to make decisions about her future.

Some families knew very little about their relative, and their involvement in establishing preferences for her was therefore problematic (see for example the account of Kirsten's mother earlier in this chapter). Bettina's parents did not know that she had been diagnosed as autistic and did not know what this meant. They found out at the CCOR meeting. In trying to understand, they were handicapped by their lack of English and by the complex terminology used by staff who had no warning of the need for explanation. Further, Bettina's mother, in halting English, tried to find out if Bettina ate well and if she ever choked. This kind of information was seen by parents as crucial in making decisions about their daughter, but in the context of the CCOR meeting it could be supplied in only a perfunctory way without any time for the families to absorb or question it before making decisions.

The sexual and physical vulnerability of the women was a key parent concern in all the CCOR meetings I attended. For example Kate's mother was concerned that she might be attacked sexually if she lived in a house in the community. She was particularly concerned that Kate not live with men, who would upset her by their very presence. She also expressed concerns about Kate's physical safety in the community. In contrast to their fears of the outside community, parents commented on the 'safety' and beauty of the grounds at Hilltop: 'It's so beautiful and peaceful here. I like to think of her walking around safe in the grounds' (Inge's father: CCOR meeting field note). Given the violence in the unit and the confinement of the women to two rooms during the day, such comments were sadly ironic.

Jane, Dora and Doris were viewed by their families or advocates as too dangerous or disruptive to go into the community. Jane was therefore forbidden a place in a community house. Dora's parents believed that other people would not be able to live with her and that she might attack 'men in the street'. And while Doris's sister would have liked her to move into the community she believed that the manic illness which Doris experienced at frequent intervals made her 'release' from an institution unlikely.

Reactivated memories of their relative as victim or oppressor sometimes influenced the way in which families established preferences, for example Dora's mother had terrible memories of her daughter's entrance to Lonsdale Lodge twenty years before and was now absolutely certain that she would not send her back there. Dora's family recollected their difficulties in living with Dora and expressed concern that others would have to do so in the community. Inge's father had similar concerns.

The majority of families saw their relative as a continuing responsibility which they were anxious about maintaining. Inge's father suggested that she live in a town close to her sisters rather than close to him because he hoped that when he died they would establish contact with her. Kirsten's mother expressed pain and guilt at her failure to visit and was seeking to involve other members of the family in visiting Kirsten and in managing her affairs.

Of the nine consultations I witnessed, only in Jodie's meeting did her advocate listen carefully to her statements about where and how she wanted to live. The advocate then actively promoted Jodie's preference.

### Staff in the Unit and CCOR

Staff in the unit decided not to obey the union bans but to participate in the CCOR process. However, the only staff involved directly were the unit manager and her deputies. They played a low-key role, only giving information when asked or when other people did not seem able to supply it. The unit manager commented that she saw her role as providing information for families to make the decision rather than being involved in it directly herself. There were times when family misperceptions of their relative or of her lifestyle could have been corrected by staff but were not. For example when Inge's father commented that she was lucky to have the grounds to walk in, the staff member present did not point out that Inge rarely went for more than a short walk each day. Outside the CCOR meetings staff were concerned about particular individuals, for example the unit manager spent a lot of time with Jane talking with her about future options and indicating strongly to her that her behaviour would need to improve if she were to live in the community. One such conversation concluded with the unit manager asking: 'Now, what do you need to do to go and live in the community?', to which Jane said: 'Be a good girl, not get angry'. The impossibility of Jane achieving this within the locked unit was acknowledged by the unit manager but she wanted to try to achieve a better solution for Jane than simply another institutional placement. The unit manager also played a role in supporting parents through CCOR. Sometimes she was the only person with whom parents felt some security. She listened to the concerns of Kate's mother about community living and reassured her about the possible consequences. In this instance the unit manager believed that Kate should move into the community. In other instances she was less certain, for example in relation to Dora.

At the conclusion of CCOR the staff in the unit were generally pleased, if surprised at the number of community preferences the women had obtained.

### The Convenors and CCOR

Nine convenors were responsible for taking the Unit N women through the eight steps of CCOR. In interviews they expressed a number of concerns about the implementation of CCOR but were positive in their views about its structure.

> I think its intentions was [sic] very good. The intention was there because the place was so enormous I don't think you could do it in the time. And it gave a structure of working which was definitely needed. If you had gone to some of those meetings without an agenda you would have walked out screaming. (Interview with convenor H.)

CCOR offered them a framework to hold onto within a very confusing world. It set clear tasks which could be worked through and then marked off.

The convenors, like the families, thought that CCOR provided an opportunity for both families/advocates and the women to have a say in the way their future lives might be lived. However, the convenors also had concerns about the process. Those who came from other regions sometimes felt caught between instructions about the kinds of people who services in their region were willing to accept and their own need to facilitate decision making by families or people living at Hilltop. They were also concerned at the implications of the union bans on the kinds of information they were able to discover about individuals.

> [B]ecause of the work bans we became responsible for making decisions about people or things about people which would have a fair bit of weight in people's future lives, based on meaningless criteria. (Interview with convenor H.)

The primary concerns expressed by the convenors centred on the degree to which they could work with families, allay their anxieties, find out what they wanted for their relative and ensure that the person living at Hilltop had a say in the development of preferences. All convenors saw these tasks as very stressful.

> A lot of people [families] were quite old ... sisters and brothers were tracked by various means and they'd be devastated ... and, well, you'd try and come up with a sort of decision out of this but you were working with people in this incredibly emotional sort of situation. People with guilt which was huge ... people would tell you what the family had gone through ... people who had never come to terms with the fact that they had had a child with an intellectual disability and they'd been told ... 'You can't look after this child, put the child away and it will be OK,' and here you come in and say to them 'Well, Hilltop is closing and where do you think they should go?' (Interview with convenor H.)

The convenors were discouraged by the lack of time available for the consultation.

> You've got over 400 people living in this centre, all with individualised needs and preferences. You can't in the space of a couple of months identify in real terms what those people want. (Interview with convenor G.)

Consequently, they relied heavily on information gained from families and from staff rather than attempting the more difficult task of finding out directly about the women. The way in which CCOR was structured also oriented convenors towards families and staff. For example much of their work involved tracing, making contact with, informing and conciliating with families. Consequently, the women were filtered through the experience and eyes of other people. The time spent by the convenors with the women was restricted to one or two short visits prior to meetings with families and staff.

> Usually on my first visit up there [to a unit] I wouldn't necessarily ask to meet the client because I wouldn't know how to interact with them or anything like that ... so I'd read the files and talk to the staff first ... I think I haven't really been given the time to come to [my] own conclusions about people, like the first major decision we have to make as convenors is whether or not the person has the ability to make the decision on their own or by representative or whatever. And the way we come to that decision is by talking to the staff, talking to the families and a [pause] little bit of contact with the client themselves. (Interview with convenor G.)

One convenor expressed despair at the limited amount of time given to work with Inge, who could not express her views:

> I mean if I had twelve months' work with them [sic], sure, you could get something of a response and she could be involved, really involved in the process to whatever extent she was capable of. But given the time constraints and the difficult working conditions you just couldn't do it. And that's what I find professionally difficult: to work under these conditions because you're not sure you're doing the right thing or getting the right power balance. (Interview with convenor H.)

The picture the convenor gained of the individual from different sources was sometimes then taken as her reality:

> Because by the end of the process you found that families from their initial outlook on things had changed their minds – sometimes quite dramatically, other times not so dramatically – but it just gave it a more solid picture of what the person [with intellectual disability] actually wanted. (Interview with convenor M.)

Convenors seconded from other regions were also constrained by their knowledge of the limited services available in the regions to which the women were going.

> Iris's epilepsy is very severe as you know, and I know that C. [unit manager] has concerns about it and at the same time she's thrilled that Iris is going to live in a house. And the main concern is that quite often [Iris] can go into stasis and she may need oxygen and intervention. (Interview with convenor T.)

In contrast, those who were members of the permanent team had little information about existing services to share with families or staff to assist in making preferences for individuals.

Although CCOR set up standardised procedures for consultation, my observations suggested differences among the convenors in the way they carried out their tasks. All developed preconceived notions of which people should go into the community and which should not. However, convenors varied widely in the degree to which such notions influenced the way they conducted the meetings. Of the six I interviewed, five were careful to ensure that all parties met together for a discussion. One placed less emphasis on this and became a broker among the interested groups, meeting each separately and conveying ideas and information among the woman, family and staff. Some convenors were highly motivated to involve the woman directly in the decision making; others were quick to remove her from the meetings. Some gave more or less credence to the files or to staff opinions, and there were also differences in how they exercised power in establishing preferences. For example one convenor indicated to me before each of her three CCOR meetings what she thought the preferences should be for that individual. Throughout the meeting she attempted to persuade families and staff to adopt her opinion. Her views were based on how disruptive the person's challenging behaviour would be in the community. She succeeded in persuading Bettina's family that Bettina should go to the community, and in Brigid and Laura's meetings she attempted to ensure that preferences for institutions were included (they were, although in both instances, because of advocacy by other members of the group, the first preference was a community one).

Other convenors saw their role as 'resource people' who attempted to clarify with families and staff what the best options were for each woman. They believed that establishing preferences was easiest when the family, the staff, the woman and the convenor were in broad agreement about the woman's possible future living situation and when she had a clear friendship network. When families expressed ambivalence about their daughter the convenors found it difficult to work effectively. For example Dora's family seemed positive about her moving to a house but then changed their minds and at the end of CCOR had not established preferences for her. Her convenor found it difficult to resolve this ambivalence. Some of the convenors were daunted by either the family or the advocate, thus in Jane's meeting the convenor did not question the right of the Public Advocate to make a decision about Jane's future living needs without discussion.

In spite of the difficulties of working with the women, convenors spoke of them often with affection and held high hopes for some of them in their new lives.

> Una I think will blossom in her relationships with people in general. I think her communication skills will increase. I think her retentive ability to stay on track will increase. (Interview with convenor G.)

## The Closure Project Team Managers

The closure project team managers were removed from the implementation of CCOR but they were responsible for its success or failure and for attempting to 'manage' the 'challenging behaviour' of the women during the process. The managers saw CCOR as offering certainty in a confused and tumultuous environment. It was the only management 'instrument' which had been developed prior to the decision to close Hilltop (see earlier this chapter). It offered opportunities for consultation and the hope of ensuring that the preferences which people established were well founded and justifiable. All managers I interviewed spoke confidently of it and were constant in its praise. The successful implementation of CCOR was important to the managers because of the opposition to Hilltop's closure from parents and the union. It was important that justice be seen to be done in the establishment of preferences. Further, the managers hoped that CCOR, if successful, could be used with other people in similar relocations.

From the beginning of CCOR, managers worked on the assumption that some people were going to be more difficult than others to take through the process. Of particular concern were those people who did not have families or advocates and those who had challenging behaviours or high support needs. The provision of a permanent client relocation team aimed to provide additional skilled support to these people, however assigning them to permanent staff led to expectations that they would be 'difficult'. It also affected the regional team convenors, who regarded them as more problematic in terms of community placement.

As CCOR got under way a committee was established to develop strategies to assist those people diagnosed as having challenging behaviours. It consisted of a staff representative from Hilltop, the Behaviour Intervention Support Team (BIST) co-ordinator, the manager of the client relocation team and a member of the regional liaison team who chaired the meetings. The committee began its work by identifying people who had varying degrees of challenging behaviours based on a survey carried out the previous year by an independent consultant skilled in behaviour intervention. The data had been gathered from interviews with unit staff. The committee followed this up with further staff interviews by two members of the BIST. They requested an assessment of individuals' challenging behaviour along two dimensions: the seriousness of the challenging behaviour in terms of danger to self, others and property; and the behaviour's frequency. Using this updated material the interviewers sometimes observed the individuals concerned, adjusted the information and added people to, or removed them from, the list. This work was carried out over three weeks. People with challenging behaviours were then placed in one of three categories: 'severe' challenging behaviours where the behaviour was perceived to be intense in both nature and frequency, and 'moderate' and 'mild' levels of challenging behaviours where the behaviour was judged to be less serious.

Because of a shortage of resources, the committee decided that the work of the BIST should be restricted to the first of these categories. They were asked to write full reports on each person with 'severe' challenging behaviour. Smaller profiles and reports were prepared for those people in the second category, and no action was taken on those in the third category.

All of the women in Unit N were noted as having 'moderate' challenging behaviours, however only two of them, Brigid and Jane, were categorised as having 'severe' challenging behaviours. It was decided by the committee to protect the rights of individuals by withholding information about their challenging behaviours until CCOR was complete, and only providing it to matching panels on request.

### The Women's Experience of Matching

During matching, life in the unit went on very much as usual. The women, as far as I know, were not told that the final decisions were being made about their futures, nor were they told how these decisions were to be made. It is possible that some of the women believed that establishing their preferences in CCOR was in effect the final decision. However although they were not present physically, their files, the client profiles developed by convenors during CCOR and their preferences were collected and gathered in great piles for discussion by the matching panels.

#### Jane's Story

I arrived in the room where Jane's preferences were being considered halfway through the afternoon. Her first preference was for a house on the grounds at Rochester. It was hot and the panel members looked exhausted and frustrated both by the work done, and that which remained.

They had spent the day attempting to juggle the more than forty people who wanted a house on the grounds at Rochester with the twenty-one places available. The decision making was made more difficult because people with places in the houses at Hilltop had first preference. Some of these people had been placed in houses because of their dangerous behaviour. Now others with a house as first preference had to be fitted into the remaining places. When I looked at the whiteboard with its names and houses I realised that Jane's name was not there. I pointed this out to the panel chairperson. The names were checked and concern was expressed by the panel members at the omission, particularly because the allocation to houses was now almost set.

A member of the relocation team was sent to look for [Jane's] file. He went reluctantly and returned to state that Jane had already been matched with a unit in another institution. He said that this solved the problem of having to consider her for a match with a house on the grounds at Rochester. One of the regional representatives stated strongly that this was unfair and that Jane should be considered for matching. The relocation team member refused to fetch the file and there was a heated argument with the panel. He finally brought it and one member of the panel quickly scanned it. The file was large, as the CCOR convenor thought Jane's best hope for a positive matching was to provide all the information available. Instead, the panel saw the size of the file and someone said: 'God, look at this: not this one.' Bits of the file were read out which described Jane's aggressive behaviour. Within three minutes the panel had decided she should not be matched to a house in the grounds. However, her convenor was called in to provide further information.

She [the conventor] was unable to reassure the panel, who took the advice of the Hilltop staff member who commented negatively on Jane's aggressive behaviour although he had not worked with her for more than twelve months. Her match with an institutional unit was retained.

The convenor stated later that she felt disadvantaged by not knowing what the discussion had been prior to her entry to the room and found it difficult to speak out against the Hilltop staff member. Jane was matched to a unit in a city institution. (Field notes)

Within the constraints of matching, the panels did try generally to consider each individual. The problematic procedures in relation to Jane's file were particularly unfortunate given her history and the commitments made to her during CCOR. But they also seemed to reflect in microcosm her experiences of the wider community.

Jane was born into a family of five children. From the age of six she was on a constant roundabout of institutions, community placements and time with her family. As mentioned in Chapter 2, she had been subjected to sexual abuse by both her father and brothers as a child and as an adult and they were now banned from visiting her by a guardianship order. Her stay in any one place rarely lasted more than twelve months. As she moved into adulthood she was evicted from community residential units, special accommodation houses and hostels. Her attempts to live in the community alone ended in attacks on neighbours or on property. She ran away from the institutions to which she was sent. She had been admitted to almost every facility in the state, both psychiatric hospitals and services for people with intellectual disability.

Jane was now thirty-three. She had a round face and short brown hair. She was articulate and clear in expressing her needs. She smoked heavily and was overweight. Her life in the unit was lonely and frustrating. Jane was able to cook and to look after herself, but there were no opportunities for this. She enjoyed drinking and partying, but there were no opportunities for this either. She had a number of friends who came to visit occasionally and she had a lover (see Chapter 4) who had visited frequently but who had been banned from contact with her because of staff fears that he might be HIV positive.

She did not associate with the other women living in the unit and although she had generally friendly relations with the staff she was treated with great wariness because of her aggression. She had her own room at the far end of the corridor and this was filled with her possessions and furniture. Poor foundations caused the room to tilt at odd angles and consequently her furniture leant around the room. Unlike the other women in the unit she had a television set and a radio in her room. Most of her days were spent in this space. Immediately after breakfast she requested permission to go to her room and she rarely reappeared till lunch time. She took her cigarettes with her and appeared to spend the time sleeping or watching television. For one half-day a week Jane was encouraged to go to work on-site at Hilltop. She went when she could be persuaded to do so and when her behaviour was judged as satisfactory. She welcomed the three dollars earned from this work, however she found it frustrating that the payment was not given directly to her but to staff at a later date.

Jane had been in Unit N (this time) for approximately twelve months. She had been admitted there from a house on the grounds because she threatened a staff member with a knife. She was one of the most heavily medicated women in the unit. She had been placed on a guardianship order which restricted her accommodation to a locked unit until 'she could demonstrate good behaviour for three months'. Jane never attacked the other women living in the unit but she did attack staff. When she did this, her 'medication' dosage was increased and she was isolated until she calmed down. Staff in the unit attempted to reduce Jane's anger and aggression by teaching her to throw 'Teddy' (a soft teddy bear) when she was angry. She was also taught some relaxation techniques, and had attended personal relationship classes and received sexual counselling (see Chapter 4). Some of these strategies worked for a while and staff had succeeded in reducing the number of violent episodes in which Jane was involved. However, they had not succeeded in securing her release from the unit and each aggressive episode ensured her a longer stay in a frustrating environment.

There were varied reasons given for Jane's violence. One psychiatrist attributed her behaviour to her 'intellectual disability', and her guardian saw it in part as a result of the restrictions and frustrations in her living environment and the exclusion of her family from her life. Staff in the unit were baffled by her behaviour and saw it as exacerbated by the frustration of her current life.

Jane's optimistic view that she would be able to live in the community when Hilltop closed was short lived. Her guardian refused to countenance such a move, and her convenor accepted this view. In compensation and in recognition of Jane's competence, her guardian suggested a house on the grounds of an institution as an interim measure. Jane had little choice but to accept this preference. Because only one institution had houses on the grounds, her second and third preferences were for institutional places. Jane was depressed about moving to another institution but had no choice. The panel's decision ended Jane's chance to live in a less institutional environment. Her guardian was angry at this decision and considered appealing it, but decided not to because she did not think it would do any good. She had discussions with Jane about which of two institutions she would prefer, and visits were made to each. Jane finally decided on the one to which she had been assigned. Even once this decision was made Jane continued to hope that she would be able to move into a flat and expressed constant anxiety about whether or not her friends and her sister would be able to visit her in the institution.

### The Final Decisions for the Women in Unit N

I observed entire panel meetings for ten of the women, and segments of another four meetings. It was impossible to attend all meetings as they were often held concurrently. Discussions with those who implemented the process, and my observations, revealed that lack of friendships, 'challenging behaviour', family or advocate ambivalence and negative service-provider attitudes were important factors determining further institutional placement of the women.

There were two groups of clearly defined friends in the locked unit. In all cases these friendships played an important part in determining a community place for the women. For example after initial doubts, Bettina and Kate were placed tentatively in a house together because of their friendship. Once this was done, all other people located there had to be compatible with them and they became more difficult to relocate than single individuals. Vera's friendship with Ilse and Elaine proved to be an even more important factor for her. During the panel discussion of Vera's future, her manic depressive illness was noted, and regional representatives instantly rejected her for community living. Her convenor and the unit manager stressed the importance of sustaining Vera's friendships. The unit manager also argued that Vera's illness was 'controllable'. Subsequently, Vera was placed in a community house with her two friends.

Prepared reports on the challenging behaviour of individuals were available on request to the matching panels. Such reports were usually requested when panels doubted the adequacy of service provision in a particular region. Lena's 'challenging behaviour', then, cost her all three preferences for community living, even though she had lived for sixty-four years in the community. She was matched to a city institution. Frantic advocacy by a sympathetic closure project team member and by me led Lena to a community placement, but one in the country 200 kilometres from her nearest relative. Assessments of Brigid's behaviour led to her rejection by all regions and institutions and she was finally placed in a country institution which could not justify her exclusion on the grounds of numbers.

Women who had a family or an advocate were advantaged in matching, as one of the criteria was to place people close to relatives or friends. Consequently, women such as Brigid and Laura who had no family or advocates found themselves displaced from regions and institutions in favour of those with family or advocates. Unfortunately Brigid and Laura were also then assigned to the less attractive options. But the presence of a family or an advocate did not guarantee a place in the community. For example the failure of Dora's family to specify preferences for her led to a delay in matching her to a new home. By the time their decisions were made, houses in her chosen region were filled by other people and her choices were limited to institutional placement.

As shown in Jane's story, the attitude of institutional staff could influence strongly what happened to an individual during matching. In another example one staff member at an institution was interested in taking Brigid into an open unit. After talking with the unit manager she changed her mind, believing Brigid's behaviour was too disruptive. She never actually met Brigid. Comments by staff members at panel meetings who might not know the woman very well could jeopardise a placement in spite of the written material provided by the CCOR convenors. Much also depended on the attitudes of the regional or institutional representatives, some of whom had quite explicit agendas. For example one regional representative commented: 'We've been caught with difficult people before. It's not going to happen this time' (Field notes). On the other hand, some regions showed great readiness to accept people. For example doubts were expressed about Laura moving into the community because she screamed. The regional representative laughed and said: 'Screaming? Is that all? We can manage that' (Field notes).

The way in which an individual's preferences were distributed made a great difference to her final matching. For example June had three preferences for North West region because this was where her advocate and only community contact lived. Unfortunately it was also the most sought-after region. Once June was excluded from it because of her behaviour all her preferences were lost and she went on the unmatched pile where her chances for institutional placement were high. Finally she was matched to a country house one hundred kilometres from her advocate.

When the final decisions were made it was found that seven of the twenty-one women were to go to institutions, one to a country institution (Brigid) and the rest to metropolitan ones (Faye, Dora, Inge, Doris, Jane and Joyce). Of the women going to institutions, two had placed an institution unambiguously as their first preference in CCOR. Inge's father changed his mind about his preference, leading to Inge's placement in an institution, and Dora's parents remained undecided about her future home. Both Faye and Brigid had placed the community as their first preference, but because of perceived deterioration in Faye's behaviour staff in the unit argued against her relocation in the community, leading to a change in her preferences. Brigid, as discussed earlier, was rejected for a community place during the matching process.

Five women went to houses in the city (Kate, Kirsten, Bettina, Iris and Jodie). In all instances these women obtained their first preference in relation to region, although they may not have obtained the particular house they wanted. Three of them formed a group of friends and another two had a close relationship together. All were matched to a house with their friends.

Eight women went to houses in the country: Lena, Una, Elaine, Vera, Rosalind, Ilse, Laura and June. Of these, four had as their first preference the regions to which they went. The other four were rejected for their first preference and were accepted either for a second or third preference or placed in the region as an alternative to an institutional setting. Three of these four people had no family and none had friendship networks among people living at Hilltop. For Lena and June, community living came at the cost of separation from their family or advocate. (As described in Chapter 5, Rhonda left Hilltop for a house in the community early in the closure process.)

### Families and Advocates: the Matching Experience

Families interviewed during and after matching indicated they had no knowledge of how it actually occurred. They were more concerned with its outcomes than with its procedures. Although they were informed that if they were dissatisfied with decisions they had the right to appeal them, few families or advocates actually did so. Most families were pleased at the decisions, expressing some surprise that so many of the women in Unit N had been matched with a community house. Four families/advocates were unhappy with the decision. Jane and Brigid's advocates thought that they had not had a fair hearing through the CCOR and matching processes. Lena's family was angry that she had been placed some 200 kilometres from her nearest relative, and Faye's sister was saddened by a decision to place Faye in another institution.

For those who were keen to see their relative live in the community, matching was a time of considerable anxiety relieved only when they received an offer for a community placement. These families then tended to see the decision as a release for their relative and as giving them some power in relation to her.

> K.: What are the good things for Una in moving to a house?'
> A.: 'Oh, having her own room. Her own room, her own bed. And good things for us from a merely selfish point of view I suppose [are] more visiting, being able to see her more often.'
> B.: 'And not having that immense trip.'
> A.: 'Yeah, because L.'s [town where Una would live] only about fifteen k down the road. And then the good thing's being able ... no medication ... and decision making; being given back those choices and options. (Interview with Una's sisters)

Some families expressed anxiety about housing arrangements for their relative, for example Kate and Kirsten's mothers were anxious about the decision which matched them to a house they would be sharing with men. The families, however, were willing to accept this as the price for not moving their relative to another institution.

Families tended to see the unit staff as influential in deciding where the women finally went. When Faye was matched to an institution, losing her community placement, her sister was upset but agreed to the decision because she trusted the staff view of Faye's suitability. Una's sisters commented that: 'It's just luck that all the staff have been for her to move into a house as well ...'

Both Brigid and Jane's advocates were extremely angry at their matching decisions but did not know how the decisions had been reached and decided not to appeal them. Lena's family appealed the decision unsuccessfully in an effort to bring her closer to them.

### Unit Staff and Matching

Staff in Unit N had very little contact with the panels and knew little about how matching was conducted. They were sometimes contacted by phone when further information about someone was needed. When such phone calls came, staff were expected to answer questions immediately without necessarily knowing the context in which the information was to be used; in some instances the information they provided was crucial in deciding what happened to an individual. Staff indicated that they felt frustrated by the way information was gathered from them, although they were also relieved that in some cases they could correct inaccurate CCOR information about an individual.

Unit staff were pleased that some Hilltop staff were panel members as they believed this enabled the panels to obtain more in-depth information about individuals and to be more sensitive to the effects of an institutional environment. However, they would have liked to have been present at the panel discussion about each of the women and to have had direct input into the decision making.

They were concerned that information obtained by panel members might be used out of context and in some cases might be inaccurate. For example, just prior to the commencement of matching, convenors visited the units at night and spoke to night shift staff about individuals' needs for active staff during the night hours. This issue was extremely important as the need for active staff at night could lead someone to be excluded from a community placement. Unit managers were angry about this process because some night duty staff were temporary and did not know the women well. They were also concerned that the context in which the women lived was not taken into account.

Following the matching decisions staff in the unit were consulted about the compatibility of people matched to the individual houses. None of the women was regarded by staff as being inappropriately placed. Staff were pleased that so many of the 'ladies' had managed to obtain a house in the community, however they did have concerns about two groups of women. The first of these included women whom staff believed had been dealt with unfairly during CCOR and matching. For example they believed that Dora should have been placed in the community and were anxious that her preferences had not been available for consideration by her panel. The second group of women included those whom staff saw as at risk of 'failing' in the community. For example staff concerns about Faye's 'deteriorating behaviour' led to her loss of a community placement. (It was later found that Faye was ill during this time, perhaps contributing to her behaviour. This did not however lead to a reconsideration of the decision.) And while Iris was matched to a house in the community, staff were anxious that her severe epileptic seizures would jeopardise her life if she were not in an institution. However, she did retain her community placement, partly because of her family contacts.

Staff therefore tended to argue on the one hand that all the women could live in the community, while on the other hand they were concerned that the supports might not be present, and that they were not given very much information about available services. They tended to react to individuals within the context in which they were currently living. For example Lena's tendency to wake at night put at risk community living even though her boredom and tendency to drop off to sleep during the day had been noted by staff.

### The Convenors and the Matching Process

Convenors had taken people living at Hilltop through CCOR and now in some instances were present as part of the panel which decided finally where individuals should live. Primarily, the convenors involved in matching were members of the permanent team based at Hilltop. People from other regions had left and although in a few instances they returned as regional representatives their role was then to represent their region at the matching panel.

The matching document allowed convenors to argue a case for individuals by providing additional information about them when this was required. However, some convenors were more ready to do this than others.

All convenors experienced anxiety about advocating for individuals they knew in case this discriminated against other, unknown people. They were caught between wanting to be 'objective' in their approach and having an interest in the future of the people with whom they had worked closely over past months.

> I know I felt very strongly about the people I'd worked with and trying to keep that under control was really really difficult. That was just ... I'm not going to let the ones I know get in the way of someone who I didn't know. The difficulty was you know what that person was capable of, whereas the other ones were an unknown quantity and you didn't trust the material. (Interview with convenor C.)

Some convenors were concerned at the failure of matching to consider all people equally. For example Dora's convenor was anxious because her preferences were not considered. Some were also anxious about the speed at which matching occurred. This was particularly the case for people relocated to other institutions.

> They only had two hours for Rochester who had fifty-four clients with a first preference, fifty-four for second preference etc. How are you supposed to go through that number of clients adequately and come up with thirty-two [placements]? I mean some of the regions ... the community placements: they took all day to work out places. (Interview with convenor T.)

They felt guilty at the way in which preferences for some of their 'clients' had been distributed. For example they did not know during CCOR that some regions were going to be highly preferred options and therefore more 'exclusive'. Nor had they realised that their ignorance of regional differences might have implications for the decisions made about individuals, for example not knowing where active night staff were available put at risk the placement of some people.

The convenors who had been involved with the women in the locked unit had little to say that was good about matching. Their primary response was one of deep anger and guilt. They thought that some of the decisions made about the women were inappropriate. Lena's convenor was very angry that Lena had been rejected for her first, second and third preferences (which were in neighbouring metropolitan regions), and perceived her final match to a house 200 kilometres from her nearest relative as inappropriate.

Some convenors were angry at the way in which information they had provided was used by the panels. For example Jane's convenor had felt powerless to change the panel's view about Jane. She did not see Jane's relocation to another institution as appropriate. All convenors expressed anxiety that information about individuals was difficult to collate on the day and that for some individuals important data were missing.

While generally convenors were satisfied when women did obtain a community placement they were also angry and upset when they felt that the woman had not received adequate or fair consideration. When this occurred convenors wanted to take action to remedy the situation. In some instances this meant consultation with other team members or the senior manager of the team, but sometimes other action was taken. For example Jane's convenor notified Jane's advocate of the matching decision prior to its formal announcement in the hope that the advocate might manage to change the decision. She did not. Although the convenors tried in a number of situations to change the matching decisions they did not succeed in doing this for any of the women.

Three convenors expressed anger at the intervention of panel members who provided new information about a particular woman. They thought that when this information was added it undermined the months of work which had been undertaken during CCOR. They were particularly concerned about the presence on the panel of institutional staff members who sometimes commented about individuals without knowing them well. And they were also concerned that when further information was called for it was given by phone to a Hilltop staff member who then relayed it to the panel.

## Closure Project Team Managers and Matching

The closure team project managers were not part of the panels making the decisions about people's lives but they did supervise the procedures and accept responsibility for their structure. They expressed concerns about both of these roles. First, they were concerned that matching was new and untried and that it had been developed quickly while the CCOR process was under way.

> So there was an intense period of activity behind the scenes to sort of produce the document and it ended up as a bit of, well, suck it and see, with the document being written as the matching process was occurring and I was very unhappy with that and that's probably the only thing in the project so far where I've felt that we haven't been looking ahead and been prepared. (Interview with closure project team manager)

Second, they were anxious about the perceived unfairness in the system which forced them to allocate half the people at Hilltop to institutions.

> I don't feel very comfortable personally about putting anybody in an institution and I don't think anybody does. I mean, you found yourself talking about things about clients' behaviours and you know … and really not knowing whether or not they'd be able to manage properly and you'd have to err on the side of caution so therefore if you were putting them at risk or setting them up to fail by taking them and so not putting them in the community and, you know, compensating by saying 'Oh well, it's not their last chance to move,' and it's not but it may be: you don't know and if they've got really extreme behaviours it probably will be their last chance to move unless something miraculous happens. (Interview with closure project team manager)

They felt guilty that some people did not receive their CCOR preferences.

> The cold hard reality was that you were dealing with people's lives and you knew that they were going to go and that you were going to end up placing people in places where you didn't want them to go and they didn't want to go. (Interview with closure project team manager)

The managers also believed that the speed with which matching occurred did not allow sufficient time to consider individual needs adequately. They were also aware that factors other than the criteria which they had established affected the process. For example people with strong advocates were more likely to have their preferences accepted and, in some instances, external political decisions determined the results.

Managers did however express some positive comments about matching. They thought that staff worked well together through a difficult procedure and that everybody was considered. There was also a view that generally those involved in matching took it seriously and gave careful consideration to the needs and wants of the individual people. And they were satisfied that the majority of people at Hilltop received one of their CCOR preferences.

None of the managers mentioned the women in the locked unit specifically in interviews, but there was concern about the fate of those people who had challenging behaviours. For some managers this concern was expressed as the tension between not wanting people to 'fail' in the community and being anxious that their placement in an institution might lead them to be there for life. Others were concerned at the potential lack of support for relocated people. As a result of the work of the 'challenging behaviour' committee, and with the support of the managers, people with severe challenging behaviours were assigned the equivalent of a full-time staff member in order to assist them in transition. However, this money was not designated for particular purposes and could be used by the service or institution in the way it thought best.

### Researcher/Advocate

The CCOR and matching processes radically changed my role as researcher. During CCOR my role ranged from a 'passive observer' to support person for individuals to provider of information. I was given permission by all parties to attend the meetings and I attempted to carry out my observer task as quietly as I could, but often this was not possible. Parents asked me questions about their daughter before staff from the unit entered the room: I gave answers, while explaining that I was not a staff member. At two meetings the convenor asked me to provide information from files since I had read them in considerable detail. I provided this information when asked and for both Laura and Brigid this information influenced the decision for a community first preference. I was with Jane and Jodie prior to their meetings and offered support and reassurance. On reflection it became clear that in some meetings I was drawn into the discussion because I was an outsider who could be approached more easily than unit staff by parents; because I was perceived as an ally by some convenors against parents; or because I was perceived as having access to information which was not held by anybody else. I found it difficult to avoid being manipulated.

Being involved in matching raised personal issues for me about the degree of participation which I could legitimately have in the process.

It confronted me with questions about the boundaries between 're-searcher' and 'advocate', and it forced me to consider ethical issues about the degree to which I should stay silent about procedures which I believed were unfair and insensitive.

Explicitly my role in matching was to watch the proceedings, however I also participated in a number of different ways. I argued for some women, sometimes suggesting further consultation and sometimes providing information which I thought should be taken into account. I listened to the concerns of project team members about matching, and in some instances I offered support to them in taking up an advocacy role in relation to individuals. At times I acted as a safety valve for the tensions which arose between individuals. As I was a silent 'ear', managers were able to express concerns and anger, secure that the information would go no further.

During these proceedings I found that my role as researcher became very blurred with that of advocate. In many of the panels I was the person who knew the woman best and at times I was a source of information about her. I was anxious that I might provide incorrect information or that I might jeopardise a person's opportunities by speaking out and thus antagonising those making the decision. There were also issues of fairness to be considered. If I argued for a particular individual then others would be disadvantaged. Because I knew the women, I was very concerned that so little attention was paid to the nature of the unit in which they lived. Yet I found it impossible to discuss their world. There was an unspoken rule in the panels that environmental or structural issues were not relevant. The focus was on 'characteristics' of the individual: their relative 'soundness' and their relative 'wholeness'.

I did act as advocate for some of the women: Brigid, Lena, Vera and Jane in particular. Such advocacy grew out of anger at perceived injustices in the process, and in these situations my research role seemed of secondary importance, at least at the time. As matching continued I felt increasingly concerned at what I saw as its injustice, lack of sensitivity and lack of concern for the individual. At its conclusion I was tempted to expose its injustices publicly or to try to reverse some of its decisions. I did not do so, as I concluded that my voice would be lost in the turmoil of closing, or if successful my complaints could jeopardise the closure process. I would also face certain exclusion from Hilltop. In the light of these considerations I sought to speak for individual women with their advocates and with closure project team managers. Like the others involved in the process, I still feel guilty and anxious about my role in it.

# CHAPTER 7

# *Leaving Hilltop*

The time has come to have a home,
Or to remain for a long time without one.
*(Primo Levi, 1988, p.13)*

The time to 'have a home' was one of turmoil, chaos and change for everyone at Hilltop and in the new services. In the six months before its final closure, the world of the institution progressively disintegrated. Simultaneously, houses and new services were finalised.

Matching decisions were sent to regions or other institutions for confirmation, then families and the women were informed about 'new homes'. The regional liaison team worked intensively with other regions and institutions to ensure that accommodation and services would be ready by due dates. Service providers were briefed about their new 'users'. Behaviour Intervention Support Team (BIST) reports on challenging behaviours were prepared and forwarded to new services.

Inside the institution, too, the activity was speeding up. Units closed: first the oldest and most distant; one, then two, then in clusters as people began to leave. People were relocated temporarily to other units, or they went to their new homes. Their assets were assessed, documented and forwarded. Staff left, and in increasing numbers so did those living at Hilltop.

After residents left they were monitored for six weeks: a transition stage. Questions were asked about the new services and accommodation, and about the quality of life of the people who had moved out. Were their living conditions 'the same or better than' Hilltop? How were they adapting to the change? After a six-week final assessment it was over: the links were broken ... unless there were problems. And there were problems, with every one of these activities. Delays, crises

130

and interruptions. The weather, recalcitrant builders, reluctant regions and institutions, parent and staff opposition, staff-rostering nightmares, disappearing assets, and individual illness and death. Through all of these, deinstitutionalisation continued, stopping only when Hilltop was empty.

## The Women and the Last Six Months

### Una's Story

A few days after the closure of Unit N, I visited the group of ten women who had moved together temporarily into a unit down the hill. Doors in the unit which had been unlocked were now firmly secured. In the dining room, Una was pacing the floor alone. Her face was bruised and she looked pale. Staff said they had separated her from the other women because June was constantly attacking her. Una did not respond to these attacks but spent a lot of time crying. (Field notes)

The attacks continued in spite of staff intervention. Una's family visited her and were upset at her appearance. Her seclusion from the other women became more permanent and she was moved early to her new home in the community after pressure from her sisters.

Una's preferences were all for community living in a town close to her family. She did not attend her Client Consultation On Relocation (CCOR) meeting as the convenor held separate discussions with her sisters in the country and with staff at the unit. Although unit staff and her family did not meet together, a great deal of informal planning and preparation went on between the unit manager and one of Una's sisters. Prior to matching, unit staff had taken Una to visit her sisters in the country in preparation for her move. She had spent some time in the house where she would be living and her family had been enthusiastic about their time with her. Her sisters were strong advocates for Una. After their first shock at the announcement of Hilltop's closure they began to work closely with staff to ensure that Una was able to take a place in the community. With these supports and because she had no 'severe' challenging behaviour, Una received her first preference of a house in a town near her family. However, as the house was one of the last to be completed, Una lived through the closure of Unit N and was moved down the hill to a unit with ten other women.

Una was third in a family of six children. The cause of her disability was not known, though one doctor suggested it might have been due to a difficult birth. She lived at home in the country with her family until she was eighteen years old. During her childhood her care was shared between her chronically ill mother and her older sisters, who gradually assumed much of her care. They regarded those years with a mixture of remembered frustration, pain and some pleasure. By the time Una was eighteen the family could no longer cope. Her mother was desperately ill and her sisters were busy with their own families. The family doctor recommended strongly that Una be admitted to an institution. Her parents agreed and she went to Hilltop.

> It was a relief [that she was going] until the day we took her in ... It was the first time I'd ever sighted Hilltop ... And it was horrific. There were so many people. I did not know that there were that many people in Australia with disabilities ... I was scared and all I could think of as we were leaving was, I wish she had died. (Interview with Una's sisters)

Una went home for frequent holidays with her parents until she began to resist leaving the institution. Her family became reconciled to Hilltop being 'her home and her family', but they continued to visit on a monthly or bimonthly basis.

> I hated going there to visit her ... yeah, even now that feeling comes over you as you start to drive up to the unit and you sort of, I think it's the rattle of the keys, the noise, the dreadful buildings that look so horrendous and antiquated. (Interview with Una's sisters)

In spite of their regular visits, Una's sisters had little knowledge of her life in the institution. For example they were shocked at the living conditions in the dormitory, which they had only recently seen. Although Una had lived in a number of units over the years at Hilltop, at no time were her family given any written information about reasons for her transfer from one unit to another. Her file reported that she had been attacked on a number of occasions by other people, but her family had discovered only one of these incidents. They visited her in hospital to discover that: 'Her nose was broken and her eye was split open, her ear was nearly torn off, she had a deep thrombosis on the leg and a prolapsed bowel' (Interview with Una's sisters). She was transferred to another unit after family complaints.

Una was a small woman of forty-two. Her hair was brown and thin and her face heart-shaped. She only spoke on rare occasions to her family or to staff. Usually dressed in a track suit, Una paced her way around an unseen track that ran around the perimeter of the day room. Sometimes she danced to music and sang wordlessly as an accompaniment. Staff encouraged her to do this, saying 'Dance Una, go on.' Una had an engaging chuckle and liked to be held by and to touch the staff.

Una's 'challenging behaviour' consisted primarily of eating inappropriate things: food scraps, dust, fluff, cigarette butts or the seeds and leaves of trees. She did not generally attack other people in the unit though she might hit or push someone as she passed by. She was more likely to be a victim, having her hair pulled or receiving a punch or hit or bite. At times Una would scream piercingly and it was difficult to stop her. Menstruation was extremely painful for her: she would moan and cry and scream for hours. Staff attempted to assist her with medication but this had little effect and they would often spend an hour on the couch stroking her head as she lay stretched out. She had been on many different medications since her admission to Hilltop: Modecate, anti-convulsants and Melleril.

Responses to Una from staff at Hilltop varied. She was very much liked in Unit N, but some earlier staff had commented that 'Her behaviour is disturbed, she bangs on walls and tables.' Her records revealed a picture which was sometimes contradicted by later entries, for example at one point in the files she was described as epileptic, but on a later page was noted as 'not being epileptic'. No reasons were given for the change in view. Reports on her level of intellectual disability varied from 'moderate' to 'severe' over the years. The files also gave a different picture of her from that given by her family.

Una's sisters recalled her skills in household chores, wiping the dishes, going to the local shops and helping with the housework. In contrast, a superintendent's report commented '... she does have a very poor degree of awareness of personal dangers in life and cannot recognise common symbols or coins etc'.

Una's family, the unit staff and the CCOR convenor were all positive about her movement from Hilltop into the community.

### Coping with Transition

The letters which arrived at the unit with formal notification of the women's future living arrangements meant little to them. Staff told them more informally about their future homes and some were taken on visits to them. This did not occur for people moving to other institutions. For some of the women, the notice that they would move to a house in the community was exciting although it involved a frustrating wait.

> I walked into the dormitory. Jodie was sitting in a chair near the door, crying. I asked what was wrong. She said 'I want to go.' I asked if she meant to her new home. She nodded. I felt terrible because I knew it was still some months before her final departure. It was very hard to explain this to her. I think she believed that once the decision had been made she would leave immediately. (Field notes)

Jane repeatedly expressed disappointment at going to another institution. The majority of the women did not know about their new homes until they arrived at them.

Matching had determined where the women would go following Hilltop's closure, however the decisions for two of the women were altered or finalised only after matching was complete. Faye's country community house was replaced with a metropolitan institution following staff reports of her increasingly aggressive behaviour. Late efforts to secure a house in the community for Dora failed because regional staff were anxious about her behaviour.

Before their final movement to new lives, the women had to live through the dissolution of the world they knew and to experience the loss of the people with whom they had lived. Unit N was one of the first units to close its doors: it was old and dilapidated, in spite of recent face lifts, and it was a long way from the administration block. Staff at Hilltop also thought that the women living in Unit N might benefit from contact with other people and from their release from the locked unit.

> On the last day of Unit N, I arrived in the morning. On the ground outside were scattered tracksuit pants, stockings, undies [briefs], jumpers, shoes, bras and plates. I discovered later that Rosalind had tossed them out of the dining room window. The front door was wide open and M. was piling boxes onto one of the dining room tables for removal to another unit.
> The rooms in the unit were echoing, as all the furniture had been removed. The women stood in the now-empty day room, with nothing to do and nowhere to sit. It was reminiscent of my first visit to the unit. (Field notes)

The closure of Unit N occurred over a two-week period in June. During this time, life became increasingly dislocated and chaotic. Clothing and furniture were packed; the group programme was abandoned; walks in the grounds became less frequent; forms on challenging behaviour were filled in for BIST; assets were transferred; and administrators were appointed. Staff had little time to spend with the women. In spite of the chaos, the women who could express themselves verbally indicated reluctance at leaving Unit N for another unit even when this offered a less restrictive environment, for example Elaine refused frequent efforts to move her to the hostel.

Some of the women did leave the unit early. Jodie went to a house on the grounds some weeks before the unit closed. She was very angry at the move, and the unit manager ensured that she was visited regularly by familiar staff. Jane too left the unit for the hostel. Staff were anxious about her reaction to the move and they visited her often. Iris spent the two months prior to the closure of Unit N in the hospital after a severe epileptic seizure. The unit manager decided that Iris should stay in the hospital until she moved into the community as she was in a 'calm and safe environment'. Doris too stayed in the hospital until she went to another institution, as she was experiencing manic episodes in quick succession and was regarded as too difficult to manage during the unit closure.

Following the completion of matching, Brigid was the first to leave. At closure project team management meetings, the client relocation team manager stressed the importance of moving Brigid early as it was expected that she would have a lot of trouble settling and that support from Hilltop staff might be needed. Brigid was also seen as less able to manage an internal shift within Hilltop and it was felt that it would be better to move her immediately to her new home rather than to another unit first. There may also have been an unspoken relief among staff at her departure. Brigid was not prepared for her move, which took her some 200 kilometres away from Hilltop to a country institution. She met the staff from the new institution once but did not make a visit to her new home before the move.

Brigid left very early one morning with the unit manager accompanying her. Later there were stories of how she had constantly pulled fellow passengers' hair on the way and had shouted and hit herself and others during the journey. She had gone by the time the women in the unit woke. Her departure made an enormous gap in the group. Some women asked where she was but no one was told unless they asked. She had simply disappeared. Her departure shifted the power balance within the group of women, with Dora becoming much more assertive. There seemed to be less energy in the group and less aggression.

Joyce left soon after Brigid to go to another institution. Staff spoke of her often with affection and sadness. She had had close relationships with the staff in the unit and was very loving with them. Her loss did not seem to mean very much to the other women and none of them mentioned her after she left. Faye was moved to her new 'home' in another institution as Unit N closed.

The twelve women who were still in the unit at its closure had no preparation for their move. They were simply grouped on the day they were to leave and taken down the hill with no introduction to their new temporary homes. Elaine joined Vera and Ilse in an open unit, as they were going to live together in the community. The remaining eleven women were moved to an open unit a little further down the hill. This raised the numbers in that unit from twenty to thirty-one. Four staff members from Unit N went with the women and joined the staff at the new unit.

I visited them in the unit several times in the first few weeks. Doors which had previously been open were locked as the women from Unit N entered the unit. Dora, who had been a leader in Unit N, sat bewildered in a chair for most of the day and there was a sense of fragmentation and confusion among the group. They were dispersed among the people who had originally lived in the unit. The change was bewildering to the women from Unit N. The environment was different, there were new people with whom they had to live and new staff to whom they had to adjust. Moreover, from the windows they could see their old home, now locked and abandoned at the top of the hill. Staff from Unit N stayed varying lengths of time in their transitional jobs, then they left, with new staff unknown to the women coming in to take their place. The transition was particularly difficult for Lena, whose mother had died just before Unit N closed. She sat in the new unit talking about her mother's death to whoever would listen.

### Advocates, Families and the Last Six Months

The role families and advocates played in the final six months of Hilltop's life depended greatly on their previous relationship with the woman and on the way they perceived her future life. I expected that the contact between the women and their families and advocates developed during CCOR would be sustained during the final six months. This did not occur. In fact, the visits from citizen advocates ceased entirely after the CCOR meetings. Some women did not comment about the loss of their advocate, but others did.

Jodie, coming into the local town with me one day, talked about her citizen advocate, showed me where she worked and wept at not seeing her. The staff rang the advocate but she did not respond. Families who had had little contact with their relatives before CCOR had little contact with them afterwards. Families who had had close contact with their relative over the years began to focus on her new life, for example Vera's sisters began to buy new clothes for her and to plan visits and excursions.

At this time, three families or advocates expressed their rejection of matching decisions to project team managers. Advocates for Brigid and Jane did not take any further action, however Lena's family appealed formally in order to bring her back to a nearby town to live. The appeal failed, as the only places available for her there were institutional ones. Although not registering a formal appeal other families did express continuing anxiety to staff about the final matching decisions and their relative. These concerns centred on safety and security issues. Staff in the unit reassured them. Some families were also concerned about the living conditions of the women after Unit N closed, in particular the crowding and the unfamiliar staff in the transitional units. For example Kate's mother was worried about her ability to cope in a new and strange environment as Kate was blind.

Families were not expected to have a role in assisting the individual to move from Hilltop, however some assumed the task of helping to prepare their relative to leave. All the families I interviewed had visited the area where their relative was to live and had seen her house or one like it. Other families had been encouraged to visit the institution to which their relative was going. Two families were heavily involved in taking their family member to their new home. Una's sisters were present when she arrived and helped her to settle in. Jodie's advocate took her to her new home and had established plans to purchase furniture and clothes with her once she moved in. She also organised ways of keeping in contact with Jodie after the move.

Some families acted as a liaison between the new service and Hilltop staff after the woman had moved into her new home. Una's sisters rang the unit manager to talk about problems which Una was experiencing in coping with her new life. They also sought help in establishing the degree of their involvement with her in her new home.

### Staff and the Last Six Months

Staff working at Hilltop found the last six months stressful and exhausting. Many were moving on to new jobs, but while they remained at the institution they had to 'cover' for those staff who had already left. The limited numbers of contract staff appointed were unable to fill the gaps and the new staff were unfamiliar with the routines of the institution and the people with whom they had to work. At the same time the administrative pressure on staff increased. They were responsible for transferring information about individuals to the project team workers, and they had to document the assets of each woman in the unit. Further, they were totally responsible for closing the unit. Staff were resentful at the additional administrative work and felt they had little time for anything else.

Many staff grieved over the closure of Hilltop and over the loss of a familiar and satisfying way of life. The majority of the staff in the unit had been at Hilltop for all or most of their working lives. It was difficult to say goodbye. The staff in Unit N were close-knit, bonded by the difficulty of their task and the length of time they had been together. There were close attachments to the unit which were born of long days and nights and known routines.

There was a period of adjustment for staff who had to work with others in new units or take up new jobs outside the institution. All of the staff in the unit were anxious about their futures. As the institution began to close, the possible future job choices of those remaining began to narrow. The unit manager had deliberately delayed in applying for jobs in order to 'see the ladies through' but now found herself with very limited choices. Consequently, staff time and emotional energy went into job applications and interviews.

While staff were generally pleased by the final matching decisions for the women they were concerned about some individuals. In Faye's case this led to a cancellation of her community placement. Staff were also concerned that Dora and Joyce had been placed in an institution but felt there was little that could be done about it. Staff did not generally feel that they could officially appeal a matching decision for fear of alienating families, both because of their public service role and because they saw it as just 'too difficult'. Staff were also concerned to ensure that women who had little contact with their families were safe-guarded in the move, so the unit manager ensured that an adminis-trator was appointed to care for the assets of those people who were moving.

The closure of Unit N was difficult for the staff. Those who moved down the hill into the transitional unit found it difficult to work with the original staff in the new unit and were uncomfortable in their new surroundings. They were also anxious about the behaviour of some of the women, particularly June, because they thought it might jeopardise their placement in the community. However, they did not attribute this behaviour directly to the anxiety of leaving the unit, nor did they develop strategies to assist the women with the stress of transition.

As the women began to leave the institution, remaining staff were keen to hear of their progress and to make contact with people who had been to see them. They discussed how particular women were settling into their new homes. Sometimes they felt that their expertise with a particular person was not taken into account and they were sometimes resentful of the attitudes of new service providers whom they perceived as patronising Hilltop staff.

### Convenors and the Last Six Months

The client relocation and regional liaison teams worked hard during the last six months of the closure project. The regional liaison team was responsible for the co-ordination and monitoring of new services with the other regions and institutions. They negotiated with regions about services and funding and they developed and implemented the final audit of new services after the institution closed. The client relocation team had responsibility for co-ordinating information about the people leaving Hilltop. They were the link between unit staff and the new services to which people were going. They were also responsible for undertaking the monitoring process, and they kept some contact with people living at Hilltop and assisted them in leaving the institution.

This work was very stressful and convenors expressed anxieties about it. Some of these related to guilt and concern about previous matching decisions. For example the convenors were aware that some families had accepted a place for their relative in the region of choice but had had to accept that the suburb was not their first preference. Convenors were frustrated at their lack of mandate to change problems which arose in the regions, both during the transitional period and the monitoring time. This frustration led to a great deal of anxiety about what changes might be made to people's quality of life after the project was complete. They were also concerned at the lack of individualised planning shown by some regions and institutions and the consequent tendency to fit people into existing programmes and services.

Because of the turmoil of the last six months and the speed with which decisions changed and shifted, convenors sometimes did not have the information which families wanted about houses and services for their relative. This left convenors feeling powerless and frustrated. They were particularly concerned about two groups of people: those who had been transferred to institutions and those who had received BIST reports about their challenging behaviour. The convenors believed that people going to institutions received less consideration than those going to the community. There was less preparation for their departure, the funding was different for them, and there was less commitment to them from the new service providers.

The convenors were conscious that few of the people going to institutions had visited their new homes, and they were concerned that some of the BIST reports on people with challenging behaviours had been prepared too late and had not provided new staff with an opportunity to read them before people arrived to take up their places. They also had stories of how the size of BIST reports for some individuals had frightened new service providers who had not yet met the person about whom the report was written.

As the months progressed there was a perceived overlap between the work of the client relocation and regional liaison teams, which sometimes led to confusion and tension between the convenors and the regions. As the closure became imminent, the convenors were aware of an increasing fragmentation in their work. They spent more time away from the institution, visiting the new services, and despite the weekly management meetings they found it more difficult to communicate with each other. More positively, the convenors expressed satisfaction with some of the services they had visited and thought that they had done well in managing the problems which had arisen in the regions.

In our discussions, the convenors expressed unease with the preparation and support the women had been given before moving into their new homes. They commented that the preparation had been a 'statistical operation' which emphasised the accumulation of materials about the women and their assets. The organisation of the women's client profiles supported this view. Thus Jane had a thick file which listed in detail her challenging behaviours and strategies for dealing with them. This file was in addition to the BIST report which was sent separately to the new service. In contrast, comments in relation to Kirsten were brief and focused primarily on her skills (and lack of them) in relation to toileting and eating. It was on these data, prepared by unit staff, that convenors had to rely in their dealings with regions. Sometimes they had been with a person during CCOR but more usually they were working with someone they did not know. As noted earlier there was little direct support for the women as they made the change.

During the transitional period convenors expressed concerns about some of the women in Unit N. For example June's convenor became increasingly concerned in the final days of closure that the region would refuse to take June because of her challenging behaviours. She spent much time on the phone and in consultation with the region in order to persuade them to give June a chance. She was very relieved when they finally accepted June. Faye's convenor was anxious about her initial unit placement in another institution and reported it as 'inappropriate' (see Chapter 6). He was relieved when she was moved to another unit within the new institution.

Convenor anxieties about the women after they left Hilltop were shown most clearly in their monitoring reports. These were prepared during the six weeks following a woman's movement to her new home. The reports about people moving into institutions were different in content and style from those for people who moved into the community. In all cases the convenor expressed reservations about the quality of life experienced by the person moving to the institution. Criticisms included that day services had not commenced, that accommodation was not of the expected standard, and that the person had been moved from her original place to somewhere less satisfactory and her behaviour had worsened.

Of the six people moving to institutions for whom monitoring reports were prepared, four were reported as having difficulties in settling into their new homes, one was perceived as gradually settling and the other appeared to have settled in quickly and happily.

> Dora has a great deal of skills [sic] which she could build on if she was placed in an environment that is suitable. To see Dora in G6 [unit in an institution] is very sad indeed. (Monitoring sheet for Dora)

While some criticisms were also made about community services and accommodation, they were usually accompanied by more positive

statements about staff attitudes and movements towards better conditions. Of those people going to the community only two were recorded as experiencing some difficulty by the convenor. Frequent
comments about the others included 'seems content', 'happy and
smiling' and 'seems happy'.

> Laura and Lena have settled into their environment well – there doesn't [sic]
> appear to be any concerns. (Monitoring sheet for Lena and Laura)

All of the monitoring reports for the women record some instances of
challenging behaviours. Two people in institutions were moved to different units because their behaviours were regarded as a threat to others
or to themselves, however in no instances were people in the community
moved. The range of challenging behaviours shown by the women
reflected their past behaviours in the unit, although two of them showed
new manifestations.

The monitoring reports and discussions with the convenors revealed
a high level of frustration at the lack of day services for people who had
moved out of Hilltop. This was most strongly expressed in relation to
institutions but was also present in relation to some of the community
placements. In relation to Faye, who had moved to an institution, the
convenor commented that:

> Day services not [present] at this point in time apart from unstructured
> informal unit based activities. Argument is that clients will receive the same
> degree of programming they received at Hilltop which in the majority of cases
> was zero. Local practice at Kingbush guarantees a minimum of 3 hours
> programming a week external to the unit. (Monitoring sheet for Faye)

In all but one of the institutions no day services were in operation at the
end of the monitoring period.

In contrast to the negative statements regarding institutional day
services, the convenors were more positive about the services provided
(or being organised) in the community. Although in the majority of
cases these services were also non-existent, the convenors commented
that they were in the process of being organised.

### Closure Project Team Managers and the Last Six Months

The six months between the completion of matching and the final
closure of the institution were exciting and tumultuous for the managers of the closure project. This period moved the project from: 'the
sort of preparatory stage of getting everything lined up and ready to go
to implementation and co-ordination' (Interview with closure project

team manager). Management team meetings were held weekly and involved a detailed review of the progress of each house towards completion and the preparations for people to leave Hilltop. When problems arose, managers were asked to deal with them and a strategy was usually developed at the meeting to allow them to do this. For the managers this stage was exciting. One manager commented that:

> [it's exciting] because it's outcome oriented. You work for so long, CCOR, matching, and I'm a results sort of person ... everyone likes to see things happen. And that's what's happened with transition and because of people moving out because that's happened at the same time. (Interview with closure project team manager)

However, the time was also very stressful. It involved sometimes protracted negotiations with other regions or institutions over the provision of services or accommodation, and preparations for the departure of people from the institution. Further, time at this point became an increasing pressure as it became clearer that the proposed closure date would coincide with a state government election.

The managers were also concerned about monitoring the movement of people from Hilltop. Checklists were used to assess the adjustment of people to their new services and to ensure that the services were operating as intended, but concerns were expressed by managers at the lack of 'teeth' which their monitoring process possessed.

The end of the closure project was stressful for all managers involved in it. The work was highly pressured and anxiety-creating. Towards the end of the closure process tensions between the different teams, particularly the client relocation and regional liaison teams, became apparent in part because of the overlap (mentioned earlier) between their work of relocating people living at Hilltop, negotiating with regional services and monitoring once people had left. In the midst of the difficult work at Hilltop, the managers were also confronting the future. None of the managers had any certainty of new or challenging positions after the project closed, and some of their energy in the last months was expended in anxiety about their own futures and in seeking new positions. Their situation was made particularly difficult since they could not leave the project to take up new positions until it was complete.

As the weeks passed and the institution began more clearly to change and shrink, the managers dealt with their own grief at the end of the project. Management meetings were moved around the grounds as buildings closed and the furniture and surroundings became more temporary. Managers talked of walking around the grounds, of the neglect and the sense of isolation that was beginning to pervade the institution.

For some of them this period was particularly poignant since it was the culmination of years of belief that Hilltop should close.

The managers had little to do with individual women at this stage of the closure except when problems arose after they left Hilltop. For example doubts were expressed about June's behaviour by the region to which she was going, and Iris's severe epilepsy led regional service providers to express doubt about her placement. In both these instances managers intervened to support convenors. Managers were responsible for approving convenors to follow up the monitoring process where this was necessary, and they reported directly to the closure project team leader when efforts to resolve problems failed. When concerns were expressed about the provision of extra staff to assist Brigid in her new home, the report went to the managers and then to the project leader, who took up the issue with the institution. Further, the managers intervened to ensure that Brigid and Jane were supported by known staff in the transitional phase. The timing of the two women's exit from Hilltop was also decided by the managers who had been given feedback by convenors about the problems these women might experience during the closure process.

### Researcher/Story Teller

For me, the last six months of the research were fragmented, chaotic and painful. Being part of the closure was an extremely intense experience, one in which close relationships were established and one which I found very difficult to 'let go'. My relationships with the women, the staff, the convenors and the managers of the closure changed radically in this time. During the last weeks of Unit N, I tried to spend as much time as possible with the women. I spent hours sitting in the unit talking with them or with the staff. Sometimes I helped with the work of the unit but I also began to take the women out on short excursions into the local town or for drives in the surrounding countryside. This relieved their boredom and gave staff more time to spend in administration. These excursions were the first time I had seen the women outside Hilltop, and I saw them differently. In some ways their disability was more pronounced: people stared or refused to talk with them, and Elaine stole fruit from the fruit shop (which I then had to pay for). Jodie burst into tears at the loss of her advocate, and we spent some happy hours choosing a housewarming gift for her new home.

Once the unit closed I tried to keep contact with the women spread across the different units in the institution. I dropped in for cups of tea, spent time sitting with them and continued to take some of them on shopping trips. I felt very stretched across the units at this time. The experience was fragmentary and alienating. My staff network had disintegrated as the Unit N staff left for new positions, and I had to renegotiate access for my visits with new staff who did not know much about my study.

While I did not have any difficulties with these negotiations I felt less comfortable in my visits to the women. I was also concerned at the difficulties some of the women appeared to be experiencing in the movement away from Unit N and at the lack of support for them. I spent a lot of time talking to the women who were verbal about their hopes and fears on the final exit from Hilltop. Those moving to the community were excited and had plans about what they would do: cooking, shopping, getting a job and doing housework seemed to be the things they were anticipating most. Dora did not speak of her movement to the new institution, but Jane hoped that it would be better than Hilltop and that she would soon be able to move into a flat in the community.

Once the women left Hilltop, it was impossible in the short term to keep in contact with them. They were scattered across the state and my attention remained fixed on the people who were left in the institution. I did visit Brigid once in her new home, but waited until the final closure of the institution to visit the other women.

For former staff of the locked unit I became a link across the units to which the women had been sent, giving news of them to the staff who were now based in different places. I was also able to act as a link between the staff team from Unit N, which was now dispersed across the institution. The convenors were my main source of information on the progress of the women after they had left Hilltop, and I spent a great deal of time talking with them either individually or in groups. By this time each convenor knew who I was interested in and would seek me out to share information about what was happening to someone in their new home. They also shared anxieties about the future in terms of their own work and about the closure of the institution.

The last six months of the closure involved a great deal of work with the closure project team managers. I attended the weekly management meetings and monitored the development of the houses for the women, noting when each person was due to leave. I interviewed finally all of the managers to obtain their views about the closure and to hear of their plans for the future. My role with these people began to change. From being a silent observer at meetings I was asked to help plan the final seminars for the management team. This included a seminar for regional managers and a debriefing session for the people involved in the closure project. For the first time I was being asked to be an active participant in the management process.

I found the transitional period the most difficult of all to work through. I wanted to see Unit N and Hilltop closed, yet I was conscious of grief at their death. On the final day that Unit N was in existence I walked through it. Without the trappings of possessions and furniture the poverty of the shell was revealed. The corrugated tin walls in the single rooms, the bareness of the bathrooms and the lack of privacy of the toilets were emphasised. The incapacity of the staff to fundamentally change the structure of the unit in spite of face lifts became glaringly obvious. Yet I still felt grief. In part it was the loss of an intense experience: one that was rarely comfortable and always distressing but also filled with intimacy and certainty. I knew the routines in the unit, the times and places for baths, meals and bed. I knew what was expected of the women and of the staff and of me. I remembered places where I had talked with an individual about her feelings or her family or her life at Hilltop, and I was conscious of the loss of relationships with the women, and also with the staff. These feelings were accompanied by concern and uncertainty about the futures of the people with whom I had worked. In the end, as the women, staff, families and managers dispersed and began new lives, I was left with what remained of Hilltop. I held their stories of the closure and of life in the locked unit.

# CHAPTER 8

# Deinstitutionalisation: Managing Subjectivities

That you are there to be found,
the disciplines agree.
*(R. S. Thomas, 1988, p.115)*

How did the disciplines which constituted deinstitutionalisation 'find' the women in the locked unit? The decision to close the institution led to the possibility that their situation would be fundamentally reviewed. It also offered the oppportunity for a change in the way in which they were constituted and 'managed'. The evidence presented in previous chapters suggests that deinstitutionalisation, as it occurred at Hilltop, did bring new knowledge and practices to focus on the women's lives. In this chapter, however, I argue that it did not fundamentally change the way in which the women's subjectivity was constituted or managed by those around them. Further, I argue that such change did not occur because of the ways in which deinstitutionalisation was constituted.

## Deinstitutionalisation and the Women

The women in the locked unit remained locked into the discourse of intellectual disability within which they had lived at the institution. In fact the process of deinstitutionalisation itself was conducted within that discourse, and its implementation served to develop the discourse further.

Although questions had been raised by staff as to whether some women in the unit actually were intellectually disabled, this was not reviewed or questioned by those closing the institution. Certainly the closure team made efforts to reassess the women's skill levels: measures of adaptive skills were used to assess the women's capacity to care for

146

themselves and to carry out household tasks. These assessments, how-ever, ignored the environment in which the women lived, which had ensured that their skills were often unknown or unused. There was no attempt to assess the women's capacity to live in new environments, nor was there any attempt to gain a view of their capacity to learn.

Intellectual disability also became a focus of attention when there were anxieties about a woman's capacity to live in the community be-cause her dependency would require high levels of staff support. Little attempt was made by those closing the institution either to cater for individual differences in skill levels or to develop programmes for in-dividuals during or after deinstitutionalisation which would increase the women's ability to live in a different environment. In fact during deinstitutionalisation even the limited efforts of the occupational thera-pists to increase the women's skills were reduced as staff moved away to new positions.

Similarly, the institutional focus on the 'challenging behaviour' of the women was not questioned during the process of deinstitutionalisation. Rather, it amplified and emphasised the focus further, a committee was established to consider this issue, reports were written about the chal-lenging behaviour of individuals, and checklists designed to assess the frequency and intensity of this behaviour were developed and dissemin-ated. Although there was unease about these processes among some of those closing the institution the information was used not only to inform the matching process but also went to service providers in the women's new homes, thus ensuring that it would remain a focus in their relationships. Such reports did not take into account the diversity camouflaged by the term 'challenging behaviour', nor did they place the behaviour within the context of the environment within which the women lived.

During deinstitutionalisation the gender of the women remained as problematic as it had been during their lives in the institution. In planning for the women's lives in the community, closure project team managers were very concerned about the adequate development of new housing and accommodation. Ironically, they paid less attention to the development of day programmes which could be expected to assist these women in coping with their new situation. Convenors also gave very limited consideration to the women's expressed interests or to finding out what these were. There was an expectation that the women would either fit into existing services or that new ones would be devel-oped some time in the future. Their desires were ignored.

As in the time before deinstitutionalisation, gender issues were in-terpreted primarily through concerns about the women's sexuality. This was a crucial factor in determining their future. The possibility of the women becoming vulnerable to sexual abuse in the wider community was a matter discussed in great detail by families. Their concerns about this issue led to Joyce and Inge being placed in other institutions rather than in the community. Jane was placed in an institution in part because of the closure team's fears about her promiscuity. Faye's physical appearance was seen as a problem which made the possibility of a life in the community more doubtful. Her convenor commented that her size, physical build and appearance 'made her appear threatening'. Closure team members also expressed concern that people in the community might react adversely to the women's inappropriate responses to men and also to their public display of sexuality. Further, in some instances the challenging behaviours shown by the women were seen through the filter of sexual vulnerability. The possibility of someone running away from a community house was given heightened consideration because of the increased vulnerability of a woman doing so.

When sexuality was not presented as a problem it was ignored. For example although some women had lived for many years in a women-only unit, the possible consequences for them (particularly for older women) of being in mixed houses were not considered as a separate factor, nor were their known anxieties or negative feelings about men taken into account. Kate, who was known to 'hate men', was placed in a house with two men and three women.

In this chapter I argue that the failure of deinstitutionalisation processes to fundamentally review or change the way the women were regarded by those around them was due to a fundamental tension between two discourses which are integral to the meanings of deinstitutionalisation. On the one hand it offers a promise of a different and more individually centred approach to people with intellectual disabilities based on their *rights as citizens*; on the other hand its knowledge and practices act to objectify and to 'discipline' them. Deinstitutionalisation provides new ways of 'managing' people with intellectual disabilities. This chapter involves a deconstruction of the meanings of deinstitutionalisation both as it is written about in the literature and in the way it was carried out in practice at Hilltop.

The closure of Hilltop met the basic requirements for the label 'deinstitutionalisation' as defined pragmatically by Willer and Intagliata (1984). It closed a large institution, replacing it with community-based services, and it involved an assessment of institutional residents ostensibly to determine if they were able to live in a 'less restrictive environment'. Those failing to meet criteria for community living moved to upgraded services in other institutions.

## Deinstitutionalisation and Rights

This was a quick and dirty process. It was not deinstitutionalisation. It was institutional closure. (Interview with closure project team manager)

The unease and anger expressed in the previous statement at the end of Hilltop's closure suggest that for this manager at least, deinstitutionalisation remained something other than what happened at Hilltop. She saw deinstitutionalisation as being about asserting the rights of those who had been living in the institution. The evidence for such a view can be found in the history of and the literature about deinstitutionalisation.

From this perspective, deinstitutionalisation has been founded on knowledge and practices which express a new and different view of people with intellectual disabilities. It has involved a shift from a medical discourse to a legal one (Gostin, 1983; N. Rose, 1985; Carney, 1991). The medical discourse diagnosed people with intellectual disabilities as 'sick' and prescribed the role of the state as providing them with treatment which aimed to cure them, to care for them and to protect them from the community – and the community from them – through institutionalisation (Wolfensberger *et al.*, 1972; N. Rose, 1979; Ryan and Thomas, 1987). In contrast, the legal discourse placed a strong emphasis on people with intellectual disability as citizens whose rights should be respected in the same manner as those of others in the community.

The evidence for this shift in discourses comes from two different sources: in particular from the focus on rights by proponents of deinstitutionalisation and from the negative view of institutional life, which was seen as incompatible with a view of people with intellectual disabilities as 'valued citizens'.

### Deinstitutionalisation: A Focus on Rights

The evidence for a shift from a medical to a rights discourse can be found in the history and practices of deinstitutionalisation. For example Whitehead (1992) traces the history of deinstitutionalisation (and normalisation) to the focus on civil rights in the 1960s and further back to concerns about rights following the Second World War.

In the United States particularly, the argument for the closure of large institutions and the relocation of residents to the community was, at least in some instances, carried out through class actions and based on the constitutional rights of people with intellectual disabilities as American citizens and on their right to adequate care and treatment

(Gostin, 1983; Rothman and Rothman, 1984; Moore and Ferleger, 1994). While legal actions of this kind have not been used to close institutions in Australia or the United Kingdom, the debates generated by them have informed government knowledge and have influenced the movement to more rights-based legislation and policies.

Proponents of deinstitutionalisation have placed a strong emphasis on the rights of people with intellectual disabilities. These rights include individual freedom, autonomy and independence and the right to live an integrated life in the community. The rights discourse reconstitutes people with intellectual disabilities as a disadvantaged group who are devalued in a community which privileges 'intelligence', 'beauty', 'competence' and 'wealth' (Wolfensberger *et al.*, 1972; Wolfensberger, 1992). Deinstitutionalisation is a means to reassert their rights as full participating members of the community.

Within the rights discourse it is not sufficient to define deinstitutionalisation in the pragmatic terms used by Willer and Intagliata (1984). Rather, deinstitutionalisation is seen in terms of a reshaping of the lives of people with intellectual disability, attitudes towards them and, more, as requiring a shift in the nature of the 'community'. In addition to the closure of such institutions, deinstitutionalisation is a philosophy which emphasises:

> the variety of needs among people with learning difficulties, their right to individual treatment, their value as individuals, their rights as citizens and the importance of integration as a guiding principle in the planning of services. (Booth, Simons and Booth, 1990, p.70)

To put this philosophy into practice requires a transfer of resources from large institutions to enable the establishment of integrated independent living situations and practices which 'promote autonomy and personal development, minimise the care-induced aspects of dependency and help to create a responsive living environment' (Booth *et al.*, 1990, p.71).

Further, deinstitutionalisation requires the acquisition of survival strategies by people with intellectual disabilities, and changes in the way they are viewed by service providers and the community. Fundamental to the description of deinstitutionalisation is a focus on the rights of people with intellectual disabilities. For example the first step to deinstitutionalisation is a right to liberty or freedom which is assumed to be denied in large institutions. Rights to autonomy, personal development, respect and dignity are then seen as goals for community living.

The link between rights and deinstitutionalisation has been given international focus by the United Nations Declarations on the Rights of Disabled Persons proclaimed in 1975 (United Nations, 1981, 1988a), the Declaration on the Rights of Mentally Retarded Persons proclaimed in 1971 (United Nations, 1988b) and by concerns expressed in a special report to the United Nations on Human Rights and Disabled Persons (Despouy, 1993). The last states that:

> It is an established fact that, while only a minority of disabled persons are institutionalized, such confinement is one of the most severe and common forms of exclusion of such persons. Many facilities, by virtue of being located in unpopulated rural areas are physically remote from the community, which only serves to increase this exclusion. Life within them bears little or no relation to the life of the community at large or even that of other disabled persons living outside. (Despouy, 1993, p.27)

Despouy goes on to list some of the rights which are denied to people in institutions, including the right of free association, the right to privacy and the right to appropriate treatment.

### Anti-Institutionalisation

By its very name, deinstitutionalisation suggests a negative focus on a site or a location. And certainly a heavy emphasis has been placed, both in its theory and practice, on the closure of large total institutions. Generally the descriptions offered of such monoliths are in terms of the high degree of power exercised over people's lives, so that 'institution' becomes synonymous with lack of choice, restrictiveness and lack of rights.

There has been a general consensus that institutions into which people are placed because of a set of 'devalued' characteristics are no longer acceptable. Over the past twenty years researchers have documented in detail the restrictions, abuse and deprivation which have been experienced by people living in institutions (see for example Wolfensberger *et al.*, 1972; Wolfensberger, 1975; Hayes, 1984; Rothman and Rothman, 1984; Potts and Fido, 1991) and which have been documented earlier in this book.

### Rights and the Closure of Hilltop

The rights discourse was fundamentally important in the closure of Hilltop. Evidence for this can be found in the motivations and goals of those responsible for the closure and in the practices which were developed during the closure.

The decision to close Hilltop was made in large part because of a growing recognition that it was not a fit place for human habitation. It was perceived as unduly restrictive on the liberty and choices of the people who resided there. The physical environment in which people lived at Hilltop was regarded as completely inadequate for their needs by all who had contact with it. Over many years the abuses and deprivations experienced by the people in Hilltop had been documented by government agencies and the media. Thus, deinstitutionalisation at Hilltop was founded on an anti-institutional view which strongly influenced the way in which it was carried out.

The goals of deinstitutionalisation at Hilltop were to provide accommodation and services equal to or better than those offered at Hilltop. Such goals were modest and compromised, but remain consistent with those prescribed in the rights discourse. They offered half the population from the institution a life in the community. The construction of new houses, the development of services and the concern expressed by those closing the institution that people should receive opportunities to live a 'normal life' were an integral part of the closure. Care was taken that those who were to go to other institutions would live in upgraded accommodation and receive better services than in the past.

The practices developed to close Hilltop were also influenced strongly by a rights discourse and reflected a view prevalent in the literature that people had the right to be consulted about their future lives (Grant, 1997). Two years of work went into the creation of Client Consultation On Relocation (CCOR). From a rights perspective it was important to involve parents, advocates and people with intellectual disabilities in making decisions about their future lives. The involvement of families or advocates was perceived to be the best means of safeguarding the rights of individuals, and it was hoped that their involvement would renew and develop relationships between them and the person with a disability, thus promoting a more 'normal' set of relationships and integration into the wider community.

Assessment by independent convenors of the individual's capacity to communicate and to make decisions was carried out so that each person could participate as fully as possible in planning for the future. The right to appeal final decisions formally and to an outside panel was available to all those connected with an individual.

For those closing the institution it was important that the practice of deinstitutionalisation as well as its goals reflected a view of people with intellectual disabilities as active participants in making decisions about their lives, who should be able to exercise their rights to their fullest potential. They were not to be treated as 'devalued' individuals but were to be valued as citizens. Their future lives were to be as 'normal' as possible and their rights were to be protected.

The commitment to rights also affected, sometimes in surprising ways, the views people had of the closure. The closure project team was committed to Hilltop's demise and was willing to accept compromises in order to achieve it. So, for example, while they were unhappy with the reinstitutionalisation of some of the women from Unit N they were prepared to allow this in order for Hilltop to close, for they believed that this was in the interests of the majority of the people living there. They were also unwilling to protest against 'quick and dirty' procedures for fear of jeopardising the whole operation. Staff justified these compromises in part because they saw 'transinstitutionalisation' as a temporary measure which would be nullified as the spotlight of deinstitutionalisation was later turned on other institutions. They also believed that life in the community for those who went there would somehow rectify any mistakes made during the closure itself. Thus the ends were seen as justifying the means.

The anti-institutional views of those closing the institution also influenced the way in which people who were placed in institutions were treated during the closure process. For example in matching, less care was given to selecting an appropriate place for people going to institutions than to those going to the community. No consideration was given to the people they would be living with. They were given few opportunities to visit their new homes, and little preparation for moving. The occupational therapists, too, restricted their work to those who were going to the community, disregarding those who were going to institutions. In contrast, those women going to the community were considered carefully in terms of house companions, had opportunities to visit their future homes and were offered some (though very limited) preparation for the move.

Anti-institutionalisation also defused resistance to the closure of Hilltop among the staff, for staff were divided into those who supported the indefinite continuation of the institution and those who wanted to see its demise. This division was crystallised in the union sub-branch, where those who were younger or professionally trained resisted the pressure from older nurses and indirect care workers to take militant industrial action. It was difficult from the beginning for the latter group to take a stand on the good life offered by Hilltop to its residents. Rather, they were forced to argue that some people could not live in the community, that they supported deinstitutionalisation with 'adequate supports' and, ironically, that they opposed the movement of people to other institutions.

### Rights: A Critique

The discourse of rights remains problematic when deinstitutionalisation is considered. Carney (1991) describes rights in the following ways:

> First, rights should be distinguished from the interests which they seek to
> secure: the legitimate interests of young people, or the disabled, in obtaining
> financial security and a reasonable standard of living does not necessarily
> found a right to the realization of those ends. Secondly, expressions of rights
> must be reasonably precise: they must rise above rhetorical statements of
> hopes or expectations. Vague platitudes are not rights. Thirdly, rights should
> carry a capacity for engendering ... compliance. A right which cannot ever
> compel (or persuade) compliance does not qualify. (Carney, 1991, p.60)

Clearly, some of the rights which are seen as being achieved through
deinstitutionalisation do not meet Carney's criteria. While liberty and
freedom to associate with others fit within his framework, others such as
the 'right to participate' do not, and are often difficult to define. The
problem of translating into practice a general 'right to participate' was
shown clearly in the difficulties which confronted the convenors involved with the women during CCOR. It was not possible to enforce
either the women's right to participate or the right to appeal the
decisions which were made about their future lives. As Ignatieff (1986)
and Green (1989) comment, relationships and quality of life may not be
amenable to a discussion of rights, for they involve subtle interactions
between individuals and cannot be legislated. Yet it was in these terms
that the needs of people at Hilltop were discussed.

Carney (1991) argues that rights must be seen as relative and as
competing with each other across groups. The 'competitive' nature of
rights impacted on the consideration of the women's futures in a number of ways. Families were not disinterested advocates and at times they
asserted their rights to 'freedom from responsibility' for their relative or
their 'right' to place her in what they saw as a secure and safe environment. When they exercised these 'rights' they inevitably succeeded,
sometimes against the 'rights' of the women to freedom and independence (for example Joyce, who went to another institution because her
family wanted her to be there in spite of staff views that she was com-
petent to live in the community). The rights of individuals to live in the
community were 'assessed' against the rights of those they would be
living with to a comfortable life-style or the rights of the 'community' to
be protected from their behaviour. Further, one set of an individual
woman's rights was sometimes in competition with another set, for
example the 'right' to freedom was evaluated against the 'right' to
appropriate services which would protect a particular woman from
herself. These issues made adherence to a rights discourse complicated
and confused in the practice of deinstitutionalisation at Hilltop.

Deinstitutionalisation had held out a promise that the women in the
locked unit would be seen through a set of lenses that were different
from the lens of 'intellectual disability', but ultimately the attribution of

'rights' did not alter the way in which the women were viewed by those around them. To exercise the right to participate they had to pass tests which would allow them this. Few of them could jump the requisite hurdles. To exercise the right to freedom and independence they had to pass as acceptable in the community. The criteria used for judging this were the same as those inherent in the intellectual disability discourse to which the women were subject. Further, the rhetoric of citizenship and rights did not lead to a reconsideration of gender issues for the women in the locked unit. In spite of the movement in the wider community towards an assertion of the rights of women, citizenship and rights were discussed during the deinstitutionalisation process as if they were gender free.

The specific interests of the women as women were not taken into account during the process, nor were they considered in framing future options for them. To have considered the women as women with rights would have required a careful consideration of how they might be involved in the process of deinstitutionalisation and of their specific needs and desires in regard to their future lives. This did not happen.

## Deinstitutionalisation and Management

Hilltop and the people living there had become an increasing problem for the government. Revelations of abuse, plus increasing media coverage of the appalling living conditions of people in institutions and the impact of the rights discourse in relation to people with intellectual disabilities exerted increasing pressure for change. At the same time the government was faced with the high cost of renovating Hilltop during an economic recession.

To solve the Hilltop problem meant finding answers to the question 'What should be done with the people and the place?' The answer was a management one involving knowledge and practices which would enable the effective and efficient management of a group of people, in this case the women (and the others living at Hilltop), their families and the site. It is perhaps significant that the person chosen to lead the Hilltop closure team was not one with a commitment to people with intellectual disabilities but a person with proven skills in managing difficult and contentious projects.

### Managing the Women

[N]ow as medicine, psychology, education, public assistance, 'social work' assume an ever greater share of the powers of supervision and assessment, the penal apparatus will be able, in turn, to become medicalized, psychologized, educationalized; and by the same token that turning-point represented by the prison becomes less useful ... In the midst of all these mechanisms of normalization, which are becoming ever more rigorous in their application, the specificity of the prison and its role as link are losing something of their purpose. (Foucault, 1979, p.306)

Foucault was writing of changes to the penal system but his argument is equally relevant in a consideration of institutions for people with intellectual disability. Hilltop was no longer necessary as a site to manage and constrain the women or to produce new knowledge and practices in relation to intellectual disability (Foucault, 1979), for now the women could be classified, categorised and disciplined within the wider community by an army of professionals.

The ways in which the management discourse played through the lives of the women is reflected in the ways they were treated during deinstitutionalisation and in their placement after the process was completed.

*Administering the Risk*

N. Rose (1994) argues that faced with the often insoluble difficulties of finding a cure for their patients' condition, psychiatrists (and their co-workers) have become involved both in a system of classification and categorisation of their clients and with an administrative task of positioning them 'safely' within society. The criterion for deciding on appropriate classification and location for people is based on an assess-ment of the risk which they are perceived as posing to others or to themselves in the community (N. Rose, 1994). The professionals in-volved in deinstitutionalisation at Hilltop carried out the same task in relation to the women in Unit N. Intellectual disability was not a medical condition which could be cured, but the professionals had the knowledge and the power to assess the risk which the women posed to themselves and to others in the community. The framework for this assessment was CCOR and matching. The use of comparative formal checklists and consultation provided assurance for professionals that the risks had been reliably and validly evaluated. During this process it was inevitable that the women would be 'objectified', for it was only those aspects of their lives which constituted their 'difference' which were of concern to those closing the institution.

*Normalisation*

Normalisation has been one of the key concepts underpinning de-institutionalisation. Although it was not explicitly referred to during Hilltop's closure it informed the way in which the women were per-ceived and classified.

Normalisation is a confused concept which historically has two meanings. The first involves:

> making available to all mentally retarded people patterns of life and conditions of everyday living which are as close as possible to the regular circumstances and ways of life of society. (Perrin and Nirje, 1989, p.220)

This definition would seem to place the concept of normalisation firmly within a rights discourse (Emerson, 1992). However, its more common usage in Australia has been based on the changed definition developed by Wolfensberger *et al.* (1972) and Wolfensberger (1982, 1983, 1984) as:

> [the] utilization of means which are as culturally normative as possible; in order to establish and/or maintain personal behaviors and characteristics which are as culturally normative as possible. (Wolfensberger *et al.*, 1972, p.28)

Wolfensberger's view of normalisation emphasised deinstitutionalisation as a means of shaping the behaviours and characteristics of people with intellectual disability in order to allow them to 'pass' as valued citizens in the community, for it was only by doing this that they could obtain their rights. Wolfensberger later abandoned the term 'normalisation' in favour of 'social role valorisation' (1987, 1992, 1995), which led to an emphasis on providing people who have disabilities with valued social roles within the community in order for them to achieve their rights as citizens and to become integrated into the community.

Wolfensberger's definition of normalisation has been attractive to managers and service providers. It has led to a focus on ways to assess and classify people and then to locate them in services along a dimension defined in terms of the 'least restrictive alternative'. Within a normalisation framework, service providers have become concerned with shaping behaviour and appearance so that a person with disabilities may 'pass' within the 'normal community'.

At Hilltop, the concept of normalisation was used very much in this way, for the women were assessed in terms of their capacity to be fitted into community life. When it seemed that their behaviour or appearance would differentiate them strongly as 'other', or when these things were regarded as not amenable to change, then they were regarded as 'unmanageable'. The process did not involve building supports around people so that they could live outside institutions, but rather judging their fitness to do so and then placing them in an appropriate service.

The positioning of normalisation (as defined by Wolfensberger) within a management discourse has led to growing criticism of the concept by those concerned with individuals' rights. Normalisation has been seen as oppressive in that it places pressure on people with intellectual disabilities to achieve 'normality', which remains generally undefined (Phillips, 1992), ignores the needs of the individual which may lie outside this ill-defined concept (Cullen, 1992), and maintains the power imbalance between those who are defined as 'able' and those labelled 'disabled' (Brown and Smith, 1992). Normalisation continues to define groups who are not 'acceptable' citizens (S. J. Taylor, 1987).

These criticisms reflect some of the concerns expressed by people involved in Hilltop's closure. Those committed to the rights of people with intellectual disabilities were angry at the need to assess people as 'able to be normalised'. They were concerned at the relocation of groups of people to restricted environments on the basis of such assessments, and they felt trapped by their own complicity in the process.

*Relocating the Women*

The rights discourse polarised institutions and the community. In the context of this discourse the community was perceived as offering the best possible life for people with intellectual disabilities and it was a place where they would be able to exercise their rights or have them protected. Evidence of the improved quality of life for people with intellectual disabilities who were living in the community had been accumulated through deinstitutionalisation research (Halpern, 1986; Edgerton, 1988; Felce and Toogood, 1988; Booth *et al.*, 1990). This evidence formed the hope and the inspiration for those people committed to the closure of Hilltop.

Contrasting with this optimistic view of community life was one which conceptualised it as risky and dangerous for people emerging from large institutions because of poor provision of services (Hope and Young, 1984). The possibility of fragmented, ill-equipped services for people with intellectual disabilities was a nightmare which managers wished to avoid. Consequently, community living was defined in narrow, 'manageable', affordable terms, which placed all eligible people in similar forms of accommodation and with similar sorts of support. There was limited opportunity to cater for individual differences, and no consideration was given to 'communities' which might have been different from the white Anglo-Saxon middle-class one within which the new or existing services were established. The management process could not take into account individual differences among people in terms of what they might want, nor could it conceive of services within a different kind of community. Rather, there was an assumption that all people, regardless of gender or class or culture, would want the same kind of life, and that all belonged in the same community. Such a view ignored the cultural diversity of 'communities' in the world outside institutions (O'Connor, 1991, 1992; Traustadottir, Lutfiyya and Shoultz, 1995) and the diversity among the women in the locked unit.

The 'community' to which people from Hilltop were to be admitted was a service system operating across the society. This was seen as involving:

> planned and tailored packages of services delivered to people with assessed needs, in cognisance of people's preferences, funded with these needs and preferences in mind, complete with built-in resource monitoring and quality assurance. (Knapp *et al.* 1992, p.4)

Such a definition integrated the idea of community living with the development of specialist services to meet people's needs within a community context.

The conception of community life which underlay deinstitutionalisation at Hilltop involved a network of fixed and already existing services which were linked by the professionals who would manage the women. Those people who did not seem as if they could adjust to the already defined community services or those that were proposed within the closure project were excluded from relocation to them. Thus the actual relocation of people was the important issue and consequently little attention was paid to what the women might do with their lives once they were living in the community. The walls of the institution were to be replaced by walls of professionals (McKnight, 1977).

The practice of deinstitutionalisation within the management discourse led to a construction of life in the community as a prize to be won by passing the appropriate tests. The question which was being asked (and answered) through many of the processes involved in Hilltop's closure was: 'Can this woman be managed or constrained within the "community"?' Some regions made a distinction between behaviours which were seen as possibly caused by institutionalisation and those which were seen as unchangeable characteristics of the woman in question. If it was decided that her behaviours were not due to the institution her placement became problematic.

Those implementing deinstitutionalisation saw the community as both dangerous for some women and also as vulnerable to attack by them. Inge's tendency to wander was therefore perceived as prohibiting her from community placement because it posed dangers to her. On the other hand, the possibility that Dora might abuse men in the street or act inappropriately sexually was perceived as making community placement difficult for her.

Ostensibly, those who failed the test for community living did so because their behaviour or their characteristics made them unsuited to community life. However, previous chapters have shown that the decisions as to where a particular woman would live were driven by issues other than her 'suitability' for community living. Half of the people living at Hilltop *had* to go to other institutions. A consideration of the actual reasons for someone being placed in another institution revealed that they had to do with choice of location for community living, the presence of active advocates or family members and the availability of services. These were primarily management issues.

### Managing Families and Advocates

Closure project managers judged family and advocate involvement as integral to protecting the rights of the women during deinstitutional-isation. Families and advocates were to advocate, to provide an independent voice and hopefully to assist in the integration of their relative into the community, but my observations suggested that involving families and advocates was also important from within a management discourse. It reflected a trend towards placing responsibility back on families for their relatives' well-being. It removed some of the decision making from the professionals and legitimised the decisions which were made about individuals.

Deinstitutionalisation has been viewed with concern by some writers who have seen the return of people from institutions to the community as providing a cheap option for governments and as placing an increasing responsibility for their care on families and particularly on women (see for example Finch and Groves, 1980; Mowbray and Bryson, 1984; Dalley, 1988; Pitkeathley, 1989; Smith and Brown, 1989; Dalley, 1992). This ideology has been labelled 'possessive individualism' (Dalley, 1988, 1992) and it emphasises:

> privacy, independence, the separation of the public domains, an acceptance of accompanying notions of gender division and women's subordination and the preaching of a creed of sturdy self-reliance. (Dalley, 1992, p.109)

Deinstitutionalisation as it occurred at Hilltop placed great emphasis on the importance of involving the private domain in decision making. Convenors traced families who had sometimes not seen their relative for years in order to involve them in CCOR, and the managers hoped that there would be an increase in family involvement with the women during and after deinstitutionalisation.

Families were not expected to care directly for the people leaving Hilltop, although some families were afraid that this might be the end result of institutional closure. They were however expected to take responsibility for deciding their relative's preferences, and there was an expectation that deinstitutionalisation might lead to closer relationships between those leaving the institution and their family members. The management of the women was perceived not only as the responsibility of those to whom they had been committed for care, but also of their families.

The involvement of families in CCOR was based partly on a view that they had a natural right to participate in decision making for their relative, for unless they were guardians, they had no legal right to do so. Only two families of the women in the locked unit were in this situation. Families (and to a lesser extent advocates) were given a large say in establishing their relative's preferences, however little support was given to them in doing so. There appeared to be an expectation that because they were family, they would make decisions in the best interests of their relative when this was required. All families were treated as though they were 'the same' and were supposed to go through the same process and have the same input regardless of their relationship with their family member. Yet some families had not seen their relative for up to six years, while others had visited regularly. Some were more informed about current ideologies and practices than others. Further, the fears and anxieties of families sometimes acted to influence their decision making. There was little opportunity to explore these issues or to assist families to work through memories and guilt in relation to their family member. This suggests that the important issue from a management position was the actual physical presence of an independent person. Managers were less concerned about what the family or advocate said than that they were there to say it.

When I interviewed the people involved in CCOR, most agreed that either the families or the convenors had most input into establishing preferences. My research experience suggested that when there was a clamour of conflicting voices families were most likely to win the argument. At one level this seemed to be because of the way other people involved in the process saw their roles: staff saw their role as giving information and the convenors tended to see their role as chairing the meetings. When the convenor did exercise power in the meetings it was usually done by attempting to manipulate family decision making. The involvement of families in CCOR absolved the professionals from taking responsibility for these decisions. Those on the closure team thought that not only did families or advocates offer an independent voice, but that they had to be involved in order for deinstitutionalisation to be carried out efficiently and effectively. One manager summed this up as: 'Justice not only has to be done. It has to be seen to be done.'

Thus families and advocates were witnesses to deinstitutionalisation. Their involvement ensured that if wrong decisions were made then the people engaged in closing Hilltop would not have to take total responsibility. Managers hoped that family involvement would also defuse some of the anxiety and anger expressed by the Parents and Friends Association at Hilltop's closure.

The power actually given to families was limited. The decisions as to where people would live were made by a group of 'professionals' who took into account but did not necessarily abide by the CCOR preferences. Those closing the institution, in hoping that family or advocate involvement with the women would increase through deinstitutionalisation, were supporting Dalley's view that in part at least deinstitutionalisation involved a re-emphasis on the importance of family relationships. For some of the women this did occur, and for some women the appointment of a specialist (action) advocate (see Chapter 6) to support them through the consultation provided them with the first outside relationship they had had in many years, or, in Brigid's case, ever. However, many of these relationships were fleeting. Action advocates were appointed only for the length of the project and their contact with a particular woman was therefore temporary. As mentioned previously, families who had little contact with their relative before CCOR did not continue their involvement after it. And significantly, all of the citizen advocates for the women ceased to visit following CCOR. The reasons for this are unclear, however it may be that the women became more difficult to visit as life at Hilltop became more chaotic and as the women began to disperse. At least three of the advocates for the women belonged to a particular church group and saw their role as intimately connected with local good works. Uncertainty about where the women would go and a sense that they may be moving away from the area may also have dampened the advocates' enthusiasm.

Morris (1993) comments that a focus on carers (or families) in considering issues affecting people with disabilities is often at the expense of the voices of the latter. The emphasis on involving families and advocates in the deinstitutionalisation of the women supports this view. It enabled those responsible for the closure of the institution to avoid a consideration of what the women themselves may have wanted or desired. Families were consulted as if they were able to speak for the women although it was clear that the interests and needs of the two groups were not always the same and were sometimes in conflict.

### Managing the Place

It is quite clear of course, that from the point of view of state expenditures, incarcerating problem populations of all descriptions in state institutions is extraordinarily costly, usually (though not universally) far more so than a deliberate policy of coping with them in the 'community'. (Scull, 1984, p.133)

The cost of maintaining and renovating institutions has been one of the underlying motivations for governments in closing them (Lerman, 1982; McKnight, 1985; Scull, 1984). This was certainly one of the issues which led the government to contemplate the closure of Hilltop. For example Naufal (1989) estimated that it would cost over $200 million to bring the state's institutions into conformity with health and safety regulations, without necessarily providing an environment conducive to the well-being of the people living in them. The government explicitly stated that Hilltop was too expensive to renovate.

The cost of the closure had been carefully calculated prior to commencing it, for at that time the state government was close to bankruptcy. Resource transfer to be achieved through the sale of Hilltop, and the one-year time-line to complete the closure, was designed to reduce the direct costs of deinstitutionalisation for the government. Similarly, the decision to move half the people living at Hilltop to other institutions was motivated largely by the government's inability to fund community living for all the former residents.

The requirement that the place and its finances be managed efficiently had varied and profound effects on the people who were subject to its closure. It limited the future living options which could be offered to people leaving the institution to either established services in the community or to one new form of housing. This precluded some people from being accommodated in the community because the accommodation and services offered were not suitable. For example regions were only able to offer very limited overnight active staff support, so those people with high physical dependency or who were likely to be 'disruptive' at night were precluded from community living. Some families too refused to countenance their relative moving into the style of community accommodation offered by the closure team. Others chose an institutional option for their relative because they were afraid that government funding for community-based services was unreliable and could not be guaranteed in the future.

However, perhaps most importantly, the need to manage the resource transfer efficiently set up a climate of competition for scarce community places among the people living at Hilltop. This competition was resolved by the professionals deciding who could go to the community and who would have to go to institutions. Management decisions made it inevitable that half the people from Hilltop would have to go to institutions, but during the closure this imperative was reconstituted as one involving the 'worth' and suitability of individuals for community living.

The processes through which the women passed during the closure were driven largely by financial imperatives and by the need to close the institution on time. CCOR was carried out quickly and the independence of the convenors was compromised by using seconded staff from the institutions and from the regions. Further, it was not possible for one person to retain the same convenor throughout the process. Similarly, matching was carried out speedily in order to ensure that the population was ready to move once the capital works were complete.

The capital works programme was based on out-of-date General Service Plans (GSPs) because it had to begin before the CCOR meeting. Consequently, the choices which people gave for future living arrangements had to be fitted into pre-existing accommodation planning rather than the housing arrangements emerging from the consultation. The closure team could not afford to maintain empty houses which might have resulted from a longer period of consultation and matching.

Finally, the very way in which the closure of the units occurred was determined primarily by cost. The older and more distant units were closed first, in part to reduce the cost of maintaining a dispersed population. The interests of the individual were subservient to the issue of finance.

### The Silence of the Women

Deinstitutionalisation at Hilltop was about rights and about management. At times these discourses were contradictory in nature. Each discourse was given different weight by different groups and individuals involved in the closure. For the politicians and some project team managers, management was the major consideration; for others the rights of those subject to deinstitutionalisation were seen to be paramount. The closure of Hilltop provides a graphic illustration of the way in which power and knowledge together govern our lives.

No one person was responsible for the way in which the discourses played through the closure, but those implementing deinstitutionalisation were caught between the two discourses of management and rights. This may explain some of the anger and stress which they experienced. For example convenors saw families as advocates for their relatives and were concerned that their views be taken seriously, but at the same time convenors were operating from a management discourse which framed the families' importance primarily in terms of their physical presence and the legitimacy which this gave to decision making. The convenors' anger at the results of the matching process is consequently understandable, for families' views formed only one small part of the information that made up the matching decision. Further, those closure project team managers who were positioned strongly within a rights discourse were frustrated by the management focus which limited their capacity to fulfil their intentions. In this situation it was tempting for individuals to reject the closure project as deinstitutionalisation in practice. Such a rejection denies the evidence that over the years these discourses have played their part in shaping and defining deinstitutionalisation. Deinstitutionalisation will always be, in the minds of some, something other than what is played out in any one instance.

In relation to the women, deinstitutionalisation at Hilltop provided a case study in 'how people constitute themselves as subjects and how they treat each other as objects' (Hoy, 1986, p.4). In the interplay of discourses which freed the women from the locked unit, they remained strangely silent and removed. The discourses moved around them. Information was gathered about them. Their lives were talked about by those exercising power over them. Their 'subjectivity' was dissected, measured and assessed according to prearranged schedules and checklists. Families and staff were consulted about them. *Because* of these very instruments ostensibly designed to reveal and free them, they remained 'objects' open to discovery within the disciplines brought to bear on them during deinstitutionalisation. Their fates were determined by the judgements of others.

> Foucault had a passionate concern for those whose ways of being cannot be spoken. But because he never told us in so many words, we do not know whether he believed that such ways of being cannot be spoken because the people who live them have not language for them or because the language in which they express their existence is politically subjugated, that is, rendered illegitimate by dominant discourses. (Cain, 1993, p.84)

Deinstitutionalisation did not enable the women in the locked unit to articulate their 'ways of being'. Perhaps for individual women there was no way for them to do so, however the important issue remains that they were not asked in any real sense to do so. The 'dominant discourses' left them silent. This chapter ends with a question: What other truths could be told about the women, truths that were not revealed by the discourse of intellectual disability?

# PART III

# *Outside*

It's not that the powerless don't have stories, and it's not
only that they don't get to tell the stories they do have.
It's that they're scarcely perceived as capable of having
stories, their stories are not so much refused as ruled
out, unimaginable to us as pieces of recognized history.
With no acceptable narrative to rely on, with no sustained permission to narrate, you feel crowded out and
silenced.

(Edward Said, cited in Wood, 1994, p.46)

# CHAPTER 9

# *Escaping Stories*

> If you think you can grasp me, think again:
> my story flows in more than one direction
> a delta springing from the riverbed
> with its five fingers spread
> *(Adrienne Rich, 1989, p.32)*

The title *Deinstitutionalising Women* has multiple meanings, and in the context of the closure of Hilltop both 'deinstitutionalising' and 'women' are problematic constructs. In this final chapter I want to explore some of the stories which escaped those involved in the process of deinstitutionalisation and to analyse some of the reasons why the women's subjectivity remained untouched throughout. For this study of the lives of a group of women has revealed that they were not only confined within a locked unit in the institution, but that they were also locked into a discourse which did not change during their deinstitutionalisation. Those who were involved with the women during this time were also locked into positions which governed the ways in which they approached the women.

The continuation of the discourse which surrounded the women of Unit N effectively wrote their subjectivity out of consideration. It screened out the expression of emotions and ambivalence felt by them and by those involved with them. It led to a focus on particular aspects of the women and disregarded the context in which the women lived. It offered a defence against the anxieties inherent in the women's lives and current situation and it legitimised the professional gaze to which they were subject. Finally, it subjected the women to a particular form of power–knowledge from which they did not escape.

In carrying out this analysis I am conscious that I too am constrained by sets of knowledge and practices which I brought with me as a researcher to the unit. The stories I have chosen to tell in this chapter are the ones of which I was aware, but beyond them is a universe of other stories which could be told. Inevitably the stories of others escape us.

## Objectification of the Women

During my research I increasingly saw the women treated as objects, as projections of others' anxieties and fears and as subject to particular organisations of power and knowledge. I saw their objectification in two major ways: the loss of their subjectivity and the failure of those involved with them to consider the environment in which the women lived.

### *Loss of Subjectivity*

Subjectivity (see Chapter 1) can be defined as: 'the conscious and unconscious thoughts and emotions of the individual, her sense of herself and her ways of understanding her relation to the world' (Weedon, 1987, p.32). The constitution of the women as revealed by my study did not include their subjectivity as defined by Weedon, for this definition of subjectivity requires such questions to be asked as: 'Who are you? Who are you as a woman? What are your desires and wants? Your history? How do you feel?' None of these questions was asked of the women in the locked unit. Rather, the women were observed and inferences were made which fitted with a particular set of knowledge and practices. However, 'subjects are (also) dynamic and multiple, always positioned in relation to particular discourses and practices and produced by these – the condition of being "subject"' (Henriques *et al.*, 1984, p.3). The women were truly 'subject' to the discourse which enveloped them (Hollway, 1989).

Life in the institution constituted the women's subjectivity in terms of a discourse of intellectual disability. This governed not only their confinement in a locked unit, but also the formal relationships which they had with staff, with their families and to some extent with each other. Deinstitutionalisation in practice continued this discourse and did not introduce essential changes in the way the women were viewed. Yet the women's subjectivity could not be contained within a consideration of their intellectual disability: their individuality 'leaked' out constantly from the edges of the formal discourse – sometimes ignored, sometimes acknowledged, but never an essential part of the formal world in which the women lived.

*Fantasies, Dreams and Desires*

> What then can we offer colleagues? First, and most basically, the conviction
> that all human beings have an inner world as well as an outer one – an
> unconscious as well as a conscious mind ... (Sinason, 1991, pp.227–8)

People with intellectual disabilities have written of their inner worlds
and their lives in the community and in institutions. Sometimes they
have done this alone and sometimes with help (Crossley and McDonald,
1980; Bogdan and Taylor, 1982; Edgerton, 1984b; Moody and Moody,
1986; Barron, 1989; Atkinson and Williams, 1990; Edgerton, 1991;
Souza and Ramcharan, 1997). Such accounts are not restricted to
people with intellectual disabilities who are able to verbalise their
experience: Goode (1989, 1992) and Gleason (1989) have provided
phenomenological accounts of what the world may be like for people
who are unable to tell us directly. Some novelists have attempted to
capture both the experience of disability and its resulting oppression
(see for example Vonnegut, 1976; Cook, 1978; Lessing, 1988; Carey,
1994; Hoeg, 1994). Many of these accounts are moving documents of
people's lives and experiences, yet the discourse of intellectual disability
effectively 'wrote out' the experiences and the inner worlds of the
women at Hilltop as individuals, for:

> To be labelled retarded is to have a wide range of imperfections imputed to
> you. One imperfection is the inability to analyse your life and your current
> situation. Another is the inability to express yourself – to know and say who
> you are and what you wish to become. (Bogdan and Taylor, 1976, p.47)

The attribution of the women's internal life was engulfed by prevailing views about the nature of intellectual disability. There were
implicit assumptions that this concept was unproblematic and that it
prevented the experience of an internal life and its expression. The
formal view of intellectual disability was firmly based on the culture
of measurement (although IQ test results for the women were not
recorded on their files, nor did I ever hear one quoted in the unit).
There was no space in the discourse to consider alternative views of
intellectual disability or its implications for the women. Although some
staff and closure team managers were aware of the confusions and dis-
tortions of the concept of intellectual disability, the unspoken view that
people with such disabilities were unable to have an internal life
continued to manifest itself in the ways they were treated.

The internal lives of people with intellectual disabilities have been
explored empirically, for example their dreams and concerns (Graffam
and Turner, 1984; Turner and Graffam, 1987), their use of memory
(Fyffe, 1994) and their perceptions of self-concept (Jahoda, Markova

and Cattermole, 1989). As noted earlier in this chapter, there is a whole literature about the way people with intellectual disabilities see the world, and psychotherapists have begun to write more extensively of their work with people with intellectual disabilities (Bates, 1992; Hollins, 1992; Symington, 1992; Szivos and Griffiths, 1992). But people's internal worlds, while acknowledged in the literature, were not part of the women's constituted subjectivity in Hilltop or during deinstitutional-isation. There was no room within the locked unit for discussions of dreams, fantasies, values or concerns which may have been experienced by the women. Conversations between staff and the women were most frequently couched in terms of immediate situations, questions and answers.

Deinstitutionalisation may have given the women an opportunity to voice some of their dreams, fantasies and experiences, for they were after all to be consulted on the kind of life they wished to lead. But this consultation was limited to their 'placement' within a location, and those closing the institution showed little interest in finding out pre-cisely what individuals might have wanted (for example the future occupations of the people leaving the institution were not of very much concern to those closing it). It should not be assumed that women who could speak could have articulated their internal lives. Many of them found it difficult to express their dreams or desires directly. It is not possible to know if this was because they did not have the ability to do so or because the discourse of intellectual disability actually offered no space for them to express such things.

The issue is not whether the women were capable of giving answers to questions about their inner lives, but that the possibility of them having an inner life was not considered at all in formal terms. In this situation staff and others involved with the women made inferences about what their behaviour meant. These inferences were based on the particular meanings given to that behaviour. Other inferences may have been possible given a different discourse. For example Brigid's final report stated that she enjoyed hurting people: a different construction of her behaviour could have been given had it been framed in terms of her need to touch or to hold others; her difficulty in separating a sense of herself from others; or that she had never had the experience of being loved or held by others (Sinason, 1992). Interpretations of behaviour were couched in narrow behaviouristic terms which did not allow for a consideration of other possibilities.

The effects of this exclusion of internal life from consideration by those involved with the women are most clearly seen in the way in which challenging behaviour was constituted both within the institution and during deinstitutionalisation. The women were observed as 'empty vessels' and the picture painted of them was restricted to observations of their behaviour only. In so far as it occurred, the attribution of desires or fantasies, or dreams which might have been involved with challenging behaviour, was restricted to motivations such as 'attention-seeking *behaviour*' or '*acting* out'. The discourse of intellectual disability provided the people involved with the women with ready and somewhat tautological answers for the questions which might have been asked about the women's internal lives.

The view taken of challenging behaviour precluded a consideration of the fantasies or motivations which the women may have been experiencing. A contrasting view is offered by Sinason (1989, 1992), who eschews the use of the term 'challenging behaviour', seeking instead to identify the underlying despair, pain and experiences of the person. Indeed, she argues cogently from psychotherapeutic experience that people may carry with them unresolved pain which they can express in no other way than through their behaviour. She also argues that such pain may in itself become a secondary disability. Her approach involves working with the individual on an emotional level to explore the sources of the pain and to resolve it. But there was no place for an exploration of this kind in the unit or during the deinstitutionalisation process. Rather, 'challenging behaviour' was constructed as a static characteristic which only the woman could change, with the help of medication or behaviour-management programmes.

Thus the women were no more than the behaviours which they displayed. In contrast, Sinason (1992) argues that an intellectual disability does not involve an emotional disability and that it is possible to explore the internal world of the individual. The behaviouristic view of the women prevented staff and the closure teams from actually examining why such behaviour was occurring or analysing the needs from which it might have sprung.

The pain which the women had experienced in the past was not considered in attempts to understand their current behaviour – sometimes because it was not known, but more often because of an assumption that their intellectual disability would preclude the effects of such experiences and because the women were not viewed as able to learn from them. Sinason (1993) and Dare (1993) have documented some of the possible effects on people with intellectual disabilities of parental and family ambivalence towards them. Nobody at Hilltop considered the effects for the women of a possible perceived rejection or abandonment by their families when they were institutionalised, even though there was evidence in their behaviour of such a response.

Efforts to change challenging behaviour involved either behaviour modification or the use of medication. During deinstitutionalisation there was an increased focus on those people categorised as having serious challenging behaviours. The existing treatment options were expanded on paper, with the Behaviour Intervention Support Team (BIST) carrying out detailed surveys and reports on individuals which focused on their challenging behaviour and which were designed to assist new service staff in working with the individual. There was no thoroughgoing reassessment as to why the women were categorised as having such behaviours.

The discourse within the institution precluded a consideration of the women in other than behavioural terms, and deinstitutionalisation continued to frame them in the same way. In order to move into the community the women had to prove that their 'behaviour' was acceptable within that context. The assumptions underlying the very construction of challenging behaviours were accepted by the closure team without question.

### Expression of Feelings

The discourse of intellectual disability did not allow for the expression of 'negative' feelings. Rather, it reframed them in terms of 'challenging behaviour', even though feelings of anger, frustration and despair were to be seen in the way the women behaved in the unit. By defining the women's behaviour in narrow mechanistic terms, these feelings were ignored by staff, who dealt with the women's easier behavioural expressions. Positive feelings such as love, affection and excitement were sometimes accepted by staff or families, but these did not become part of the formal picture presented of the women. It seemed that the focus on behaviour which could be 'managed' was less anxiety-creating for staff and those involved with the women than confronting strong feelings which required interpretation and inference.

This denial of feelings became particularly obvious during the closure of Hilltop. While there was general acknowledgement that stress was an inevitable part of institutional closure, the only concession to this was a management decision that the women should only move once during Hilltop's final closure. To be uprooted from an environment in which they had lived for many years, and to lose relationships and routines, was stressful and difficult. The effects of this on people with intellectual disabilities have been well documented (see for example Heller, 1984; Dulley, 1990; Firth, Holtom, Mayor and Woods, 1990; Holtom, Firth and Wood, 1990; Wood, Firth and Holtom, 1990), however, during deinstitutionalisation, the feelings which the women might have experienced during the process were also ignored or written out of the discourse.

Deinstitutionalisation workers were driven by their concern to shift the women from the institution and also by their view that the institutional closure was to be celebrated as a victory for the rights of the people living there. There was no space within the discourses for the women to express their feelings of anxiety about their future lives (although some did try), nor was it easy for them to express their grief about parting from their home and those with whom they had lived. Information about the closure was relayed to the women by staff who were upset by its imminence, and while staff informally acknowledged the possibility of the women's anxiety or grief, the women's behaviour was ignored or explained in terms of their disability or challenging behaviour. There was no provision for counselling or support for those women who found the move away from the 'secure' locked unit to a different environment upsetting. There was no preparation of the women for the departure of people with whom they had lived, sometimes for years. In contrast, counselling was readily available for staff at the institution who found the experience of deinstitutionalisation anxiety-creating or painful. Families, later in the process, were also given some limited counselling support.

### Relationships

Increasingly it is recognized that the quality of life of people with learning disabilities is not only about the physical environment in which they live. Nor is it only about the choice and value derived from work, training, education or other activities. Different kinds of social life suit different people. But for almost everyone, with or without a disability, the relationships with the people with whom they live, together with other social relationships are a major contribution to the quality of their lives. (Firth and Rapley, 1990, p.16)

The possibility of the women developing relationships was restricted within the locked unit to the other women, to staff and to occasional visits by families or advocates. Yet even the limited relationships available to the women were given little attention within the discourse. Relationships which were articulated (Vera and Ilse, see Chapters 2, 5 and 6) or which were physically close (Kate and Bettina, see Chapters 2, 4 and 6) were acknowledged by staff and also by those closing the institution. Relationships which were negative, such as that between Dora and June (see Chapter 2), were acknowledged and the women were separated after disputes but there was no consideration of their possible need to live apart. Further, during Client Consultation On Relocation (CCOR) when Jodie expressed a desire to live with Lena after the institution closed, her stated preference was ignored on the basis of staff input (see Chapter 6).

Relationships between staff and the women were ambiguous. Staff were tentative about expressing liking for an individual as they thought they should 'like all of them the same', yet individual staff had formed strong attachments with particular women. No acknowledgement of these relationships was made in the way staff were allocated to the unit itself. There was also a limit to the closeness of the relationships which could be developed within the unit. For example an ex-staff member who had formed a close relationship with Brigid while working in the unit was regarded with some concern by other staff members who felt that this was 'unprofessional'. The relationship was however acknowledged when the staff member became Brigid's action advocate during deinstitutionalisation. Further, individual women's anxieties about, or dislike of, some staff were not taken into account except under extreme circumstances. Staff with close relationships or a great deal of knowledge about a particular woman were not consulted as part of CCOR. Rather, the consultation relied on the input of the unit manager or her deputies, thus losing a possible important source of information about some women.

With deinstitutionalisation the friendships of some of the women were taken into account when they were relocated to houses, but when there was doubt about the nature of a relationship it tended to be dismissed. Certainly the strength of the relationships between the women and staff were not taken into account when the women were moved to other units within the institution.

### Skills

The way in which intellectual disability was defined by staff, families and advocates shaped the way in which the women were regarded. The use of tests of adaptive skills during deinstitutionalisation was also shaped by the prevailing discourse around intellectual disability. Consequently, some of the skills which the women had were disregarded by those around them or were reinterpreted (see Chapters 2 and 6 for more detailed discussion).

The skills of the women were narrowly defined during deinstitutionalisation because those closing the institution were interested only in the extent to which the women could maintain some measure of independence. Because there was no examination of the environment in which the women lived and no independent study of its effects on the women, their skills were treated in isolation.

### A Voice

Benn (1981), writing about poverty, describes how people are disadvantaged in our community by their lack of power over resources, relationships, information and decision making. She argues that the extent to which people can obtain power over the first three of these determines the power they will be able to exercise over decision making. The women in the locked unit were powerless in relation to all four of Benn's issues. They had no power over their resources, since their money was held for them in trust, and they had access to few services which they needed. They had little power over relationships which were governed by their physical isolation and the rules which dictated professional conduct of staff, nor did they have access to information about their situation even if they could use it. Few of them had independent advocates, and advocates involved with the women saw their role as a companion or 'friend' rather than someone who might change the situation in which a particular woman lived. Consequently, even if they were judged capable, the decision making which the women could exercise over their own lives was extremely limited.

Women in the unit who could speak were listened to in terms of basic requests – for relocation in space, a cup of coffee or a walk. Others who found it less easy to articulate their needs verbally tended to be ignored. Signing was not used in the unit and there was no provision for teaching the women to signal even basic needs without using behaviour which was then treated as 'challenging'.

Although deinstitutionalisation was seen by the managers and policy workers as giving the women a voice in decision making about their future lives, a verbal group consultation to establish preferences denied a voice to many of them. Some of the women could not speak; others were not able to manage the formal processes of a meeting. There were no other options for these people, and it was not possible to avoid the process altogether by, for example, purchasing a house of one's own.

As the process continued, the voices of the women became even weaker as it became apparent that their preferences were only one component in the decision making about their future lives. Matching removed the women as people from the process entirely, leaving the panels with documents about them which listed their skills and their behaviours. The women's powerlessness remained untouched by de-institutionalisation in practice.

*Individual Histories*

Green and Wunsch (1993) comment that attitudes to people with intellectual disabilities change markedly when their histories are known and appreciated. Without an acknowledged history, it is difficult to relate to others. We become our appearance at the particular time at which we are encountered, and important tools which we use to explain our behaviour and which others use to understand us are not present.

A denial of histories or denying permission to reminisce about the past leaves unresolved feelings and confusions connected with past events (Fensome, 1992).

The women were located firmly in the present by those involved with them both before and during deinstitutionalisation. Although there were detailed records on each woman, these provided only a fragmented picture of her, emphasising the problems which she posed for management. The women lost their histories as they entered the institution; cultural differences and the uniqueness of family relations were ignored or lay outside the possibility of consideration. Further, a family had only glimpses of the life of their relative after she entered the institution, so a large part of the women's lives was not known to people outside the unit. Staff rarely initiated conversations with the women about their past and responded only superficially when such issues were raised by the women themselves. One staff member stated that she deliberately did not read the files of the women lest these influence her interaction with members of the group.

This perspective did not change with deinstitutionalisation. Closure team staff sometimes read the files of the women, which offered only reinforcement for the prevailing view. The closure team relied on families and staff for input in relation to the women's history but saw this as relevant only in empowering these two groups, not in terms of what it might offer in helping to make decisions about the woman concerned.

### The Women's Living Environment

> Normalization keeps watch over the excessive and the exceptional, delimiting the outcasts who threaten the order of normalcy. There are institutions to contain these outcasts, and – if possible, this is at least the idea – to redirect their course to the latitudes of the normal. Institutions will form and well adjust the young into supple, happy subjects of normalization. Institutions will reform the abnormal who stray beyond the limits. (Caputo and Yount, 1993, p.6)

Until the women were perceived to be within the limits of normality there was little chance for them to move outside the locked unit or the institution. The women had to change and were to be assisted to do so with medication or with behavioural programmes. The discourse in which they were positioned provided explanations for their behaviour and for 'who they were' which took little regard of their environment.

Although staff openly acknowledged the paucity of the environment in the unit for the women and the possibility that the women's behaviours were made worse by living there, within the formal discourses proposals for a change in this environment were restricted to hopes expressed in General Service Plans (GSPs). Thus within an environment which restricted choice and increased frustration the women were expected to show significant changes in behaviour before that environment could be radically changed. Again during the deinstitutionalisation process the onus was placed firmly on the women to show their skills, their adaptability and their passivity. None of the staff closing the institution had time to spend in the unit and anyway this was not part of their brief. They relied heavily on the unit staff to tell them about the women and did not spend time observing the environment from which the women came.

Institutions have been conceptualised as having as their goal the disciplining of citizens (Foucault, 1979; Cohen, 1985), which includes surveillance, classification, examination and ordering. Further, the institutions generate new forms of behaviour to be disciplined. Thus in Unit N, which was ostensibly designed to rehabilitate the women who entered it, the women's behaviours developed new permutations which were recorded and classified. A study of the files of the women reveals that new forms of 'challenging behaviour' would emerge, be recorded and be added to over the years. There was a concentration on such recording, and on the basis of it the women were reassigned to new locations within the institution. As mentioned in Chapter 4, staff gained status and skills from dealing with such behaviour, and the institution itself took some of its *raison d'être* from the behaviour exhibited by the women. The discourse of intellectual disability enabled the institution to continue its work which was sanctioned by the community. Deinstitutionalisation continued this work, it did not change it.

## Functions of the Intellectual Disability Discourse

The intellectual disability discourse continued to frame the women, in part because it served useful functions for those involved with them. My observations suggested that for the people involved with the women in Unit N, these included a defence against the anxiety of working with them, the continuing legitimisation of professional regard and the maintenance of power and knowledge about them.

### *Defence Against Anxiety*

Patients and relatives have very complicated feelings towards the hospital which are expressed particularly and most directly to nurses, and often puzzle and distress them. Patients and relatives show appreciation, gratitude, affection, respect; a touching relief that the hospital copes; helpfulness and concern for nurses in their difficult task. But patients often resent their dependence; accept grudgingly the discipline imposed by treatment and hospital routine; envy nurses their health and skills; are demanding, possessive and jealous. Patients, like nurses, find strong libidinal and erotic feelings stimulated by nursing care, and sometimes behave in ways that increase the nurses' difficulties ... Relatives may also be demanding and critical, the more so because they resent the feeling that hospitalization implies inadequacies in themselves. They envy nurses their skill and jealously resent the nurse's intimate contact with 'their' patient. (Lyth, 1988a, p.48)

The women in the locked unit were not sick. They were however subject to nursing care, and families had made a decision to institutionalise their relative because they found it too stressful to live with her at home. The feelings and anxieties aroused by hospitalisation were made more complex by the long-term nature of institutionalisation and by the difficulties which the women had in expressing their feelings directly to those around them.

By constituting the women as 'other', families, staff and those closing the institution were able to deal with the often unconscious needs and anxieties aroused in them by the women and their situation. It can also be argued that these unconscious needs and anxieties led to the constitution of the women as 'other'. The process was therefore interactive. In particular these needs included:

the need to avoid painful feelings, the need to diffuse responsibility for difficult decisions, the need to shield themselves from the intensity of demands on their time and energy and their need to evoke a familiar framework which glosses over the lack of reciprocity in a paid caring relationship. (Smith and Brown, 1992, p.90)

Lyth (1988a,b,c) outlines a number of ways in which organisational defences operate to distance nurses from their patients. Many of these applied also to the staff in Unit N at Hilltop, to the people who came to close the institution and to families. One of the key ways in which people defended themselves against the anxieties created by the women was to prevent contact with the 'whole person', and the reduction of the women's subjectivity to a discourse of intellectual disability served this in a number of ways. The women could be contained through formal measurements of their behaviour, their internal life could be ignored on the basis that intellectual disability precluded the existence of such a thing, and their feelings could be attributed to their disability. Constituting the women in such a way enabled people to make decisions which they may otherwise have found unbearable.

Once the women were established as 'other', relationships with them could be restricted by professional codes of conduct which determined the ways in which staff 'should' relate to them. Relationships could also be limited by the time which people could spend with the women. For example families rarely spent more than two hours in visits to their relative and usually had developed routines about the nature of these visits; convenors had little time during CCOR to get to know the women in the unit; and staff were in charge of a group of twenty-one people whom they had to 'manage'.

Decision making about the women during their lives in the institution and during deinstitutionalisation was diffused: responsibility was shared, limiting the sense of intimacy which might otherwise have resulted. Families were required to meet only once with their relative (although encouraged to do so more often) in order to make decisions about her future, and CCOR convenors rarely stayed with the same person throughout the closure.

The focus on the discourse of intellectual disability led to a formal denial and suppression of the feelings which staff and families had towards the women. Staff in the unit were valued for their capacity to work in a stressful environment and to be 'strong'. Expressing feelings of anger, anxiety or distress was seen as a sign of an inability to cope rather than as a legitimate response to an unbearable situation. Staff were 'counselled', given leave or removed from the unit when they expressed such feelings.

As discussed in Chapter 3, my interviews with families revealed that the process of coming to a decision to institutionalise a relative had been accompanied by profound feelings of ambivalence and that the decision itself engendered still more. Although twenty years on, parents still cried in memory of this experience, once the woman was in the institution the feelings that were directed towards her could also be put away. Families all expressed the belief that their relative was there for life. Their ambivalence and their pain did not have to be examined but were locked with her behind the institutional walls. Deinstitutional-isation broke down the walls, offering families the prospect not only of the release of their relative but of the strongly ambivalent feelings they had about her. Consequently, as described in this book and in other literature on institutional closure (Meyer, 1980; Farlow and Lord, 1987; Reece, 1987; Ursprung, 1990; Tossebro, 1993), families were angry, anxious and distressed at the announcement of Hilltop's closure. For some of them, deinstitutionalisation also involved the emotional experience of sudden reacquaintance with a daughter or sister, while at the same time they were required to make decisions in her best interests.

All of these complex feelings were ignored formally by those closing the institution who were concentrating on the task of moving the women. Some convenors did spend time with families, talking with them and attempting to reduce their anxiety. But my observations of the

CCOR meetings suggested that families' decisions were strongly influenced by the unresolved feelings which they held about their relative.
There was no space to deal with these.

Finally, the convenors and managers closing the institution informally
expressed strong and persistent feelings during its closure. There was
excitement at the prospect of seeing the end of Hilltop, but there were
also periods when the compromises made to reach this goal and the
personal betrayals which were involved led to expressions of anger and
frustration. This was particularly so following matching. As noted in
Chapter 6, my interviews with convenors and managers revealed high
levels of anger and anxiety about particular individuals and about the
process as a whole. Some convenors channelled this anger into advocating strongly for individuals (and consequently experienced guilt
that they had thereby disadvantaged someone else), while others found
little space other than in informal sharing to voice their anger. A
debriefing session was held for staff involved in matching, but this was
not seen by them as offering an appropriate forum to release their
feelings. In fact, the deinstitutionalisation placed the convenors in a
difficult position: they were required by CCOR to make contact with
families and to familiarise themselves with individuals living in the
institution (some had repeated contact with families over time), yet the
feelings of 'protectiveness' or 'affection' which resulted had to be
suppressed during matching as the convenors were forced to consider
groups rather than individuals. Their role was therefore ambiguous.

### Legitimisation of Professional Regard

> So the test results were always related to time. Thereby producing a new figure
> – a measurement of intelligence. A calculated figure, and hence quite
> objective. All the psychologist had done was to let the children read and
> answer the questions, record them on a tape, note the times, double-check the
> figures and refer to the evaluation table. Everything clear and obvious. So that
> the result was, by and large, exempt from human uncertainty. Almost
> scientific. (Hoeg, 1994, p.96)

While we may all live within a carceral society, subject to its disciplinary
techniques (Foucault, 1979), no group of people can have been so
openly subjected to disciplinary procedures as people with intellectual
disabilities. The use of IQ tests or later substitutes established them as
'other'. The seemingly objective assessments of intelligence did not
allow for doubt but promulgated a professional certainty about the
nature of the people subjected to them. Once a person's 'low intelligence' was established, the discourse precluded from consideration all
other aspects of their subjectivity which could not be observed and in

turn measured. Within the unit the women's challenging behaviour was rated in terms of its incidence and 'severity'. Its nature was not considered except in these terms. The women's physical well-being was subjected to careful coding and surveillance. Their movements, their relationships and their sexuality were subject to professional regard, and this was justified in terms of their intellectual disability. The voices of the women, even when raised in anger and frustration, were heard through the distorting prism of objective measurement.

There is also a paradox in professional regard, for it created the women as 'other' through its formal assessments, knowledge and practices. Yet efforts to restore to the women their rights and privileges were also constituted through the same professional gaze. The checklists of skills, the tests of intelligence and social adaptiveness and the professional psychological reports which had located the women in the institution and in the locked unit were being used during deinstitutionalisation to establish their bona fides as citizens in the community. The context changed but the discourse remained the same.

*Power–Knowledge*

> More than any other social critic, Foucault asserted the deep connection between knowledge and power, that is the point that the modern mode of domination is based on a combination of scientific disciplines and professional and administrative practices, which penetrate each and every socialized subject of society. In Havel's words, it is as if the regime had an outpost inside every citizen, and consequently the regime is hard to locate within a particular institution or social group. Consequently Foucault rejects the idea of class or state power, and talks instead of a knowledge-power and the social discourse through which it manifests itself, a knowledge-power regime. (Soderquist, 1992, p.145)

This book demonstrates repeatedly the integral relationship between knowledge and power in the lives of the women who lived in the locked unit. The intellectual disability discourse differentiated them from the rest of the population as 'intellectually disabled'. Once so categorised on the basis of 'scientific knowledge' they became subject to practices and relationships which served to sustain and heighten this difference. These practices and relationships shaped their lives, determined their futures and constituted their subjectivity.

New approaches to the women were taken, new drugs introduced to change their 'challenging behaviours', and new information was introduced to assist staff in managing the women's disability and its consequences. Over the years, the women were increasingly talked about: their lives were documented in files, they became legends within the institution, the media recounted the horror of their lives in the locked unit, and parliamentarians expressed concern at their living conditions. They remained the still centre of a burgeoning set of knowledge and practices.

Deinstitutionalisation as it occurred at Hilltop did nothing to change this underlying discourse. It introduced a knowledge of people with intellectual disabilities as citizens with rights. On the basis of this knowledge, it was decided that the women should be given the chance to live in the community, to have access to generic services and the right to a better quality of life than that offered in the institution and, where possible, to have a say in their own future. In the closure process the rights discourse found expression in the stated requirements that the women participate in the decision-making process, that there be rights of appeal against decisions made about them and that their situations should be reviewed before further decisions were made. In practice, deinstitutionalisation established a set of structures, for example the CCOR and appeal mechanisms. However, the information used to fill these structures came from the discourse of intellectual disability. The people consulted about the women's futures were the staff in the unit, who were positioned as professionals within the discourse of intellectual disability and who had known the women only within the context of the locked unit, and families who viewed their relative through the professional knowledge of intellectual disability or through fragmented pictures of her over the years. Advocates appointed to assist those who had no families relied on staff for information and had ready-formed pictures of people with intellectual disability. All of these people had firmly positioned the women within the discourse of intellectual disability, so the only information available during the process was that which locked the women into their former position.

Far from challenging or reshaping the discourse in which the women were positioned, the deinstitutionalisation process sustained it and even amplified it (Foucault, 1979). The women's resistance to their positioning within this discourse was either unheard or reconstituted as part of it.

Foucault (1979; see also Ramazanoglu, 1993) discusses how each discourse offers opportunities for resistance. Those people whose sexual preference defined them as 'different', for example, could utilise the difference to argue with or turn back the discourse on itself. But unlike other such groups, the women in the locked unit had a voice which had no strength against the discourse in which they were positioned. They were silent, talked about and objectified with no capacity to voice their opposition or their desires in ways that would be acknowledged or heard.

The people who closed the institution did so in the name of values such as freedom, liberty and rights. No one person sought to oppress or to ignore the women – on the contrary, concern was expressed at their living conditions and there was a view that these should be better. But the managers and the closure team were themselves positioned within discourses which ensured a continuation of the knowledge and practices which enveloped the women.

Normalisation underpinned the closure of Hilltop in both intended and unintended ways. In its conceptualisation as part of a rights discourse it offered the possibility of the women living within the 'normal' community and leading lives as similar as possible to those of 'normal' people. However, it also involved an assessment of the women's behaviour to determine to what extent they met social norms. When it was decided that certain women did not do so and that their behaviour was not likely to be changed by shaping to make them acceptable, then these women were excluded from the possibility of living in the wider community. For this group deinstitutionalisation led to a continuation of institutional life, plus the addition to their files of the information that they had been judged unable to live in the community. The professional regard continued and was confirmed by the decisions made during institutional closure. New lives began for the women who were judged able to live in the community, yet questions remain about the degree to which the shift from institutional to community life changed the way in which the women were constituted by those around them.

## Conclusion

> The role of an intellectual is not to tell others what they have to do. By what right would he [sic] do so? And remember all the prophecies, promises, injunctions, and programs that intellectuals have managed to formulate over the last two centuries and whose effects we can now see. The work of an intellectual is not to shape others' political will; it is through the analyses that he carries out in his own field, to question over and over again what is postulated as self-evident, to disturb people's mental habits, the way they do and think things, to dissipate what is familiar and accepted, to reexamine rules and institutions and on the basis of this reproblematization (in which he carries out his specific task as an intellectual) to participate in the formation of a political will (in which he has his role as a citizen to play). (Foucault, 1988a, p.265)

This book has described the lives of a group of women who lived in a locked unit and has documented the processes and decision making involved in their deinstitutionalisation. The account has been shaped from my experience and concerns as a researcher involved with them. Many other stories could have been told, from many different perspectives, both of the women and of deinstitutionalisation. In writing this study, I have at times been tempted to take other paths, yet in the end the story I have told was the one that *I* had to tell.

The stories I gathered, the pain and confusion, the excitement and anticipation, and the intensity of the experience of closing the institution led me to have increasing concerns about what deinstitutionalisation left out. The question 'Who are these women?' was one which confronted me early in my encounters with them; it was also one which preoccupied those who worked with the women, particularly their families and those who closed the institution. The discourse of intellectual disability gave one set of answers to this question: they were answers which enabled the women to be managed, and they were answers which I found increasingly unsatisfactory over the months I sat with the women in the locked rooms or watched the meetings and the discussions about them during deinstitutionalisation. My conclusion, that there was no final answer as to who the women were, is unsatisfying and inevitable.

The experience challenged my existing mental habits and practices which were based on an assumption that an answer was possible. Being part, and yet not part, of the institution and its closure dislocated my previous values, assumptions and firmly held views of the world. It was not a comfortable experience.

Deinstitutionalisation was shaped out of contrasting, contradictory views of people with intellectual disability and the lives they should lead. It was a reform. It was meant to make the lives of the people who had been institutionalised better, to return to them rights which had previously been taken away or which they had never had. On the surface it offered a different and conflicting view of the women from that which had led to their lives in the locked unit. But it did not succeed in changing the fundamental ways in which they were viewed. It was overwhelmed by the existing discourse which objectified the women. In being denied as individuals they were also denied as women. *Their* stories continue to escape us.

> ... life in its brief play
> was a bit rough.
> Some fumble
> with thick tongue for words,
> and are deaf;
> shouting their faint names
> I listen;
> they are far off,
> the echoes return slow.

(R. S. Thomas, 1988, p.63)

# Glossary

**Behaviour Intervention Support Team (BIST)** Formed to work specifically with people with challenging behaviours or high dependency needs. They usually consisted of a psychologist/trained mental retardation nurse and workers with experience of people with intellectual disabilities. Their focus was on behavioural and environmental analysis and the design of behaviour modification programmes. Their key task was defined as follows: 'BISTs provide intensive intervention, consulting, training and education services to clients, families and service providers. The core business of BIST is to address highly complex, high intensive and deeply entrenched behaviours in a strategic manner by managing and reducing inappropriate behaviour and through positive programming techniques enabling clients to develop replacement skills' (Community Services Victoria, 1992a).

**client** The name used to refer to people living at the institution or to those who used services provided by the relevant government department. It superseded the older term 'resident' when referring to people living in the institution.

**Client Consultation On Relocation (CCOR)** An eight-step process, implemented throughout the closure of Hilltop, by which residents of Hilltop established their preferences for future living arrangements.

**convenor** A member of the client relocation team and responsible for taking people through CCOR. In this book the term also applies to members of the regional liaison team, both for the sake of convenience and because their work at various points in the closure overlapped.

**field note** Notes made by the author during her field work.

**files, file note** Institutional files kept in the unit on the women living there. These included medical assessments, incident reports and nursing notes.

**General Service Plans (GSPs)** These were required under the state's *Intellectually Disabled Persons Services Act*. They were defined in the Act as 'a comprehensive plan prepared for an eligible person which specifies the area of major life activity in which support is required and the strategies to be implemented to provide that support' (*Intellectually Disabled Persons Services Act 1986*, p.2). GSPs were to be developed for people in institutions every twelve months in consultation with staff, family or advocate and the person with intellectual disabilities.

**Individual Program Plans (IPPs)** These were required under the state's *Intellectually Disabled Persons Services Act*. They were defined in the Act as 'a plan prepared by a service provider for an eligible person which specifies activities and methods to achieve goals in areas identified in the General Service Plan' (*Intellectually Disabled Persons Services Act 1986*, p.2). IPPs were to be developed in consultation with staff, family or advocate and the person with an intellectual disability.

**institution** This book uses Goffman's definition of a total institution: 'A place of residence and work where a large number of like-situated individuals, cut off from the wider society for an appreciable period of time, together lead an enclosed, formally administered round of life' (Goffman, 1961, p.11). Steer (1986, p.2) defines an institution for people with intellectual disability more specifically as: 'a twenty four hour State operated long term care residential facility, usually constructed prior to the Second World War, with more than 100 residents who are labelled mentally retarded'. Considered together these definitions provide an accurate description of Hilltop.

**medications** The following medications are mentioned in the text as being taken by individual women in the locked unit:

*Largactil* – Trade name for chlorpromazine, a phenothiazine derivative and major tranquilliser.

*Lithium* – Used to treat manic-depressive symptoms.

*Melleril* – Trade name for the psycho-relaxant thioridazine, a major tranquilliser and neuroleptic.

*Modecate* – Trade name for fluphenazine decanoate, a major tranquilliser with often severe side-effects such as Parkinsonism and oculo-gyric crisis.

*Neulactil* – Trade name for pericyazine, a phenothiazine derivative and neuroleptic.

*Stelazine* – Trade name for trifluoperazine hydrochloride, a phenothiazine-type major tranquilliser.

*Valium* – Trade name for diazepam, a member of the benzodiazepine family. A minor tranquilliser, anxiolytic, muscle-relaxant and anti-convulsant.

**Superintendent** This was the name previously given to the Chief Executive Officer at the institution. Although traditionally the superintendent had been a psychiatrist, at the time of the study the person was usually a senior manager within the public service.

**unit** This term had replaced the older one of 'ward'. Most units at Hilltop consisted of old bluestone or timber buildings which housed between fifteen and thirty people.

**Unit N** The pseudonym given to the locked unit at Hilltop.

# Bibliography

Alaszewski, A. 1988, 'From villains to victims', in A. Leighton (ed.), *Mental Handicap in the Community*, Cambridge: Woodhead-Faulkner, 3–13.

Aman, M. G. 1985, 'Drugs in mental retardation: Treatment or tragedy?', *Australia and New Zealand Journal of Developmental Disabilities*, 11 (94), 215–16.

Aman, M. G. and Sing, N. N. (eds) 1988, *Psychopharmacology of the Developmental Disabilities*, N. Y.: Springer-Verlag.

American Association on Mental Retardation (AAMR) 1991, *Classification in Mental Retardation*, draft document, Washington D. C.: American Association on Mental Retardation.

American Association on Mental Retardation 1992, *Mental Retardation. Definition, Classification and Systems of Support*, (9th Edition), Washington D. C.: American Association on Mental Retardation.

Armstrong, J. 1990, 'And the walls come tumbling down', *Community Quarterly*, 17, 7–13.

Asch, A. and Fine, M. 1992, 'Beyond pedestals: revisiting the lives of women with disability', in M. Fine (ed.), *Disruptive Voices. The Possibilities of Feminist Research*, Ann Arbor: University of Michigan Press, 139–71.

Atkinson, D. and Williams, F. 1990, *Know Me as I Am. An Anthology of Prose, Poetry and Art by People with Learning Difficulties*, London: Hodder and Stoughton.

Bailey, S. 1983, 'Extraneous aversives', in S. Axelrod and J. Apsche (eds), *The Effects of Punishment on Human Behaviour*, N. Y.: Academic Press, 247–84.

Barnes, M. 1997, 'Families and empowerment', in P. Ramcharan, G. Roberts, G. Grant and J. Borland (eds), *Empowerment in Everyday Life. Learning Disability*, London, Jessica Kingsley Publishers Ltd., 70–87.

Barron, D. 1989, 'Locked away. Life in an institution', in A. Brechin and J. Walmsley (eds), *Making Connections. Reflections on the Lives and Experiences of People with Learning Difficulties*, London: Hodder and Stoughton, 121–24.

Bates, R. 1992, 'Psychotherapy with people with learning difficulties', in A. Waitman and S. Conboy-Hill (eds), *Psychotherapy and Mental Handicap*, London: Sage Publications, 81–98.

Bayley, M. 1973, *Mental Handicap and Community Care*, London: Routledge and Kegan Paul.

Beer, P. 1993, *Friend of Heraclitis*, London: Carcanet.

190

Benn, C. 1981, *Attacking Poverty through Participation. A Community Approach*, Melbourne: Preston Institute of Technology Press.

Berkman, K. and Meyer, C. 1988, 'Alternative strategies and multiple outcomes in the remediation of severe self injury', *Journal of the Association for People with Severe Handicaps*, 13(2), 76–86.

Biklen, S. K. and Moseley, C. R. 1988, 'Are you retarded? No, I'm Catholic. Qualitative methods in the study of people with severe handicaps', *Journal of the Association for Persons with Severe Handicaps*, 13, 155–62.

Bicknell, J. 1994, 'Psychological process: the inner world of people with mental retardation', in N. Bouras (ed.), *Mental Health in Mental Retardation*, Cambridge: Cambridge University Press, 48–56.

Binstead, N. 1995, 'Women with intellectual disabilities. Silent in the women's movement', paper presented at the Australian Association for the Scientific Study of Intellectual Disability, Melbourne.

Blatt, B. 1970, *Exit from Pandemonium*, Boston: Allyn and Bacon.

Blatt, B. 1981a, 'Purgatory', in B. Blatt, *In and Out of Mental Retardation. Essays on Educability, Disability and Human Policy*, Baltimore: University Park Press, 139–59.

Blatt, B. 1981b, 'Exodus from Pandemonium', in B. Blatt, *In and Out of Mental Retardation. Essays on Educability, Disability and Human Policy*, Baltimore: University Park Press, 161–205.

Blatt, B. 1981c, 'The family papers. A return to Purgatory', in B. Blatt, *In and Out of Mental Retardation. Essays on Educability, Disability and Human Policy*, Baltimore: University Park Press, 259–69.

Blatt, B. and Kaplan, F. 1966, *Christmas in Purgatory: A Photographic Essay on Mental Retardation*, Boston: Allyn and Bacon.

Blunden, R. 1990, 'Services for people with learning difficulties and challenging behaviour. A brief review of recent developments', *International Review of Psychiatry*, 2(1), 5–10.

Blunden, R. and Allen, D. 1987, *Facing the Challenge. An Ordinary Life for People with Learning Difficulties and Challenging Behaviour*, London: Kings Fund Centre.

Bogdan, R. 1988, *Freak Show*, Chicago: Chicago University Press.

Bogdan, R. and Biklen, S. K. 1992, *Qualitative Research for Education: An Introduction to Theory and Methods*, Boston: Allyn and Bacon.

Bogdan, R. and Taylor, S. J. 1976, 'The judged, not the judges. An insider's view of mental retardation', *American Psychologist*, 31(1), 47–52.

Bogdan, R. and Taylor, S. J. 1982, *Inside Out. The Social Meaning of Mental Retardation*, Toronto: University of Toronto Press.

Bogdan, R. and Taylor, S. J. 1989a, 'Relationships with severely disabled people. The social construction of humanness', *Social Problems*, 36, 135–48.

Bogdan, R. and Taylor, S. J. 1989b, 'What's in a name?', in A. Brechin and J. Walmsley (eds), *Making Connections. Reflecting on the Lives and Experiences of People with Learning Difficulties*, London: Hodder and Stoughton, 76–81.

Booth, T. 1996, 'Sounds of still voices. Issues in the use of narrative methods with people who have learning disabilities', in L. Barton (ed.), *Disability and Society. Emerging Issues and Insights*, London: Harlow Addison Wesley Longman Ltd, 237–54.

Booth, T., Simons, K. and Booth, W. 1990, *Outward Bound: Relocation and Community Care for People with Learning Difficulties*, Milton Keynes: Open University Press.

Borthwick, C., Kennedy, K., Mallia, P. and Marshall, W. 1988, *Community Visitors' Report to the Minister*, Melbourne: Office of the Public Advocate.

Bowman, D. 1991, 'Public policy, private lives of women as mothers of children with disabilities', *Interaction*, 5(4), 16–22.

Bowman, D. and Virtue, M. 1993, *Public Policy Private Lives*, Canberra: Australian Institute on Intellectual Disability.

Brantley, D. M. and Gemill, P. A. 1991, 'Mental retardation', in A. Glitterman (ed.), *Handbook of Social Work Practice with Vulnerable Populations*, N. Y.: Columbia University Press, 265–85.

Brantner, J. P. and Doherty, M. A. 1983, 'A review of time out: A conceptual and methodological analysis', in S. Axelrod and J. Apsche (eds), *The Effects of Punishment on Human Behaviour*, N. Y.: Academic Press, 87–132.

Brothers, C. R. 1958, *Early Victorian Psychiatry, 1835–1905*, Melbourne: Department of Mental Health.

Brown, H. 1994, 'An ordinary sexual life. A review of the normalisation principle as it applies to the sexual options of people with learning disabilities', *Disability and Society*, 9, 123–44.

Brown, H. and Barrett, S. 1994, 'Understanding and responding to difficult sexual behaviour', in A. Craft (ed.), *Practice Issues in Sexuality and Learning Disability*, London: Routledge, 50–80.

Brown, H. and Smith, H. 1992, 'Postscript', in H. Brown and H. Smith (eds), *Normalisation. A Reader for the Nineties*, London: Routledge, 172–7.

Brown, H. and Turk, V. 1995, 'Sexuality: towards a more balanced view', in N. Bouras (ed.), *Mental Health in Mental Retardation. Recent Advances and Practices*, Cambridge: Cambridge University Press, 168–84.

Brown, L. D. and Tandon, R. 1983, 'Ideology and political economy in inquiry: action research and participatory research', *Journal of Applied Behavioral Science*, 19(3), 277–94.

Burgess, R. G. 1982, 'Approaches to field research', in R. G. Burgess (ed.), *Field Research: A Sourcebook and Field Manual*, London: Allen and Unwin, 1–11.

Burgess, R. G. 1984, *In the Field. An Introduction to Field Research*, London: George Allen and Unwin.

Burman, E. and Parker, I. (eds) 1993, *Discourse Analytic Research. Repertoires and Readings of Texts in Action*, London: Routledge.

Cain, M. 1993, 'Foucault, feminism and feeling. What Foucault can and cannot contribute to feminist epistemology', in C. Ramazanoglu (ed.), *Up against Foucault. Explanations of some Tensions between Foucault and Feminism*, London: Routledge, 73–96.

Caputo, J. and Yount, M. 1993, 'Institutions, normalization and power', in J. Caputo and M. Yount (eds), *Foucault and the Critique of Institutions*, Pennsylvania: Pennsylvania State University Press, 3–23.

Carey, P. 1994, *The Unusual Life of Tristan Smith*, Brisbane: University of Queensland Press.

Carney, T. 1991, *Law at the Margin*, Australia: Oxford University Press.

Carr, E. G. and Lovaas, O. I. 1983, 'Contingent electric shock as a treatment for severe behaviour problems', in S. Axelrod and J. Apsche (eds), *The Effects of Punishment on Human Behaviour*, N. Y.: Academic Press, 221–45.

Carr, W. and Kemmis, S. 1986, *Becoming Critical: Knowing through Action Research*, Melbourne: Deakin University.

Cashin, C. 1992, *CCOR Manual*, Melbourne: Community Services Victoria.

Cattermole, M., Jahoda, A. and Markova, I. 1988, 'Life in a mental handicap hospital', *Mental Handicap*, 16, 28–31.

Chein, I., Cook, S. and Harding, J. 1990, 'The field of action research', in S. Kemmis and R. McTaggart (eds), *The Action Research Reader*, Melbourne: Deakin University Press, 57–65.

Cherns, A. B. 1976, 'Behavioural science engagements', *Human Relations*, 29(10), 905–10.

Clark, A. W. 1976, *Experimenting with Organizational Life*, N. Y.: Plenum Books.

Clark, P. A. 1972, *Action Research and Organizational Change*, N. Y.: Harper and Row.

Clements, J., Clare, I. and Ezelle, L. 1995, 'Real men, real women, real lives? Gender issues in learning disabilities and challenging behaviour', *Disability and Society*, 10(4), 425–35.

Client Relocation Team 1992, *Client Relocation: Planning and Implementation Document*, Melbourne: Community Services Victoria.

Cocks, E. 1985, 'Roadblocks to appropriate services for persons with an intellectual disability in Australia', *Australia and New Zealand Journal of Developmental Disabilities*, 11(2), 75–82.

Cohen, S. 1985, *Visions of Social Control*, Cambridge: Polity Press.

Collins, J. 1992, *When the Eagles Fly. A Report on the Resettlement of People with Learning Difficulties from Long-Stay Hospitals*, London: Values into Action.

Commonwealth Government 1986, *Disability Services Act*, Canberra: Australian Government Printing Service.

Commonwealth Government 1992, *Disability Discrimination Act*, Canberra: Australian Government Printing Service.

Community Services Victoria (undated), 'Brief History of the Centre', pamphlet in K. Johnson's private collection, Melbourne.

Community Services Victoria 1989, *The State Plan and the Redevelopment of Intellectual Disability Services, 1990–1992*, Melbourne: Community Services Victoria.

Community Services Victoria 1990, *CCOR Implementation Package*, Melbourne: Community Services Victoria.

Community Services Victoria State Plan Implementation Team 1990, *Client Consultation on Relocation*, Melbourne: Community Services Victoria.

Community Visitors Board 1990, *Annual Report of the Community Visitors*, Melbourne: Victorian Government Printing Office

Conroy, J. W. and Bradley, V. J. 1985, *The Pennhurst Longitudinal Study. A Report of Five Years of Research and Analysis*, Philadelphia: Temple University Developmental Disabilities Center.

Conway, J. B. and Bucher, B. D. 1974, 'Soap in the mouth as an aversive consequence', *Behaviour Therapy*, 5(1), 154–6.

Cook, D. 1978, *Walter*, Harmondsworth: Penguin.

Crabbe, H. F. 1995, 'Pharmocotherapy in mental retardation', in N. Bouras (ed.), *Mental Health in Mental Retardation. Recent Advances and Practices*, Cambridge: Cambridge University Press, 187–204.

Crawford, D. 1983, *Review of Training Centres*, Melbourne: Mental Retardation Division, Department of Community Services.

Crossley, R. and McDonald, A. 1980, *Annie's Coming Out*, Melbourne: Penguin.

Cullen, C. 1992, 'Bridging the gap between treatment techniques and service philosophy', in J. Harris (ed.), *Service Responses to People with Learning Difficulties and Challenging Behaviour*, BIMH Seminar Papers No. 1. Kidderminster: BIMH, 55–7.

Cummins, R. and Dunt, D. 1990, 'The deinstitutionalization of St Nicholas Hospital II. Lifestyle, community contact and family attitudes', *Australia and New Zealand Journal of Developmental Disabilities*, 16(2), 19–32.

Cummins, R., Polzin, U. and Theobald, T. 1990a, 'The deinstitutionalization of St Nicholas Hospital III. Four-year follow-up of life-skill development', *Australia and New Zealand Journal of Developmental Disabilities*, 16(3), 219–32.

Cummins, R., Polzin, U. and Theobald, T. 1990b, 'Deinstitutionalization of St Nicholas Hospital IV. A four-year follow-up of resident life-style', *Australia and New Zealand Journal of Developmental Disabilities*, 16(4), 305–21.

Cunningham, B. 1976, 'Action research: Towards a procedural model', *Human Relations*, 29: 215–38.

Daley, P. 1991, 'Second inquiry into disabled deaths', *The Age*, 5 May.

Dalley, G. 1988, *Ideologies of Caring: Rethinking Community and Collectivism*, London: Macmillan.

Dalley, G. 1992, 'Social welfare ideologies and normalisation', in H. Brown and H. Smith (eds), *Normalisation. A Reader for the Nineties*, London: Tavistock/Routledge, 100–11.

Danziger, K. 1990, *Constructing the Subject. Historical Origins of Psychological Research*, Cambridge: Cambridge University Press.

Danziger, K. 1996, 'The practice of psychological discourse', in C. F. Graumann and Kenneth J. Gergen (eds), *Historical Dimensions of Psychological Discourse*, Cambridge: Cambridge University Press, 17–35.

Dare, C. 1993, 'The family scapegoat', in V. Varma (ed.), *How and Why Children Hate. A Study of Conscious and Unconscious Sources*, London: Jessica Kingsley, 186–98.

Dartington, T., Miller, E. and Gwynne, G. 1981, *A Life Together. The Distribution of Attitudes around the Disabled*, London: Tavistock Publications.

Daston, L. 1996, 'The naturalized female intellect', in C. F. Graumann and Kenneth, J. Gergen (eds), *Historical Dimensions of Psychological Discourse*, Cambridge: Cambridge University Press, 165–92.

Davies, B. 1992, 'Women's subjectivity and feminist stories', in C. Ellis and M. G. Flaherty (eds), *Investigating Subjectivity. Research on Lived Experience*, Newbury California: Sage Books, 53–76.

Deaux, K. 1993, 'Sex or gender. Commentary: Sorry, wrong number – A reply to Gentile's call', *Psychological Science*, 4(2), 125–26.

de Beauvoir, S. [1949] 1988, *The Second Sex*, translated by H. M. Parshley, London: Pan.

De Board, R. 1990, *The Psychoanalysis of Organizations. A Psychoanalytic Approach to Behaviour in Groups and Organizations*, London: Routledge.

Despouy, L. 1993, *Human Rights and Disabled Persons*, N. Y.: United Nations.

Dixon, R. 1988a, 'Violence alleged at centre for disabled', *The Age*, 27 April.

Dixon, R. 1988b, 'When will I be going home? Soon?', *The Age*, 20 June.

Dokecki, P. R., Anderson, B. J. and Strain, P. S. 1977, 'Stigmatisation and labelling', in J. L. Paul, D. J. Stedman and R. G. Neufeld (eds), *Deinstitutionalisation*, Syracuse: Syracuse University Press, 37–52.

Donnellan, A. M. and Cutler, B. C. 1991, 'A dialogue on power relationships and aversive control', in L. H. Meyer, C. A. Peck and L. Brown (eds), *Critical Issues in the Lives of People with Severe Disabilities*, Baltimore: Paul H. Brookes, 617–24.

Dulley, H. 1990, 'Relocation within institutions', *Mental Handicap*, 18 December, 172.

Dunt, D. 1988, *The St Nicholas Project. The Evaluation of a Deinstitutionalization Project in Victoria*, Melbourne: Community Services Victoria.

Dunt, D. and Cummins, R. 1990, 'The deinstitutionalization of St Nicholas Hospital. I. Adaptive behaviours and physical health', *Australia and New Zealand Journal of Developmental Disabilities*, 16(1), 5–18.

Edgerton, R. B. 1963, 'A patient elite. Ethnography in a hospital for the mentally retarded', *American Journal of Mental Deficiency*, 68 (Supplement), 372–85.

Edgerton, R. B. 1971, *The Cloak of Competence*, Berkeley: University of California Press.

Edgerton, R. B. 1984a, 'The participant observer approach to research in mental retardation', *American Journal of Mental Deficiency*, 86(5), 498–505.

Edgerton, R. B. 1984b, *Lives in Process. Mildly Retarded Adults in a Large City*, Washington D. C.: American Association on Mental Deficiency.

Edgerton, R. B. 1984c, 'Introduction', in R. B. Edgerton, *Lives in Process. Mildly Retarded Adults in a Large City*, Washington D. C.: American Association on Mental Deficiency.

Edgerton, R. B. 1988, 'Community adaptation of people with mental retardation', in J. E. Kavanagh (ed.), *Understanding Mental Retardation: Research Accomplishments and New Frontiers*, Baltimore: Paul H. Brookes, 311–18.

Edgerton, R. B. 1991, *Lives of Older People with Mental Retardation in the Community*, Maryland: Paul H. Brookes.

Edgerton, R. B. and Bercovici, S. M. 1976, 'The cloak of competence years later', *American Journal of Mental Deficiency*, 80(5), 485–97.

Edgerton, R. B., Bollinger, M. and Herr, B. 1984, 'The cloak of competence after two decades', *American Journal of Mental Deficiency*, 83(4), 345–51.

Emerson, E. 1992, 'What is normalisation?', in H. Brown and H. Smith (eds), *Normalisation. A Reader for the Nineties*, London: Tavistock/Routledge, 1–18.

Emerson, E., Barrett, S., Bell, C., Cummings, R., McCool, C., Toogood, A. and Mansell, J. 1987, *Developing Services for People with Severe Learning Difficulties and Challenging Behaviours*, Canterbury: University of Kent at Canterbury, Institute of Social and Applied Psychology.

Estroff, S. 1981, *Making it Crazy. An Ethnography of Psychiatric Clients in an American Community*, Berkeley: University of California Press.

Evans, J. 1966, 'A training centre for mentally retarded adults', *The Medical Journal of Australia*, 1(596), April 2, 596–8.

Fairclough, N. 1992, *Discourse and Social Change*, Cambridge: Polity Press.

Farlow, D. and Lord, J. 1987, *Reuniting Families. A Resource Guide for Family Involvement in the Closing of Institutions*, Vancouver: Family Support Institute.

Felce, D. and Toogood, S. 1988, *Close to Home*, London: British Council on Mental Retardation.

Fensome, H. 1992, 'Sharing memories: the role of reminiscence in managing transition', in A. Waitman and S. Conboy-Hill (eds), *Psychotherapy and Mental Handicap*, London: Sage Publications, 171–84.

Ferguson, K. E. 1984, *The Feminist Case Against the Bureaucracy*, Philadelphia: Temple University Press.

Ferguson, P. M., Ferguson, D. L. and Taylor, S. J. 1992a, 'Disability at the edges of life', in P. M. Ferguson, D. L. Ferguson and S. J. Taylor (eds), *Interpreting Disability. A Qualitative Reader*, N. Y.: Teachers College Press, Columbia University, 13–17.

Ferguson, P. M., Ferguson, D. L. and Taylor, S. J. 1992b, 'Introduction: inter-
pretivism and disability studies', in P. M. Ferguson, D. L. Ferguson and
S. J. Taylor (eds), *Interpreting Disability. A Qualitative Reader*, N. Y.: Teachers
College Press, Columbia University, 1–11.

Finch, J. and Groves, D. 1980, 'Community care and the family: A case for equal
opportunities', *Journal of Social Policy*, 9(4), 387–511.

Fine, M. and Gordon, S. M. 1992, 'Feminist transformations of/despite
Psychology', in M. Fine (ed.), *Disruptive Voices: The Possibilities of Feminist
Research*, Ann Arbor: University of Michigan Press, 1–25.

Finger, M. 1990, 'Heinz Meier's concept of action research', in S. Kemmis and
R. McTaggart (eds), *The Action Research Reader*, Melbourne: Deakin
University, 259–65.

Firth, H., Holtom, R., Mayor, J. and Wood, A. 1990, 'The effects of relocation',
*Mental Handicap*, 18, 145–9.

Firth, H. and Rapley, M. 1990, *From Acquaintance to Friendship. Issues for People with
Learning Disabilities*, Kidderminster: BIMH Publications.

Flax, J. 1990, *Thinking Fragments. Psychoanalysis, Feminism and Postmodernism in the
Contemporary West*, Berkeley: University of California Press.

Foucault, M. 1967, *Madness and Civilization. A History of Madness in the Age of
Reason*, London: Tavistock Publications.

Foucault, M. 1970, *The Order of Things. An Archaeology of the Human Sciences*,
London: Tavistock Publications.

Foucault, M. 1976, *The Birth of the Clinic. An Archaeology of Medical Perception*,
London: Tavistock Publications.

Foucault, M. 1978, *The History of Sexuality. An Introduction*, Harmondsworth:
Penguin.

Foucault, M. 1979, *Discipline and Punish. The Birth of the Prison*, London:
Penguin.

Foucault, M. 1980, 'Two lectures', in C. Gordon (ed.), *Power/Knowledge. Selected
Interviews and Other Writings 1972–1977 by Michel Foucault*, N. Y.: Pantheon
Books, 78–108.

Foucault, M. 1988a, 'The concern for truth', in L. D. Kritzman (ed.), *Michel
Foucault. Politics, Philosophy, Culture. Interview and Other Writings 1977–1984*,
London: Routledge, Chapman and Hall, 255–67.

Foucault, M. 1988b, 'On power', in L. D. Kritzman (ed.), *Michel Foucault. Politics,
Philosophy, Culture. Interviews and Other Writings 1977–1984*, London:
Routledge, Chapman and Hall, 96–109.

Foucault, M. 1988c, 'Critical theory/intellectual history', in L. D. Kritzman
(ed.), *Michel Foucault. Politics, Philosophy, Culture. Interviews and Other
Writings*, London: Routledge, Chapman and Hall, 17–46.

Foucault, M. 1991a, 'Politics and the study of discourse', in G. Burchell, C.
Gordon and P. Miller (eds), *The Foucault Effect with Two Lectures and an
Interview with Michel Foucault*, London: Harvester Wheatsheaf, 53–72.

Foucault, M. 1991b, 'Questions of method', in G. Burchell, C. Gordon and
P. Miller (eds), *The Foucault Effect with Two Lectures and an Interview with
Michel Foucault*, London: Harvester Wheatsheaf, 73–86.

Foucault, M. 1997a, 'Psychiatric power', in P. Rabinow (ed.), *Michel Foucault.
Ethics. The Essential Works 1*, Harmondsworth: Penguin Books, 39–50.

Foucault, M. 1997b, 'Subjectivity and truth', in P. Rabinow (ed.), *Michel Foucault.
Ethics. The Essential Works 1*, Harmondsworth: Penguin Books, 87–92.

Foucault, M. 1997c, 'The abnormals', in P. Rabinow (ed.), *Michel Foucault. Ethics.
The Essential Works 1*, Harmondsworth: Penguin Books, 51–9.

Frankenberg R. 1982, 'Participant observers', in R. G. Burgess (ed.), *Field Research: A Source Book and Field Manual*, London: George Allen and Unwin, 50–2.

Fraser, S. (ed.) 1995, *The Bell Curve Wars. Race, Intelligence and the Future of America*, N. Y.: Basic Books.

Freud, S. 1984, *On Metapsychology. The Theory of Psychoanalysis. Beyond the Pleasure Principle, The Ego and the Id and Other Works*, The Pelican Freud Library. Vol. 11, Harmondsworth: Pelican Books.

Frosh, S. 1987, *The Politics of Psychoanalysis. An Introduction to Freudian and Post-Freudian Theory*, London: Macmillan Education Ltd.

Fuss, D. 1990, *Essentially Speaking. Feminism, Nature and Difference*, London: Routledge.

Fyffe, C. 1994, 'Intellectual disability: further support for distinguishing between conscious and unconscious memory processes', paper given to the Victorian State Conference of Australian Society for the Scientific Study of Intellectual Disability (ASSID), Melbourne, March, ASSID Collected Conference Papers, Melbourne.

Gans, R. J. 1982, 'The participant observer as a human being: observations on the personal aspects of field work', in R. G. Burgess (ed.), *Field Research: A Source Book and Manual*, London: George Allen and Unwin, 53–61.

Gardner, W. I. and Graeber, K. L. 1995, 'Use of behavioural therapies to enhance personal competency: a multimodal diagnostic and intervention model', in N. Bouras (ed.), *Mental Health in Mental Retardation. Recent Advances and Practices*, Cambridge: Cambridge University Press, 205–23.

Gavagan, S. 1991, *CCOR: Summary Document*, Melbourne: Community Services Victoria.

Gentile, D. A. 1993, 'Just what are sex and gender, anyway?', *Psychological Science*, 4(2), 120–2.

Gilman, S. L. 1991, *Inscribing the Other*, Lincoln: University of Nebraska Press.

Glaser, B. and Strauss, A. L. 1967, *The Discovery of Grounded Theory: Strategies for Qualitative Research*, N. Y.: Aldine De Gruyter.

Gleason, J. J. 1989, *Special Education in Context. An Ethnographic Study of Persons with Developmental Disabilities*, Cambridge: Cambridge University Press.

Goffman, E. 1961, *Asylums. Essays on the Social Situation of Mental Patients and Other Inmates*, London: Peregrine Books.

Goldstein, A. P. and Keller, H. 1987, *Aggressive Behavior. Assessment and Intervention*, N. Y.: Pergamon Press.

Goleman, D. 1996, *Emotional Intelligence. Why It Can Matter More Than IQ*, London: Bloomsbury Publishing Co.

Goode, D. A. 1989, 'The world of the congenitally deaf-blind: towards the ground for achieving human understanding', in A. Brechin and J. Walmsley (eds), *Making Connections. Reflecting on the Lives and Experiences of People with Learning Difficulties*, London: Hodder and Stoughton, 133–9.

Goode, D. A. 1992, 'Who is Bobby? Ideology and method in the discovery of a down syndrome person's competence', in F. M. Ferguson, D. L. Ferguson and S. J. Taylor (eds), *Interpreting Disability. A Qualitative Reader*, N. Y.: Teachers College Press, Columbia University, 197–212.

Gostin, L. 1983, 'The ideology of entitlement: the application of contemporary legal approaches to psychiatry', in P. Bean (ed.), *Mental Illness: Changes and Trends*, London: John Wiley and Sons, 327–64.

Gostin, L. 1986, *Institutions Observed. Towards a New Concept of Secure Provision in Mental Health*, London: King Edward's Hospital Fund for London.

Graffam, J. and Turner, J. L. 1984, 'Escape from boredom. The meaning of eventfulness in the lives of clients at a sheltered workshop', in R. B. Edgerton (ed.), *Lives in Process. Mildly Retarded Adults in a Large City*, Washington D. C.: American Association on Mental Retardation, 121–44.

Graham, H. 1984, 'Surveying through stories', in C. Bell and H. Roberts (eds), *Social Researching. Politics, Problems, Practices*, London: Routledge and Kegan Paul, 104–24.

Grant, G. 1997, Consulting to involve or consulting to empower', in P. Ramcharan, G. Roberts, G. Grant and J. Borland (eds), *Empowerment in Everyday Life. Learning Disability*, London: Jessica Kingsley, 121–43.

Green, D. 1989, 'Can We Legislate for Respect in Homes for the Aged?', draft article in K. Johnson's private collection.

Green, J. and Wunsch, A. 1993, 'The lives of six women', *Interaction*, 7(4), 11–15.

Grunberg, F. 1977, 'Willowbrook: A view from the Top', in J. Wortis (ed.), *Mental Retardation and Developmental Disabilities*, Vol. IX, N. Y.: Brunner/Mazel, 46–52.

Halpern, A. S. 1986, *On My Own. The Impact of Semi-Independent Living Programs for Adults with Mental Retardation*, N. Y.: Paul Brookes.

Hammersley, M. and Atkinson, P. 1992, *Ethnography. Principles in Practice*, London: Routledge.

Hand, J. E., Trewby, M. and Reid, P. M. 1994, 'When a family member has an intellectual handicap', *Disability and Society*, 9(2), 167–84.

Hansen, C. 1977, 'Willowbrook', in J. Wortis (ed.), *Mental Retardation and Developmental Disabilities*, Vol. IX, N. Y.: Brunner/Mazel, 6–45.

Hanson, F. A. 1994, *Testing Testing. Social Consequences of the Examined Life*, Berkeley: University of California Press.

Harding, S. 1987, 'Introduction. Is there a feminist method?', in S. Harding (ed.), *Feminism and Methodology. Social Science Issues*, Milton Keynes: Open University Press, 1–14.

Harris, J. 1991, 'A challenge to services', in J. Harris (ed.), *Service Responses to People with Learning Difficulties and Challenging Behaviour*, BIMH Seminar Papers No. 1, Kidderminster: BIMH, 1–15.

Hattersley, J., Hosking, G. P., Morrow, D. and Myers, M. (eds) 1987, *People with Mental Handicap. Perspectives on Intellectual Disability*, London: Faber and Faber.

Hayes, S. C. 1984, 'Out of the frying pan – Making deinstitutionalization work', *Australia and New Zealand Journal of Developmental Disabilities*, 10(4), 87–90.

Hayes, S. C. and Hayes, R. 1982, *Mental Retardation. Law, Policy and Administration*, Sydney: The Law Book Company.

Heistad, G. T., Zimmermann, R. L. and Doebler, M. I. 1982, 'Long term usefulness of thioridazine for institutionalized mentally retarded people', *American Journal of Mental Deficiency*, 87, 243–51.

Heller, T. 1984, 'Issues in the adjustment of mentally retarded individuals to residential location', *International Review of Research into Mental Retardation*, 12, 123–42.

Helstetter, E. and Durand, V. M. 1991, 'Nonaversive interventions for severe behaviour problems', in L. H. Meyer, C. A. Peck and L. Brown (eds), *Critical Issues in the Lives of People with Severe Disabilities*, Baltimore: Paul H. Brookes, 559–600.

Henriques, J., Hollway, C., Urwin, V. and Walkerdine, C. (eds) 1984, *Changing the Subject. Psychology, Social Regulation and Subjectivity*, London and New York: Methuen.

Hernstein, R. J. and Murray, C. 1996, *The Bell Curve. Intelligence and Class Structure in American Life*, N. Y.: The Free Press.

Heyman, B. and Huckle, S. 1995, 'Sexuality as a perceived hazard in the lives of adults with learning difficulties', *Disability and Society*, 10(2), 139–55.

Hills, S. 1991a, *Client Consultation on Relocation (CCOR). Summary Document*, Melbourne: Community Services Victoria.

Hills, S. 1991b, *Client Consultation on Relocation (CCOR). Evaluation Report*, Melbourne: Community Services Victoria.

Hills, S. 1991c, *Client Consultation on Relocation. Report on the Kew Project*, Melbourne: Community Services Victoria.

Hills, S. 1992a, *The CCOR Process. Step by Step*, (Appendices), Melbourne: Community Services Victoria.

Hills, S. 1992b, *Client Matching. Planning and Implementation*, Melbourne: Community Services Victoria.

Hillyer, B. 1993, *Feminism and Disability*, University of Oklahoma Press, Norman: Publishing Division of the University.

Hoeg, P. 1994, *Borderliners*, London: Harvill.

Hollins, S. 1992, 'Group analytic therapy for people with mental handicap', in A. Waitman and S. Conboy-Hill (eds), *Psychotherapy and Mental Handicap*, London: Sage Publications, 139–49.

Hollins, S., Sinason, V. and Thompson, S. 1995. 'Individual, group and family psychotherapy', in N. Bouras (ed.), *Mental Health in Mental Retardation. Recent Advances and Practices*, Cambridge, Cambridge University Press, 233–43.

Hollway, W. 1989, *Subjectivity and Method in Psychology. Gender, Meaning and Science*, London: Sage Publications.

Holt, G. 1995, 'Challenging behaviour', in N. Bouras (ed.), *Mental Health in Mental Retardation. Recent Advances and Practices*, Cambridge: Cambridge University Press, 126–32.

Holtom, R., Firth, H. and Wood, A. 1990, 'An evaluation of the effects of relocation within institutions', *Mental Handicap*, 18(2), 60–3.

Hope, M. and Young, Y. 1984, 'From back wards to back alleys. Deinstitutionalization and the homeless', *Urban and Social Change Review*, 80–4.

Horner, R. H. 1991, 'The future of applied behavior analysis for people with severe disabilities, Commentary 1', in L. H. Meyer, C. A. Peck and L. Brown (eds), *Critical Issues in the Lives of People with Severe Disabilities*, Baltimore: Paul H. Brookes, 607–15.

Howe, F. (ed.) 1993, *With Wings. An Anthology of Literature by and about Women with Disabilities*, London: The Feminist Press.

Hoy, D. C. 1986, 'Introduction', in D. C. Hoy (ed.), *Foucault: A Critical Reader*, Oxford: Basil Blackwell, 1–25.

Hubert, J. 1992a, *Too Many Drugs. Too Little Care. Parents' Perceptions of the Administration and Side-effects of Drugs Prescribed for Young People with Severe Learning Difficulties*, London: Values into Action.

Hubert, J. 1992b, 'A spoonful of sugar', *Community Care*, 13 February, 16–17.

Huizer, G. 1991, 'Participatory research and healing witchcraft: an essay in the anthropology of crisis', in L. Nencel and P. Pels (eds), *Constructing Knowledge. Authority and Critique in Social Science*, London: Sage Publications, 40–58.

Ignatieff, M. 1986, *The Needs of Strangers. An Essay on Privacy, Solidarity and the Politics of Being Human*, N. Y.: Penguin Books.

Jacoby, R. and Glauberman, N. (eds) 1995, *The Bell Curve Debate. History, Documents, Opinions*, N. Y.: Times Books.

Jahoda, A., Markova, I. and Cattermole, M. 1989, 'Stigma and the self-concept of people with mild mental handicap', in A. Brechin and J. Walmsley (eds), *Making Connections. Reflecting on the Lives and Experiences of People with Learning Difficulties*, London: Hodder and Stoughton, 147–56.

Jennings, L. 1996, 'Converging discourses. Action learning and action research', *Action Learning Action Research Journal*, 1(1), 3–13.

Jensen, A. R. 1972, 'The heritability of intelligence', in P. Zimbardo and C. Maslach (eds), *Psychology for Our Times*, Illinois: Scott, Foresman and Co., 129–34.

Jewell, M. 1984, 'The implication of normalization for families of intellectually handicapped children in residential care', in AGSSOMD, *Beyond Normalization*, Vol. 2, Perth: University of Western Australia.

Johnson, K. 1992a, *Client Consultation on Relocation: A Case Study of the Implementation of the CCOR Process*, Melbourne: Community Services Victoria.

Johnson, K. 1992b, 'The Matching Process', policy paper prepared for closure management team [Hilltop], in K. Johnson's private collection, Melbourne.

Johnson, K., Andrew, R. and Topp, V. 1987, *Silent Victims. A Study of People with Intellectual Disabilities as Victims of Crime*, Melbourne: Office of the Public Advocate.

Johnson, K. and O'Brien, S. 1989, *The Need for Nursing Home Accommodation for Children with Severe Disabilities*, Melbourne: MOIRA Nursing Home for Children with Severe Disabilities.

Jones, W. E. 1905, *Hospitals for the Insane: Report of the Inspector-General of the Insane*, Report presented to both Houses of Parliament, Victoria.

Jorgensen, D. 1989, *Participant Observation. A Methodology for Human Studies*, Newbury Park California: Sage Publications.

Jorgensen, J. 1992, 'Co-constructing the interviewer/co-constructing "family"', in F. Steier (ed.), *Research and Reflexivity*, London: Sage Publications, 210–25.

Kamin, L. J. 1974, *The Science and Politics of I.Q.*, N. Y.: John Wiley and Sons.

Kelly, H. 1991, '"Am I doin' alright?"', in R. B. Edgerton and M. Gaston (eds), *I've Seen It All. Lives of Older Persons with Mental Retardation in the Community*, Maryland: Paul H. Brookes, 239–67.

Kemmis, S. 1990, 'Action research in retrospect and prospect', in S. Kemmis and R. McTaggart (eds), *The Action Research Reader*, third edition, Melbourne: Deakin University, 27–39.

Knapp, M., Cambridge, P., Thomason, C., Beecham, J., Allen, C., Leedham, D. and Durton, R. 1992, *Care in the Community. Challenge and Demonstration*, Aldershot: Ashgate Publishing.

Korman, N. and Glennerster, H. 1985, *Closing a Hospital. The Darenth Park Project. Occasional Papers on Social Administration*, No. 78, London: Bedford Square Press/NCVO.

Korman, N. and Glennerster, H. 1990, *Hospital Closure. A Political and Economic Study*, Milton Keynes: Open University Press.

Leighton, A. 1988, 'Introduction', in A. Leighton (ed.), *Mental Handicap in the Community*, Cambridge: Woodhead-Faulkner, xvii–xxi.

Lerman, P. 1982, *De-institutionalization and the Welfare State*, New Brunswick: Rutgers University Press.

Lessing, D. 1988, *The Fifth Child*, London: Cape.

Levi, P. 1988, *Collected Poems*, London: Faber and Faber.

Linscheid, T. R. and Landau, R. J. 1993, 'Going all out pharmacologically? A re-examination of Berkman and Meyer's alternative strategies and multiple outcomes in remediation of severe self injury', *Mental Retardation*, 31(1), 1–6.

Lord, J. and Hearn, C. 1987, *Return to the Community. The Process of Closing an Institution*, Kitchener: Center for Research and Education in Human Services.

Lord, J., MacNaughton, E., Occhocha, J. and Roth, D. 1993, 'Research and evaluation of the support clusters project. Findings and themes', *Double Vision*, 4, 1–6.

Lord, J. and Pedlar, A. 1990, *Life in the Community. Four Years after the Closure of an Institution*, Kitchener: Center for Research and Education in Human Services.

Lyth, I. Menzies 1988a, 'The functioning of social systems as a defence against anxiety (1959, 1961, 1961b, 1970)', in I. Menzies Lyth, *Containing Anxiety in Institutions. Selected Essays. Vol. 1*, London: Free Association Books, 43–85.

Lyth, I. Menzies 1988b, 'Nurses under stress', in I. Menzies Lyth, *Containing Anxiety in Institutions. Selected Essays. Vol. 1*, London: Free Association Books, 100–14.

Lyth, I. Menzies 1988c, 'Action research in a long stay hospital', in I. Menzies Lyth, *In Containing Anxiety in Institutions. Selected Essays. Vol. 1*, London: Free Association Books, 103–52.

Lyth, I. Menzies 1988d, 'The psychological welfare of children making long stays in hospital: an experience in the art of the possible', in I. Menzies Lyth, *Containing Anxiety in Institutions. Selected Essays. Vol. 1*, London: Free Association Books, 153–207.

McBrien, J. and Felce, D. 1992, *Working with People who have Severe Learning Difficulty and Challenging Behaviour. A Practical Handbook on the Behavioural Approach*, Kidderminster: BIMH.

McClelland, D. C. 1972, 'Do I.Q. tests measure intelligence?', in P. Zimbardo and C. Maslach (eds), *Psychology for Our Times. Readings*, Illinois: Scott, Foresman and Company, 134–7.

McCubbery, J. and Fyffe, C. 1991, 'Deinstitutionalization in a rural community', *Interaction*, 5(5), 4–9.

MacFarlane, A. 1994, 'Subtle forms of abuse and their long term effects', *Disability and Society*, 9(1), 85–8.

McGee, J. J. and Menolascino, F. J. 1991, *Beyond Gentle Teaching. A Non-aversive Approach to Helping Those in Need*, N. Y.: Plenum Press.

McGee, J. J., Menousek, P. E. and Hobbs, D. 1987, 'Gentle teaching: An alternative to punishment for people with challenging behaviors', in S. J. Taylor, D. Biklen and J. Knoll (eds), *Community Integration for People with Severe Disabilities*, N. Y.: Teachers College Press, Columbia University, 147–63.

McGill, P. and Cummings, R. 1990, 'An analysis of the representation of people with mental handicaps in British newspapers', *Mental Handicap Research*, 3(1), 60–9.

McKnight, J. 1977, 'On good works and good work', paper presented at Conference on New Strategies for Education, Work and Retirement, Center for Policy, Washington D. C.

McKnight, J. 1985, 'Regenerating community', paper presented at Canadian Association on Mental Health Search Conference, Canadian Association on Mental Health, Ottawa.

MacMillan, J. 1967, *A History of Nurse Training and Nursing at Sunbury Mental Hospital*, research paper in K. Johnson's private collection, Melbourne.

McTaggart, R. 1991, *Action Research. A Short Modern History*, Melbourne: Deakin University.

Meyer, L. H. and Berkman, K. A. 1993, 'What's straw and what's real: A reply to Linschied and Landau', *Mental Retardation*, 31(1), 7–14.

Meyer, R. J. 1980, 'Attitudes of parents of institutionalized mentally retarded individuals towards deinstitutionalization', *American Journal of Mental Deficiency*, 85, 184–7.

Miller, E. J. and Gwynne, G. V. 1972, *A Life Apart. A Pilot Study of Residential Institutions for the Physically Handicapped and the Young Chronic Sick*, London: Tavistock Publications.

Money-Kyrle, R. 1988, 'Normal counter-transference and some deviations', in E. Bott Spillius (ed.), *Melanie Klein Today. Mainly Practice*, Vol. 2, London: Routledge, 22–33.

Moody, P. and Moody, R. 1986, *Half Left. The Challenges of Growing Up 'Not Quite Normal'*, Oslo: Dreyers Forlag.

Moore, K. and Ferleger, D. 1994, 'Evolutions in advocacy: 1960–1994 for people with developmental disabilities', *Paper Presented at Conference: Beyond Normalization. Towards One Society for All*, Reykjavik, Iceland.

Morris, J. 1993, *Pride Against Prejudice. Transforming Attitudes to Disability*, London: The Women's Press.

Morris, J. (ed.) 1996, *Encounters with Strangers. Feminism and Disability*, London: The Women's Press.

Morris, P. 1969, *Put Away. A Sociological Study of Institutions for the Mentally Retarded*, London: Routledge and Kegan Paul.

Mowbray, M. and Bryson, L. 1984, 'Women really care', *Australian Journal of Social Issues*, 19(4), 261–71.

Munro, J. D. 1977, 'Attitudes of adult institutionalized retardates towards living in the community', *The Social Worker*, 45, 130–6.

Naufal, R. 1989, 'The ten year plan for the redevelopment of intellectual disability services', *Policy Issues Forum*, April, 21–7.

Neilson Associates 1987a, *Ten Year Plan for the Redevelopment of Intellectual Disability Services, Interim Report. Part 1, The Form of the Task*, Melbourne: Community Services Victoria.

Neilson Associates 1987b, *Ten Year Plan for the Redevelopment of Intellectual Disability Services, Interim Report. Part 2, Quantification of the Task*, Melbourne: Community Services Victoria.

Neilson Associates 1988a, *The Ten Year State Plan for the Redevelopment of Intellectual Disability Service, The Final Report, Data Book*, Melbourne: Community Services Victoria.

Neilson Associates 1988b, *Ten Year Plan for the Redevelopment of Intellectual Disability Services, Final Report*, Melbourne: Community Services Victoria.

Norton, J. 1991, 'My love she speaks like silence: men, sex and subjectivity', *Melbourne Journal of Politics*, 20, 148–88.

Oakley, A. 1990, 'Interviewing women: A contradiction in terms', in H. Roberts (ed.), *Doing Feminist Research*, London: Routledge, 30–61.

O'Brien, S. and Johnson, K. 1987, *Having a Real Say. Strategies for Developing Consumer Participation in Services for People with Intellectual Disabilities*, Melbourne: AMIDA.

O'Brien, S. and Johnson, K. 1993, 'Improving consumer participation', in J. Ward (ed.), *Australian Community Development. Ideas, Skills and Values for the Nineties*, Melbourne: Community Quarterly, 24–7.

O'Connor, S. 1991, *I'm Not Indian Anymore. The Challenge of Providing Culturally Sensitive Services to American Indians*, Syracuse University: Center on Human Policy.

O'Connor, S. 1992, *What Would Really Help They Won't Do. The Meaning of Services and Their Cost to Families of Children with Disabilities*, Boston: Federation for Children with Special Needs.

Office of the Public Advocate 1990, *Annual Report of the Community Visitors, 1990*, Melbourne: Office of the Public Advocate.

Oliver, M. 1996, *Understanding Disability. From Theory to Practice*, London: Macmillan.

Outhwaite, W. 1985, 'Hans-Georg Gadamer', in Q. Skinner (ed.), *The Return of Grand Theory in the Human Sciences*, Cambridge: Cambridge University Press, 23–39.

Owen, L., Cooper, B. K. and Barber, J. G. 1994, *Relocation of People with Intellectual Disabilities in Victoria. Final Report*, Melbourne: The Human Resource Centre, Graduate School of Social Work, Latrobe University.

Perrin, B. and Nirje, B. 1989, 'Setting the record straight: A critique of some frequent misconceptions of the normalisation principle', in A. Brechin and J. Walmsley (eds), *Making Connections. Reflections on the Lives and Experiences of People with Learning Difficulties*, London: Hodder and Stoughton, 220–7.

Personal Social Services Research Unit 1987, 'A home visit', *Care in the Community*, Spring, 11.

Petterman, D. M. 1991, 'A walk through the wilderness. Learning to find your way', in W. B. Shaffir and R. A. Stebbins (eds), *Experiencing Fieldwork. An Insider View of Qualitative Research*, Newbury Park: Sage Publications, 87–96.

Pfeiffer, D. 1994, 'Eugenics and disability discrimination', *Disability and Society*, 9(4), 481–99.

Phillips, M. J. 1992, 'Try harder. The experience of disability and the dilemma of normalization', in P. M. Ferguson, D. L. Ferguson and S. J. Taylor (eds), *Interpreting Disability. A Qualitative Reader*, N. Y.: Teachers College Press, Columbia University, 213–27.

Pitkeathley, J. 1989, *It's My Duty, Isn't It? The Plight of Carers in Our Society*, London: Souvenir Press.

Pool, R. 1991, ' "Oh research, very good!": On fieldwork and representation', in L. Nencel and P. Pels (eds), *Constructing Knowledge. Authority and Critique in Social Science*, London: Sage Publications, 59–77.

Potter, J. and Wetherell, M. 1987, *Discourse and Social Psychology. Beyond Attitudes and Behaviour*, London: Sage Publications.

Potts, M. and Fido, R. 1991, *A Fit Person to be Removed. Personal Accounts of Life in a Mental Deficiency Institution*, Plymouth: Northcote House.

Presland, J. L. 1989, *Overcoming Difficult Behaviour. A Guide and Sourcebook for Helping People with Severe Mental Handicap*, Kidderminster: BIMH Publications.

Radford, J. P. and Tipper, A. 1988, *Starcross: Out of the Mainstream*, Toronto: The G. Allan Roeher Institute.

Ramazanoglu, C. 1993, 'Introduction', in C. Ramazanoglu (ed.), *Up Against Foucault. Explorations of Some Tensions Between Foucault and Feminism*, London: Routledge, 1–25.

Rapoport, R. N. 1970, 'Three dilemmas in action research', *Human Relations*, 23(6), 499–513.

Reece, D. 1987, 'Viewpoint from a parent', *Care in the Community Newsletter*, Spring: 7.

Reed, C. and Reed, M. 1992/1993, 'Looking for adaptive in maladaptive behaviour', *Interaction*, 6(4), 26–9.

Rich, A. 1981, *A Wild Patience Has Taken Me This Far. Poems 1978–1981*, N. Y.: W. W. Norton and Co.

Rich, A. 1989, *Time's Power. Poems 1985–1988*, N. Y.: W. W. Norton and Co.

Richardson, J. T. 1991, 'Experiencing research on new religions and cults. Practical and ethical considerations', in W. B. Shaffir and R. A. Stebbins (eds), *Experiencing Fieldwork. An Inside View of Qualitative Research*, Newbury Park: Sage Publications, 62–71.

Rilke, R. M. 1981, *Selected Poems of Rainer Maria Rilke. A Translation from the German and Commentary by Robert Bly*, N. Y.: Harper and Row.

Roberts, H. 1990, 'Women and their doctors', in H. Roberts (ed.), *Doing Feminist Research*, London: Routledge, 7–29.

Rose, D. 1990, *Living the Ethnographic Life. Qualitative Research Methods. Series 23. A Sage University Paper*, Newbury Park, California: Sage Publications.

Rose, N. 1979, 'The psychological complex: mental measurement and social administration', *Ideology and Consciousness*, 5, 5–68.

Rose, N. 1985, 'Unreasonable rights: mental illness and the limits of the law', *Journal of Law and Society*, 12(2), 203–19.

Rose, N. 1990, *Governing the Soul. The Shaping of the Private Self*, London: Routledge.

Rose, N. 1994, 'Psychiatry as a political science: advanced liberalism and the administration of risk', paper given at History of Human Sciences Conference, Melbourne, September.

Rosenham, D. L. 1973, 'On being sane in insane places', *Science*, 179, 250–8.

Roth, D. 1992, 'Living on the edge: Families' experiences of developmental disability and mental illness across the lifecycle', *MA thesis submitted to Wilfrid Laurier University*, Kitchener.

Rothman, D. J. 1990, *The Discovery of the Asylum. Social Order and Disorder in the New Republic*, (revised edition), Boston: Little, Brown and Company.

Rothman, D. J. and Rothman, R. 1984, *The Willow Brook Wars*, New York: Harper and Row.

Ryan, J. and Thomas, F. 1987, *The Politics of Mental Handicap*, London: Free Association Press.

Said, E. 1984, 'Permission to narrate', *London Review of Books*, 29 February.

Sanford, N. 1970, 'Whatever happened to action research?', *Journal of Social Issues*, 26(4), 3–23.

Schratz, M. and Walker, R. 1995, *Research as Social Change*, London: Routledge.

Schwartz, L. 1989, 'Centre for intellectually disabled a "snake pit"', *The Age*, 29 May.

Schwartz, M. 1964, 'The mental hospital. The research person in the disturbed ward', in A. Vidich, K. Bensen and M. Stein (eds), *Reflections on Community Studies*, N. Y.: Harper and Row, 85–117.

Schwier, K. M. 1994, *Couples with Intellectual Disabilities Talk about Living and Loving*, Rockville, Maryland: Woodbine House.

Scull, A. 1979, *Museums of Madness. The Social Organization of Insanity in 19th Century England*, London: Allen Lane.

Scull, A. 1984, *Decarceration. Community Treatment and the Deviant. A Radical View*, Cambridge: Polity Press.

Seltzer, M. S., Sherwood, C., Seltzer, G. B. and Sherwood, S. 1981, 'Community adaptation and the impact of deinstitutionalization', in R. H. Bruninks and C. Meyers (eds), *Deinstitutionalization and the Community Adjustment of Mentally Retarded People*, Monograph No. 4, Washington D. C.: American Assocation on Mental Deficiency.

Shakespeare, P. and Atkinson, D. 1993, 'Introduction', in P. Shakespeare, D. Atkinson and S. French (eds), *Reflecting on Research Practice. Issues in Health and Social Welfare*, Buckingham: Open University Press, 1–10.

Sinason, V. 1989, 'Barry: A case study', in A. Brechin and J. Walmsley (eds), *Making Connections. Reflecting on the Lives and Experiences of People with Learning Difficulties*, London: Hodder and Stoughton, 140–6.

Sinason, V. 1991, 'Psychoanalytical psychotherapy with the severely, profoundly, and multiply handicapped', in R. Szur and S. Miller (eds), *Extending Horizons. Psychoanalytic Psychotherapy with Children, Adolescents and Families*, London: Karnac Books, 225–42.

Sinason, V. 1992, *Mental Handicap and the Human Condition. New Approaches from the Tavistock*, London: Free Association Books.

Sinason, V. 1993, 'Hate and learning disability. Issues in psychoanalytical psychotherapy', in V. Varma (ed.), *How and Why Children Hate. A Study of Conscious and Unconscious Sources*, London: Jessica Kingsley, 186–98.

Sinason, V. 1994, 'Working with sexually abused individuals who have a learning disability', in A. Craft (ed.), *Practice Issues in Sexuality and Learning Disabilities*, London: Routledge, 156–75.

Smith, H. and Brown, H. 1989, 'Whose community? Whose care?', in A. Brechin and J. Walmsley (eds), *Making Connections. Reflecting on the Lives and Experiences of People with Learning Difficulties*, London: Hodder and Stoughton, 229–36.

Smith, H. and Brown, H. 1992, 'Inside-out: a psychodynamic approach to normalisation', in H. Brown and H. Smith (eds), *Normalisation. A Reader for the Nineties*, London: Tavistock/Routledge, 84–99.

Sobsey, D. 1994, 'Sexual abuse of individuals with intellectual disability', in A. Craft (ed.), *Practice Issues in Sexuality and Learning Disabilities*, London: Routledge, 93–115.

Soderquist, T. 1992, 'Biography or ethnobiography or both? Embodied reflexivity and the demonstration of knowledge-power', in F. Steier (ed.), *Research and Reflexivity*, London: Sage, 143–62.

Souza, A. and Ramcharan, P. 1997, 'Everything you ever wanted to know about Down's Syndrome, but never bothered to ask', in P. Ramcharan, G. Roberts, G. Grant and J. Borland (eds), *Empowerment in Everyday Life. Learning Disabilities*, London: Jessica Kingsley, 3–14.

Spelman, E. V. 1990, *Inessential Woman. Problems of Exclusion in Feminist Thought*, London: The Women's Press.

Stainton, T. 1992, 'A terrible danger to the race', *Community Living*, 5(3), 18–20.

Steedman, P. H. 1992, 'On the relations between seeing, interpreting and knowing', in F. Steier (ed.), *Research and Reflexivity*, London: Sage Books, 53–62.

Steier, F. 1992, 'Introduction. Research as self-reflexivity, Self-reflexivity as Social Process', in F. Steier (ed.), *Research and Reflexivity*, London: Sage Books, 1–11.

Steer, M. 1986, 'Closing mental retardation institutions. Recent developments in the United States', *Options*, 5(1), 2–3.

Stokes, J. and Sinason, V. 1992, 'Secondary mental handicap as a defence', in A. Waitman and S. Conboy-Hill (eds), *Psychotherapy and Mental Handicap*, London: Sage Publications, 46–58.

Stone, D. 1991, 'State to widen disabled abuse investigations', *The Age*, 12 May.

Stringer, E. 1997, *Action Research. A Handbook for Practitioners*, Thousand Oaks, California: Sage Publications.

Susman, G. I. and Evered, R. D. 1978, 'An assessment of the scientific merits of action research', *Administrative Science Quarterly*, 23, 582–601.

Symington, N. 1992, 'Counter transference with mentally handicapped clients', in A. Waitman and S. Conboy-Hill, (eds), *Psychotherapy and Mental Handicap*, London: Sage Publications, 132–8.

Szivos, S. and Griffiths, E. 1992, 'Coming to terms with learning difficulties: The effects of group work and group processes on stigmatised identity', in A. Waitman and S. Conboy-Hill (eds), *Psychotherapy and Mental Handicap*, London: Sage Publications, 59–80.

Taylor, C. 1986, 'Foucault on freedom and truth', in D. C. Hoy (ed.), *Foucault. A Critical Reader*, Oxford: Basil Blackwell, 69–192.

Taylor, S. J. 1977, 'The custodians. Attendants and their work at state institutions for the mentally retarded', PhD thesis submitted to University of Michigan, Ann Arbor: University Microfilms.

Taylor, S. J. 1987, 'Introduction', in S. J. Taylor, D. Biklen and J. Knoll (eds), *Community Integration for People with Severe Disabilities*, N. Y.: Teachers College Press, Columbia University Press, xv–xx.

Taylor, S. J., Bogdan, R. and Lutfiyya, Z. M. (eds) 1995, *The Variety of Community Experience. Qualitative Studies of Family and Community Life*, Baltimore: Paul H. Brookes.

Thomas, R. S. 1983, *Later Poems 1972–1982*, London: Macmillan.

Thomas, R. S. 1988, *The Echoes Return Slow*, London: Macmillan.

Tossebro, J. 1993, 'Why this opposition? Family attitudes to deinstitutionalization', paper given to the symposium Dissolution of Institutions; Development of Community Services, Uppsala, Sweden.

Tossebro, J. 1996, 'Deinstitutionalisation in Norway. Continuity and change', paper given at the 10th World Congress of the International Association for the Scientific Study of Intellectual Disability, Helsinki, Finland, 8–13 July.

Throne, J. M. 1979, 'Deinstitutionalization. Too wide a swath', *Mental Retardation*, August, 19(1), 171–5.

Traustadottir, R. 1991, 'Mothers who care: Gender, disability and family life', *Journal of Family Issues*, 12(2), 211–28.

Traustadottir, R., Lutfiyya, Z. M. and Shoultz, B. 1995, *Community Living. A Multicultural Perspective*, Baltimore: Paul H. Brookes.

Trent, J. R. 1995, *Inventing the Feeble Mind. A History of Mental Retardation in the United States*, Berkeley: University of California Press.

Turner, J. L. and Graffam, J. H. 1987, 'Deceased loved ones in the dreams of mentally retarded adults', *American Journal of Mental Retardation*, 92(5), 282–9.

Tyne, A. 1992, 'Normalisation from theory to practice', in H. Brown and H. Smith (eds), *Normalisation. A Reader for the Nineties*, London: Tavistock/Routledge, 35–46.

Unger, R. K. and Crawford, M. 1993, 'Commentary: Sex and gender – The troubled relationship between terms and concepts', *Psychological Science*, 4(2), 122–4.

United Nations 1981, 'Declaration of the rights of the disabled', *Technical Aid to the Disabled Journal*, 1(1), 13.

United Nations 1988a, 'The declaration on the rights of disabled persons', in United Nations, *Human Rights. A Compilation of International Instruments*, N. Y.: United Nations, 400–2.

United Nations 1988b, 'The declaration on the rights of mentally retarded persons', in United Nations, *Human Rights. A Compilation of International Instruments*, N. Y.: United Nations, 391–2.

Ursprung, A. W. 1990, 'Family crisis related to the deinstitutionalization of a mentally retarded child', in M. Nagler (ed.), *Perspectives on Disability*, Palo Alto: Health Markets Research, 302–8.

Venn, C. 1984, 'The subject of psychology', in J. Henriques, W. Hollway, V. Urwin and C. Walkerdine (eds), *Changing the Subject. Psychology, Social Regulation and Subjectivity*, London: Methuen, 119–52.

Victorian Government 1986, *Intellectually Disabled Persons' Services Act*, Melbourne: Victorian Government Printing Office.

Victorian Government 1986, *Guardianship and Administration Board Act*, Melbourne: Victorian Government Printing Office.

Victorian Government 1987, *People and Opportunities: Victoria's Social Justice Strategy*, Melbourne: Victorian Government Printing Office.

Vonnegut, K. 1976, *Slapstick Or Lonesome No More*, N. Y.: Dell Publishing.

Waitman, A. and Conboy-Hill, S. (eds) 1992, *Psychotherapy and Mental Handicap*, London: Sage Publications.

Wallace, J. 1991, *Pleasant Creek Training Centre. Report to the Director General Community Services Victoria*, Melbourne: Victorian Government Printing Service.

Warren, C. and Johnson, K. 1992, *Putting a Good Idea into Practice. An Evaluation of a Group Programme in a Locked Unit*, Melbourne: Community Services Victoria.

Wearing, B. 1996, *Gender. The Pain and the Pleasure of Difference*, Melbourne: Addison Wesley Longman.

Weedon, C. 1987, *Feminist Practice and Poststructuralist Theory*, Oxford: Basil Blackwell.

Weiner, R. 1990, 'Looking for quality', *Mental Handicap*, 18(4), 166–8.

Whitehead, S. 1992, 'The social origins of normalisation', in H. Brown and H. Smith (eds), *Normalisation. A Reader for the Nineties*, London: Tavistock/Routledge, 47–59.

Whittaker, J. K. 1987, 'The role of residential institutions', in J. Garbarino, P. E. Brookhouser, K. J. Authier and Associates (eds), *Special Children Special Risks. The Maltreatment of Children with Disabilities*, N. Y.: Aldine De Gruyter, 83–100.

Wilkinson, S. and Kitzinger, C. (eds) 1995, *Feminism and Discourse. Psychological Perspectives*, London: Sage Publications.

Willer, B. and Intagliata, J. 1984, 'An overview of the social policy of deinstitutionalization', *International Review of Research in Mental Retardation*, 12, 1–23.

Wilkinson, J. 1989, '"Being there": Evaluating life quality from feelings and daily experience', in A. Brechin and J. Walmsley (eds), *Making Connections. Reflecting on the Lives and Experiences of People with Learning Difficulties*, London: Hodder and Stoughton, 54–62.

Wilmuth, M. and Holcomb, L. (eds) 1993, *Women with Disabilities. Found Voices*, Binghampton N. Y.: Harrington Park Press.

Wing, L. 1989, *Hospital Closure and the Resettlement of Residents. The Case of Darenth Park*, Aldershot, London: Gower.

Wolfensberger, W. 1975, *The Origin and Nature of Our Institutional Models*, Syracuse: Syracuse Policy Press.

Wolfensberger, W. 1982, 'A brief outline of the principle of normalization', *Rehabilitation Psychology*, 27(3), 131–45.

Wolfensberger, W. 1983, 'Social role valorisation: A proposed new term for the principle of normalisation', *Mental Retardation*, 21(6), 234–9.

Wolfensberger, W. 1984, 'A reconceptualisation of normalisation as social role valorisation', *Canadian Journal on Mental Retardation*, 34(7), 238–9.

Wolfensberger, W. 1987, 'Values in the funding of social services', *American Journal of Mental Deficiency*, 92(2), 141–3.

Wolfensberger, W. 1992, *A Brief Introduction to Social Role Valorisation as a High-Order Concept for Structuring Human Services*, revised edition, Syracuse N. Y.: Syracuse University.

Wolfensberger, W. 1995, 'Social role valorization is too conservative. No, it is too radical', *Disability and Society*, 10(3), 365–7.

Wolfensberger, W., Nirje, B., Olshansky, S., Perske, R. and Rose, P. 1972, *The Principle of Normalisation of Human Services*, Toronto: National Institute on Mental Retardation.

Wolfensberger, W. and Tullman, S. 1989, 'A brief outline of the principle of normalisation', in A. Brechin and J. Walmsley (eds), *Making Connections. Reflecting on the Lives and Experiences of People with Learning Difficulties*, London: Hodder and Stoughton, 210–19.

Wood, M. 1994, 'Lost paradises', *New York Review of Books*, 3 March, 46.

Wood, A., Firth, H. and Holtom, R. 1990, 'An evaluation of the effects of relocation within institutions. Part 2. Implementation at Proudhoe Hospital', *Mental Handicap*, 18(3), 114–17.

Woolf, V. [1929] 1994, *A Room of One's Own*, London: HarperCollins Publishers.

Zetlin, A. G. and Turner, J. L. 1984, 'Self-perspectives on being handicapped: Stigma and adjustment', in R. B. Edgerton (ed.), *Lives in Process. Mildly Retarded Adults in a Large City*, Washington D. C.: American Association on Mental Deficiency, 93–120.

# Index

AAMR *see* American Association on Mental
    Retardation
absconding 54
action research 9–10
activities *see* Unit N
adaptive skills 71, 159–60, 176
admission *see* reasons for
advocates 82, 86, 87, 177
    action 100, 109, 111, 121, 122–3, 162
    and deinstitutionalisation 160, 162
    and the last six months 136–7
    citizen 85, 100, 136, 162
    in CCOR process 110–11
    public 58, 80, 100, 109
    researcher 121, 128–9
    women's relationships with 41
affection between staff and women 42
aggressive behaviour 38, 39, 40, 42, 48,
    53–4, 64, 74, 88, 118, 119
    *see also specific women*
American Association on Mental
    Retardation (AAMR) 70, 71
anti-institutionalisation 151, 153
Asch, A. and Fine, M. 64
attention-seeking behaviour 26, 39

Beer, Patricia (poet) 45
behaviour *see* challenging behaviour *or*
    *specific behaviours*
Behaviour Intervention Support Team 76,
    116, 130, 139
behaviour modification strategies 76–7,
    174
Benn, C. 176–7
Bettina (Junisov) xi, 28, 40, 50, 53, 55, 63,
    67, 175
    community placement 109, 120, 122

convenor's views 115
    parents 110
Blunden, R. and Allen, D. 73
Bogdan, R. 8, 10, 65, 72, 171
Booth, T., Simons, K. and Booth, W. 150,
    158
Brigid (Anderson) x, 27, 71, 115, 176
    advocate's reaction to placement
        decision 123, 136
    behaviour 4, 25–6, 29, 41, 57, 121, 172
    behaviour modification 76
    CCOR meeting 108–9
    departure 135
    General Service Plan 26
    institutional placement 121, 122
    management support during transition
        143
    medication 26
    researcher advocacy 128, 129
    researcher attitude to 29
    staff attitude to 26–7, 31
    story 24–7
Brown, H. 65, 73, 158, 180

Cain, M. 165
Carney, T. 153–4
CCOR *see* Client Consultation on
    Relocation
challenging behaviour
    and attribution of dreams or desires 173
    and deinstitutionalisation 147, 173–4,
        179
    and discourse 72–7
    and expression of feelings 174–5
    and gender 77
    and placement 120–1
    and psychiatric illness 54–5

challenging behaviour *cont.*
  and underlying pain and despair 173
  behaviour modification strategies 76–7,
    173–4
  CCOR committee assessment 116–17
  critique of 75
  definition 73–4
  medication use for 26, 34, 76
  staff attitudes to 31, 57–8, 74–5
  variety of 26, 38–40, 57, 132–3, 179
  women's views of 75
  *see also specific behaviours*, e.g. aggressive
    behaviour
citizen advocates *see* advocates
Client Consultation on Relocation 82,
    98–100, 156, 164, 175
  action advocates 100
  advocate participation 110–11
  and client's rights 152
  closure project team manager's role
    116–17
  committee, assessment of challenging
    behaviours 116–17
  constraints
    availability of services in the
      community 104–5
    staff availability 103–4
    staff involved 102–3
    time 102
  consultation process 108–10
  convenors' responsibilities 99–100,
    112–15
  family participation 105–7, 110–11, 161
  Kirsten's story 105–8
  researcher's role 128
  steps 99
  unit staff involvement 111–12
  women's experience of 105–10
  *see also* matching
client relocation team 82, 100, 101, 138,
    139
clients 43
  community placement of 81
  *see also* 'ladies'; women
closure
  institution 2–3, 5–6, 79–83, 84
    and rights 151–3
    closure project team managers'
      responses 91–2
    costs of 163–4
    families' responses 181
    Hilltop Parents and Friends
      Association responses 89, 93–4
    management responses 90–1
    physical process of 130–1
    researcher response 94, 96

  union response 92–3, 95–6
  last six months of
    closure project team managers 141–3
    convenor anxieties 138–41
    families' and advocates' roles 136–7,
      160–2
    researcher/story teller 143–5
    staff concerns and anxieties 137–8
    Una's story 131–3
    women's coping with transition 133–6
  stages of 5–6, 81–3
  Unit N
    families' responses 88–9
    researcher banned by union from
      95–6
    staff responses 87–8, 89–90, 137–8
    women's responses 84–8
closure decision 80–1
  and staff powerlessness 7
  industrial bans 6, 88, 92–3, 103
closure project team 6, 103
  commitment to rights 152–3
  formation 82
closure project team managers 5, 165, 182
  and CCOR 116–17
  and matching 127–8
  and the last six months 141–3
  concerns over women's sexuality 148
  interviews with 127
  lack of concern over day programmes
    147
  managing families and advocates 160–2
  researcher role 144
  views on closure 91–2
cluster village, campaign for 93–4
community living
  and improved quality of life 158
  and specialist services 159
  tests for 71, 159–60, 176
community placement 81, 88
  family anxiety about 123
  monitoring reports on 141
  outcomes 122, 136
  Parents and Friends Association
    concerns over 94
  preferences 106, 109, 110, 111, 112, 120,
    122
  union concerns over 93
convenors 99–100
  and CCOR 112–15
  and matching process 125–6, 139, 164
  anxieties about people leaving Hilltop
    138–41, 182
  concerns over institutional day services
    141, 147
  constraints 113–14

interviews with 112–15, 125
monitoring reports 140, 141
perception of their role 115
view of families as advocates 164
work with families 113, 114, 181–2

daily routines *see* Unit N
Dalley, G. 160, 162
Danziger, K. 61, 69
Daston, L. 67
deinstitutionalisation 1, 3, 6–7, 8, 16, 21,
  148, 186
  'administering the risk' 156
  and challenging behaviour 147, 173–4,
    179
  and families 160–2, 181–2
  and furthering of institutional life 185
  and gender discourse 147
  and improved quality of life 158
  and management 155–64
  and objectification of women 178–9
  and rights 149–55
  and sexuality 147–8
  and the women 146–8, 165
  and women's feelings 174–5
  as philosophy 150
  at Hilltop, goals 151–3
  definition 148
  government commitment to 80
  normalisation 156–8
  transition stage 130–1
Despouy, L. 151
difficult behaviour *see* challenging
  behaviour
discourse 14–16
  and challenging behaviour 72–7
  and subjectivity 14, 15–16
  gender 61–8, 77, 147, 155
  intellectual disability *see* intellectual
    disability discourse
  power/knowledge 68–77, 164–5, 169,
    183–5
Dora (Craig) x, 23, 28, 37, 41, 43, 56, 57,
  63, 68, 88, 159, 175
  aggressive behaviour 48
  convenor's concerns 125
  coping with transition 135
  family contact 47
  institutional placement 110, 115, 121,
    124, 134
  medication 48
  monitoring report 140
  parents' views 46–7, 48–9, 52, 111
  staff approach to 48
  staff concerns over matching decision 138
  story 45–9

Doris (Smith) xii, 28, 56, 110, 111, 122
  hospitalisation 134–5

Edgerton, R. B. 8, 158, 171
Elaine (Stone) xii, 28, 34, 40, 51, 55, 64,
  71, 90, 122, 134
  friendships 86, 120
  move into open unit 135
Emerson, E. 73, 157
Estroff, S. 8
ethnography 10

Fairclough, N. 15
families
  and deinstitutionalisation 160–2, 181–2
  and institutionalisation 19, 46–7, 52,
    61–2, 63, 69, 87, 179–80, 181
  and the last six months 136–7
  attitudes towards sexuality 63, 65
  CCOR visits 105–6, 108–9
  confusion about intellectual disability
    46, 61
  confusion about their daughters 61–4
  interviews with 5, 45–52, 181
  involvement in CCOR process 105–7,
    110–11
  responses to unit closure 88–9
  visits 48, 50, 51, 63, 132, 181
  women's relationships with 41
Faye (Morris) xii, 27, 49, 63, 148
  convenor's concerns 140
  departure 135
  monitoring report 141
  placement 122, 123, 124, 134, 138
feminist
  approach to research 12–13
  theory 11, 61–8
  *see also specific theorists*
Fine, M.
  and Gordon, S. M. 12, 13
  *see also* Asch, A. and Fine, M.
Foucault, Michel 14, 79, 155–6, 165, 179,
  182, 183, 184, 185
friendships 86, 87, 120, 175, 176

gender discourse *see* discourse; sexuality
General Service Plans (GSPs) 5, 26, 36, 57,
  71, 93, 164, 179
genital touching 25, 66
gentle teaching 76
Gilman, S. L. 1
glossary 188–9
Goffman, E. 19
Gordon, S. M. see Fine, M. and
  Gordon, S. M.
Guardianship and Administration Board 58

guardianship order 50, 53, 56

Harding, S. 12
Henriques, J. 14
Hilltop see institution
Hilltop Parents and Friends Association 106, 162
    response to closure 89, 93–4
Hoeg, P. 182
Hollway, W. 13, 14, 170

Ilse (Lane) xi, 27, 40, 54, 86
    move into open unit 87, 90, 135
    placement 120, 122
'immorality' 50
independent living skills see adaptive skills
Individual Programme Plans (IPPs) 36, 71, 76, 93
industrial bans
    convenor concerns 113
    over closure decision 6, 88, 92–3, 103
    staff disobey over CCOR involvement 111
    staff polarisation over 89, 93, 153
Inge (Roberts) xii, 28, 49, 63, 109, 114, 122, 148, 159
    father's concerns 109, 111, 112
institution 1, 2
    closure see closure
    financial costs 163–4
    geography of 20
    going into 3–4
    history of 19–21
    management 3, 57–8, 72, 162–4
        response to closure 90–1
    women's paths to 45–52
institutional day services, lack of 141
institutional placement
    convenor's concerns 138–41
    outcomes 122
    preferences 110, 111, 120, 121–2
    staff concerns 138
institutionalisation
    and families 19, 46–7, 52, 61–2, 63, 69, 87, 179–80, 181
    and nursing care 180
    as family's best option 69–70
    of researcher 96
    reasons for 20, 45–52
        allegations of abuse 50
        appeals against 58
        'at moral risk' 54–5
        birth of another child 50
        death of a parent 51
        Dora's story 45–9
        increasing age of parents 50–1

problems with a difficult daughter 49–50
        unknown causes 51
intellectual disabilities 1
    and expression of feelings 174–5
    and individual histories 177–8
    and lack of voice 13, 176–7, 184
    and low IQs 20
    and skill levels 147, 176
    as discourse (legal, medical) 149
    diagnosis and assessment 61, 69–71, 146–7
    family views of 46
    internal worlds of people with 171–4
    researcher knowledge of 7–8
    rights of people with 80, 149–51
    stereotyped views 72
intellectual disability discourse 69–72, 77–8, 186
    functions 179–85
Intellectual Disability Review Panel 58
Intellectually Disabled Persons' Services Act 1986 58, 80
intelligence measurement 69, 70, 182
interviews
    with convenors 112–15, 125
    with families 5, 45–52, 181
    with managers and staff 5, 31–2, 127
    with women 5
IQ tests 171, 182
    basis for assessment 70
    validity of 69, 70
Iris (James) x, 27, 40
    hospitalisation 134
    placement 122, 124, 143

Jane (King) xi, 28, 31, 41, 42, 63, 68, 74, 77, 88, 111, 115
    advocate's reaction to placement decision 123, 136
    aggressive behaviour 118, 119
    at industrial workshop 64, 119
    CCOR meeting 109
    convenor's concerns 126, 140
    departure to hostel 134
    family history 118–19
    guardianship order 50, 53, 56, 119
    management support during transition 143
    matching experience 117–20
    placement preference 112, 120, 122, 133
    promiscuity 55, 66, 148
    researcher advocacy 128, 129
    sexual relationship 66, 68, 119
    staff attitude to 119
    story 117–20

Jodie (Ryan) xii, 27, 40, 51, 57, 68, 88
  accommodation preference 109, 110, 122
  advocate 111, 128, 136, 137
  coping with transition 133
  early departure from unit 134
  relationships 175
Joyce (Thames) xiii, 23, 27, 38, 44, 55, 64,
    66, 68, 88, 148, 154
  departure 135
  institutional preference 110, 122
  staff concern over matching decision
    138
June (Miles) xi–xii, 27, 38, 39, 41, 42, 48,
    51, 131
  accommodation preferences 109, 121–2
  closure project team managers'
    concerns 143
  convenor's concerns 140

Kate (Surrey) xiii, 27, 40, 53, 57, 63, 67,
    109, 120, 122, 148, 175
  mother's concerns 111, 112, 123
Kirsten (Jones) xi, 27, 29, 33, 38, 41, 51,
    54–5, 57, 66, 140
  CCOR meeting 105–8
  community living preferences 106, 122,
    123
  family history 107, 108
  meeting with mother 105–7
  parents' responsibility 61–2, 111
  sexually at risk 54–5, 66, 108
  staff views of 107–8
  story 105–8
knitting 37, 39
knowing the women
  challenging behaviour 72–7
  intellectual disability 69–72
knowledge/power discourse see
    power/knowledge discourse

'ladies' 43
  staff attitudes to 32, 37, 68
  see also clients; women
last six months see closure
Laura (Mitchell) xii, 28, 55, 64, 109, 115,
    121, 122, 128, 141
Lena (Johnson) x–xi, 27, 35, 37, 39, 41,
    44, 64, 68, 71, 110, 175
  aggressive behaviour 54, 64
  community placement 121, 122, 123, 125
  convenor's concerns 126
  coping with placement 141
  coping with transition 136
  family appeals matching decision 136
  guardianship order 56
  researcher advocacy 129

Levi, Primo (poet) 130
locked unit 1, 2, 48
  legality of 58
  see also Unit N
Lonsdale Lodge 46–8, 111
Lyth, I. Menzies 11–12, 179–80

management
  and deinstitutionalisation 155–64
  closure team see closure project team
    managers
  institutional 3, 57–8, 72, 162–4
  of the women 155–6
  relocating the women 158–60
  Unit N 30, 31, 90, 111–12
matching 82, 100–2, 156
  advocates' responses to placement
    decisions 122–3
  appeal against decisions 136, 152
  client preferences 100–1, 104, 120
  closure project team managers'
    concerns 127–8
  constraints
    availability of services in the
      community 104–5
    competition for scarce community
      places 104
    staff availability 103–4
    staff involved in 103
    time 102
  convenors' role 125–6
  decision-making panels 101–2, 103
  establishing preferences 108–10
  families' reactions to placement
    decisions 122–3, 136, 152
  Jane's story 117–20
  placement decisions 122, 134, 136
  preference criteria 101
  researcher/advocate role in 128–9
  unit staff role in 123–5
  women's experiences of 117–22
medication
  and challenging behaviour 26, 34, 76
  Largactil 34, 54, 56, 76
  list of 189
  lithium 86
  management of 34, 35
  Melleril 26, 34, 48, 54, 76, 133
  Modecate 26, 48, 56, 133
  Neulactil 34
  side effects 76
  Stelazine 26, 48, 56
  Valium 34
mental retardation, definition 70
monitoring reports 140, 141
Morris, J. 162

normalisation 156–8, 178
  and rights 158, 185
  definition 157
nursing care 180

Oakley, A. 11
observation, participant 4, 10, 69
occupational therapy 34, 47
Office of the Public Advocate 58, 80, 100,
  109, 115

parents *see* families
Parents and Friends Association *see* Hilltop
  Parents and Friends Association
placement *see* community placement;
  institutional placement
possessive individualism 160
power/knowledge discourse 68–77, 169,
  183–5
  and Hilltop closure 164–5, 184
powerlessness *see* women
preferences *see* matching
professional regard, legitimisation of
  182–5
psychiatric illness 54–5
psychoanalysis 11–12
psychotherapeutic methods 76

qualitative research 8–9
quality of life 21, 153, 154, 158

Ramazanoglu, C. 14, 15, 184
Rapoport, R. N. 9
reasons for admission
  to Hilltop 45–52
  to Unit N 53–8
  researcher investigation of 58–9
reflexivity, rationale for 10–11
regional liaison team 130, 138, 139
relationships 175–6
  between women living in the unit 40–1,
  175
  of women with people outside the
  institution 41
  of women with staff 42–3, 176, 180–1
relocating the women
  and rights 158–60
  appeals concerning 136, 152
research
  feminist approach 12–13
  methodology 3–7
researcher
  advocacy 121
  as author 16–17
  as participant 43–4
  in management process 144

attitude to women 68
banned by union from unit 95–6
contact with women after closure 143–4
conversations with the women 43, 44
feelings about closure 145
investigates women's admission 58–9
last six months 143–5
observation 4, 10, 69
positions of 7–16
reaction to closure 94, 96
reinstatement after unit staff lobbying
  96
relationship with staff and managers
  42–3, 97, 144
relationship with women 143
staff attitudes to 2, 3
Unit N activities 4–5
*see also* interviews
Rhonda (Lee) xi, 27, 43, 50, 65
  family secures her release 58
  move into community 88, 90
Rich, Adrienne 22, 169
rights 80
  and closure of Hilltop 151–3
  and deinstitutionalisation 149–51, 154
  and gender issues 155
  and normalisation 158, 185
  and relocating the women 158–60
  competition across groups 154
  critique of 153–5
  relationships and quality of life 153, 154
Rilke, Rainer Maria (poet) 19, 98
Rosalind (Maitland) xi, 27–8, 40, 50, 56,
  122
Rose, N. 9, 10, 15, 20, 61, 65, 69, 149, 156

Said, Edward 167
screaming 23, 38, 55, 57, 107, 108, 121, 133
self-injury 56–7
sexual abuse 30, 39, 41, 50, 55, 65, 66, 77,
  148
sexual counselling 66
sexual expression 66
sexual preference 184
sexual relationships 66–7
sexual vulnerability 55, 67, 108, 111, 148
sexuality
  and subjectivity 64–7, 147–8
  and women 30, 54–5, 57
  families' attitudes towards 63, 65
  management 65–6
  staff attitudes towards 65, 66, 67
Sinason, V. 8, 11, 63–4, 76, 171, 172, 173
smashing windows/furniture 48, 55, 57
Soderquist, T. 183
Spelman, E. V. 61

staff
and group programme 35–6, 71–2
and the last six months 137–8
assessment of women 71
caring behaviours 68
concerns over placement decisions
124–5, 138
control over women 43
duties 32–3
frustration with women's behaviour 31
in Unit N 2, 4, 30–3, 74, 137
interviews with 5, 31–2
lack of knowledge about women's
history 63
lobby for researcher's reinstatement 96
polarisation over industrial action 89,
93, 153
qualifications 32
redundancy packages/redeployment
opportunities 81, 82
relationships with women 42–3, 176,
180–1
response to unit closure 87–8, 89–90
role in CCOR process 111–12, 176
role in matching process 123–5
shocked at ban on researcher 95
staff attitudes
and matching 121
to challenging behaviour 31, 57–8, 74–5
to researcher 2, 3, 96
to sexuality 65, 66
to women 4, 26–7, 31, 32, 42, 67–8
Steier, F. 11
study, the
assumptions 9
ethnography 10
goal 8
rationale for 1–3
subjectivity 13, 14
and discourse 14, 15–16
and sexuality 64–7, 147–8
and the women 13–14, 64–7, 146–8, 169,
170
definition 14
loss of 170
management 146–65
problematic nature of 14

Taylor, S. J. 8, 9, 72, 158, 171
theory development from research
experience 10
Thomas, R. S. 146, 187
'time out' 76
transinstitutionalisation 93, 94, 153
transition, coping with 131, 133–6, 145
Traustadottir, R. 52, 159

Una (Harris) x, 27, 32, 57
challenging behaviour 40, 57, 132–3
community placement 115, 122, 123,
131, 133
family advocacy 131
family assistance in settling in 137
family history 50–1, 131–2
family visits 132
medication 133
staff responses to 133
story 131–3
union
bans researcher from unit 95–6
concern over staff job losses 92
reaction to closure 88, 89, 90, 92–3
staff disobey bans in CCOR process 111
see also industrial bans
Unit N
activities 37–40, 44
as punishment 58
bath times 34
bed time 35
closure
families' responses 88–9
staff responses 89–90, 137, 138
women's responses 84–8
daily routines 33–5
families' views of 48–9, 53
formal life of 4–5, 33–7
geography 22–3
group programme 35–6, 71–2
informal life in 37–43
meal times 33–4, 35
music in 37
noise in 23–4
physical closure 134, 145
reasons for admission 45–59
absconding 54
administrative 56
aggressive behaviour 53–4
'at moral risk' 54–5
diagnosed psychiatric illness 55–6
guardianship order 56
screaming or making noise 55
self-injury 56–7
smashing windows/furniture 55
recording life in 37
relationships
between women living in 40–1, 175
with family or advocates 41
with staff 42–3
researcher activities in 4–5, 58–9
smell in 24
snapshot 27–30
staff in 2, 4, 30–2, 74, 111–12, 123–5
teeth cleaning in 34, 35

Unit N *cont.*
  television 28, 37, 47
  toileting in 34, 35
  women living in 2, 24–30
  women's path to 53–8
  *see also specific women*
United Nations
  Declarations on the Rights of Disabled
    Persons 150
  Declaration on the Rights of Mentally
    Retarded Persons 151

Vera (Waters) xiii, 27, 40, 64, 71
  aggressive behaviour 87
  family history 85–6
  friendships 86, 87, 120, 175
  'going home' 85, 86–7, 88
  move into open unit 87, 90, 135
  placement 120, 122
  psychiatric diagnosis 55–6, 85–6
  researcher advocacy 129
  story 85–7
violence 4, 25, 35, 39, 40, 41, 42, 74

walks 35, 47
Weedon, C. 13, 15, 170
Willer, B. and Intagliata, J. 80, 148, 150
Wolfensberger, W. 19, 21, 70, 72, 149, 150,
  157
women, the 16–17
  activities 37–40
  and deinstitutionalisation 146–8, 165,
    172–3
  as 'failed' daughters and sisters 61–4
  as 'failed women' 61–8
  behaviouristic view 172–3
  caring behaviours 68
  communication problems 28–9, 44
  contact with/feelings towards men 66, 68
  employment 64
  establishing preferences 108–10
  experiences of CCOR 105–10
  experiences of matching 117–22
  expression of feelings 174–5
  family ambivalence towards 173
  fantasies, dreams and desires 171–4
  home visits 64
  independence 34
  interviews with 5
  lack of voice 13, 176–7, 184
  last six months 131–6
  living environment 178–9
  objectification of 165, 170–9
  placement outcomes 122, 134
  powerlessness 176–7
  relationships 175–6
    between women living in the unit
      40–1, 175
    with people outside the institution 41
    with staff 42–3, 176, 180–1
  reluctance to leave Unit N 134
  responses to unit closure 84–8
  skills 71, 87, 176–7
  views on challenging behaviour 75
  *see also specific women*
Woolf, Virginia 60